INVISIBLE HANDS

INVISIBLE HANDS

VOICES FROM THE GLOBAL ECONOMY

COMPILED AND EDITED BY

CORINNE GORIA

FOREWORD BY

KALPONA AKTER

Assistant editors

DELMI ARRIAZA, JOAN FLORES, RYAN FORSYTHE, FRANCOIS GUIDON, DAVID HILL, AARON MCMULLIN, LUIPA MONDOKA, ALBERTO REYES MORGAN, MARCY REIN, RAYMUNDO SANDOVAL, GABRIEL THOMPSON, NATHAN WELLER

Research editor

ALEX CARP

VOICE OF WITNESS

Additional interviewers

BRANDON LUSSIER, CLIFF MAYOTTE,
UZBEK–GERMAN FORUM FOR HUMAN RIGHTS

Transcribers

CHARLOTTE CROWE, BRENDAN DALY, YANNIC DOSENBACH,
ARIADNA FERNANDEZ, CARMEN GONZALES, JILL HABERKERN, VICTORIA
HAVLICEK, PHIL HOOVER, KATE IRICK, RACHEL KOBASA, NATE MAYER,
MAGNOLIA MOLCAN, SOPHIE NUNBERG, NAOKI O'BRYAN, SAM RILEY,
REBECCA RUBENSTEIN, ZACK RUSKIN, LISA SCHRETER,
SARAH ANN MARIE SHEPHARD, EM-J STAPLES

Translators

STEPHANIE CASLER, NATALIE CATASÚS, KATRINA KOVALEVA,
EDGAR QUEZADA, RIKI GARCIA REBEL, LISA SCHRETER,
DANIELLA URETA-SPONTAK, VALERIE WOOLARD

Copy editor

ANNE HOROWITZ

Fact checker

HANNAH MURPHY

Proofreaders

NATALIE CATASÚS, KERRY FOLAN, NATASHA FRIEDMAN, KAYE HERRANEN

Additional assistance

BRENDAN DALY, MICHAEL GALVIS, NAOKI O'BRYAN, GABRIEL URIAS

This book is dedicated to the women, men, and children who shared their experiences with us. And to all those who courageously fight to be heard.

VOICE OF WITNESS

McSWEENEY'S BOOKS
SAN FRANCISCO

For more information about McSweeney's, see www.mcsweeneys.net
For more information about Voice of Witness, see www.voiceofwitness.org

Map and illustrations by Julien Lallemand

Front cover photo by Daniel Kestenholz
Back cover photos by Julien Harneis (top), Jurvetson (middle),
US Department of Agriculture (bottom)

ISBN: 978-1-938073-90-8

VOICE OF WITNESS

Voice of Witness is a non-profit organization that uses oral history to illuminate contemporary human rights crises in the U.S. and around the world. Its book series depicts these injustices through the oral histories of the men and women who experience them. The Voice of Witness Education Program brings these stories, and the issues they reflect, into high schools and impacted communities through oral history-based curricula and holistic educator support. Visit www.voiceofwitness.org for more information.

VOICE OF WITNESS FOUNDING ADVISORS

STUDS TERKEL
Author, Oral Historian

ROGER COHN
Executive Editor, Yale Environment 360; former Editor-in-Chief, Mother Jones

MARK DANNER
Author; Professor, UC Berkeley & Bard College

HARRY KREISLER
Executive Director, Institute of International Studies, UC Berkeley

MARTHA MINOW
Dean, Harvard Law School

SAMANTHA POWER
Author; Professor, Founding Executive Director, The Carr Center for Human Rights Policy

JOHN PRENDERGAST
Co-chair, ENOUGH Project; Strategic Advisor, Not On Our Watch

ORVILLE SCHELL
Arthur Ross Director, Asia Society

WILLIAM T. VOLLMANN
Author

EXPERT CONSULTATION AND ASSISTANCE FOR THIS BOOK

BAMA ATHREYA
International Labor Rights Forum

DEBBIE CHAN
Students and Scholars Against Corporate Misbehaviour

ALLISON COOK
Story of Stuff

CAITLIN DUNKLEE
Network in Solidarity with the People of Guatemala

KATE FERRANTI
AFL-CIO and author, Diet for a Hot Planet

YAEL FALICOV
Pesticide Action Network North America Regional Center

LIANA FOXVOG
International Labor Rights Forum

ALISTAIR FRASER
Cambridge University

MARCIA ISHII-EITEMAN
Pesticide Action Network North America Regional Center

REUBEN KALABA
Miners' Union, Kitwe, Zambia

JEONG OK KONG
Supporters for the Health And Rights of People in the Semiconductor industry

MILES LARMER
Sheffield University

CHING KWAN LEE
University of California, Los Angeles

JOHN LUNGU
Copper Belt University

CRAIG MERRILEES
International Longshore & Warehouse Union

DENISE MITCHELL
AFL-CIO

KIRSTEN MOLLER
Global Exchange

TIM NEWMAN
International Labor Rights Forum

UMIDA NIYAZOVA
Uzbek-German Forum for Human Rights

PETER OLNEY
International Longshore & Warehouse Union

LORENZO OROPEZA
California Rural Legal Assistance

PAULINE OVEREEM
Good Electronics

JIM PUCKETT
Basel Action Network

LISA ROFEL
University of California, Santa Cruz

JOAN SEKLER
Locked Out 2010

PETER SINKAMBA
Citizens for a Better Environment

TED SMITH
International Coalition for Responsible Technology

PHILIP THOMAS
Employment Attorney

TRINA TOCCO
International Labor Rights Forum

STEVE TRENT
Environmental Justice Foundation

CONTENTS

FOREWORD

STORIES THAT DEMAND CHANGE

by Kalpona Akter

When I was twelve, my family in Dhaka, Bangladesh, fell into poverty, and I started working in a garment factory. The life I had then is difficult to remember and nearly impossible to describe. For years, I worked day and night among other exhausted children, some as young as eight. I earned less than $7 a month, yet often worked eighteen hour days in a chaotic, unhygienic, and unsafe environment.

Becoming an activist has taken finding my voice and learning to speak up about my experience: the opposite of what women are taught in my country. Just a couple of years after I started working at the garment factory, I spoke up to my bosses because my co-workers and I were being denied overtime pay we were owed. Some of my co-workers and I decided to strike in protest. I was fired, but I kept speaking up. I could never have overcome my fear without my fellow workers who believed in me, who listened to my stories, and who shared stories of their own. I am also indebted to the union that took me in and gave me the labor rights training I needed.

My fellow workers helped me find the courage to stand up and speak out—the same courage that it has taken every person in this book to share his or her story. Through telling our stories we connect, we believe, and we might even come to care so much that we can no longer be silent.

As an adult, I've traveled around the globe, and I've spoken to audiences of thousands about the working conditions in my home country. I've spoken up to multinational corporations like Walmart and my own government, and my name has been in newspapers around the world. Even after I was jailed and tortured by agents of the state, and even after my friend and colleague was assassinated for standing up for workers' basic rights, I kept raising my voice.

Every week I hear of struggle, but I also hear of victories. Sometimes the successes are really small, but sometimes they are big enough that I can glimpse the changes that come when enough of us overcome fear and speak truth to power. The courageous narrators in this book are speaking their truth. Like myself, they have given their time, not just so that you would listen—although I hope that you listen carefully—but also so that you will seek change.

Around the world, workers and communities in crisis are standing up for their rights, against all odds, and winning. I feel connected to them even though I've never met them, even though I don't speak their language. There may be differences in our circumstances but we're united in our common struggle to seek justice, whether from our employers, multinational corporations, or the state.

Whenever I see workers or communities who are fighting for justice, and women who are fighting for their empowerment, I feel I'm part of the same struggle. When workers in other countries are jailed, it scares me but it also tells me that I'm not alone. When organized workers stay strong despite facing repression, it gives me inspiration. Each victory I hear of gives me courage to act. We are not alone in our struggle for human rights.

It was hard for me to tell my story for this book and to make my life so public. But I ask myself: How do I want to live? Suffer in silence from the trauma I have faced and the stories I hear from workers every day? Or speak out, be passionate, love and celebrate the beauty in life, believe in the goodness of humanity, and do what I can to inspire others to act? If my story touches someone's heart—maybe yours—if it lets another woman who has faced exploitation and repression feel that she is not alone, and even encourages her to speak up, then it is worth it.

We share our stories in this collection to engender outrage but also to cultivate an imagination of what is possible. Tell your own story. And take time to listen to workers that you encounter every day. For it is through story that we come to care, come to believe, and are ultimately transformed until we can no longer be silent.

Kalpona Akter
2013

Kalpona Akter is an internationally recognized labor rights advocate. She is the executive director of the Bangladesh Center for Worker Solidarity (BCWS) and is herself a former child garment worker. BCWS is regarded by the international labor rights movement as among the most effective grassroots labor organizations in Bangladesh. Kalpona's work has been covered extensively by local and international media, including ABC, the BBC, the New York Times, *and the* Wall Street Journal.

INTRODUCTION

MEETING IN THE MARKETPLACE

by Corinne Goria

I first met Kalpona Akter in 2011 in Los Angeles. Her stop in L.A. marked the end of her tour of the United States, during which she'd spoken at a Walmart shareholders' meeting and various union meetings about the dire conditions garment workers face in her home country of Bangladesh. She explained that thousands have died in Bangladeshi factories like those where she herself worked as a child. Fires and workplace accidents are common due to negligent safety standards. While the majority owners of Walmart—a single family—took home more than $2 billion in stock dividends in 2010, Bangladeshi workers making clothes for the retail giant were unable to feed their families on wages of less than $45 per month.

During our first interview at the airport hotel where she was staying, Kalpona was confident, thoughtful, and even full of humor as she told me about her life growing up in Bangladesh's crowded capital, her struggle as a child garment worker, her journey into human rights activism, and her brief imprisonment for her work the previous year. Along with stories of her work life, she also talked about her desire to have children, her goal of opening a small snack stand, and her hope that there might be time to pursue these dreams once conditions improved for her friends and fellow garment workers in Bangladesh.

A year after our meeting in L.A., I woke up early one November morning in 2012 to Skype Kalpona. We chose to talk over the Internet because she'd been warned her phone was tapped. She was regularly receiving calls from anonymous government agents warning her to stop going to work, that something terrible might happen to her or her family if she didn't stand down. In Dhaka, Bangladesh, it was late at night, and on Kalpona's end, apart from the blue glow of the computer screen illuminating her face, it was dark. She spoke into the microphone quietly so as not to wake her parents or siblings, asleep in the other room, but she also spoke with greater trepidation than in our first meeting. Every word was chosen carefully, and her easy self-assurance was less apparent.

Between our two interviews, Kalpona's situation had taken a turn. In April 2012, her colleague, Aminul Islam, had been kidnapped. The incident had followed numerous threats to silence their campaign to raise workers' wages and improve workplace conditions countrywide. Kalpona remembered when Aminul's wife had called to tell her that he was missing. His body was found two weeks later. When Kalpona spoke of the photos of her friend's mutilated body, showing signs of torture, her voice broke. Still, we spoke late into the night for her, late into the morning for me, her voice growing hoarse as she told her story. Kalpona's last words to me that morning were, "Pray for us."

When I was a child, *Sesame Street* aired a segment on how crayons were made. It was a short montage that showed orange wax being poured into molds, and then thousands of crayon-shaped sticks being wrapped in paper and stacked in boxes. The manufacture was carried out in seamless cooperation between many machines and a couple of workers in hairnets and aprons. The montage was fascinating to me as a child in that it showed the origin, the creation, of something I used every day. Of course it raised questions: *Where was the factory? Who were the people? What did they do when they weren't at work?*

This book started with that simple aim of getting to know the people who produce the things we use every day. Our jeans, our coffee, our gasoline, our cell phones. We wanted to know what their work was like, what hardships they faced, and what hopes they had. As we spoke with the narrators, their pride in the work they did became clear. As one narrator, a garment worker named Ana Juárez, explained: "The work we're doing is very worthy. Every time I see a pair of pants I say to myself, 'How proud I am that I made those pants. It was my work. It was my effort. It was my night shifts when I didn't sleep.'"

As we continued to seek stories, we discovered that nearly every potential narrator we spoke with was leading some fight, large or small, to make life better in his or her workplace and community. And like Kalpona, so many of our storytellers were faced with an impossible dilemma, one oft repeated in economic debates: Can workers bargain for better job conditions—including the banning of child labor—without losing their jobs altogether? Can communities speak out against environmental degradation, political corruption, and unfair land acquisition without losing economic investment? And perhaps most importantly, can those individuals most negatively impacted by the global economy ask for change without facing dire consequences? After dozens of interviews, the guiding question of this collection shifted from *Who are the people in the factories?* to *How are workers and communities putting their futures at risk when they demand something better?*

In Kalpona's case, she stands against Bangladeshi officials who are not keen on raising wages, as many of them are factory owners themselves, or have run election campaigns bankrolled by factory owners. The garment industry makes up the bulk of Bangladesh's export economy, and some authorities fear that a higher minimum wage will force foreign corporations to move operations elsewhere to maintain a profit margin. That fear leads politicians and factory owners alike to stifle efforts to better workers' rights and wages. Still, Kalpona sees sharing her story as her best hope for informing consumers and drawing international pressure that could lead to positive change.

Many of our narrators, such as Terri Judd, a miner from Boron, California, and Ana Juárez, the garment worker from Tehuacán, Mexico, were at first reluctant to fight for better working conditions. Only after years of frustration from being left out of the conversation about their work contracts, their compensation, and their day-to-day health and safety did they feel compelled to speak out.

For some narrators, serious injuries from unsafe working conditions have been the catalysts for activism. Hye-kyeong Han of Seoul, South Korea, speaks, in the limited ways allowed by her brain tumor, to other semiconductor workers throughout the world about the dangers of their work—something about which most semiconductor manufacturers have remained silent. Albert Mwanaumo of Chambishi, Zambia, chose to speak out after officials of the company that employed him shot him during a wage protest.

Still, for others, participation in the global market does not present a balance of reward and risk; it represents existential threat. For Sanjay Verma of Bhopal, India, the struggle began when, as an infant, he lost both of his parents and five of his siblings to a devastating chemical leak near his home. Decades later, Bhopal is still plagued by contamination from the leak, and those who survived the disaster or were born after it have continued to suffer debilitating health problems. Sanjay has dedicated his adult life to fighting for adequate compensation for the survivors, demanding a cleanup of the still-contaminated lands around the former chemical factory, and forcing the former executives of the chemical company to face legal responsibility for the accident. Of his activism, Sanjay says, "The people of Bhopal have fought for almost twenty-nine years, and I strongly believe that we'll get justice one day even if we have to fight for another twenty-nine years."

The task of assembling this book has not been simple. It has taken several years to gather and edit this collection of narratives. We've chosen to highlight four broad industrial sectors—the garment industry, agriculture, natural resource extraction, and electronics—because the struggles of workers in these sectors are so representative of the economic battles being staked out across the marketplace every day around the globe. To find storytellers from these economic sectors, the book's team of interviewers, translators, and volunteers from various nongovernmental organizations reached out to dozens of potential interviewees in places including China, Mexico, Guatemala, India, Bangladesh, Zambia, Nigeria, and the United States. The rapid spread of digital communications made our job more manageable in some ways, but even though our world has been drawn tightly together by jet travel, satellites, and the Internet, some distances are still carefully guarded. For many workers, the pressure to remain silent is strong. Some chose not to return our calls and other attempts to make contact. Some potential narrators declined to continue their involvement after an initial interview. Many workers feared retaliation from their employers or even their own governments for speaking out.

For those who chose to speak, the motivation was often simple connection—to potential readers, and to other workers who shared their stories. The scope of this book allows us to show some of the surprising ways the global economy links workers and communities in vastly different parts of the world—sometimes through the complexities of the supply chain, sometimes through common challenges and goals, and sometimes through struggles with the same transnational business entities. The same mining company mired in labor rights battles in Boron, California, arguably fomented civil war in Papua New Guinea decades earlier. The same garment brands now in the news for sourcing their goods through low-paying, unsafe factories in Bangladesh were in the news a decade ago for contracting with low-paying, unsafe factories in Mexico.

The narrators here have diverse perspectives and voices, and no easy conclusions can be drawn from their experiences: "do not buy consumer goods," "unions are always effective," and "foreign corporations are destructive" are not lessons that we—or most of our narrators—hope that readers draw from these stories. Instead, perhaps the most important lesson the majority of our narrators would agree on is the necessity to speak up at all costs, to have all voices in the global economy heard, to have all raised hands counted.

Corinne Goria
2013

EXECUTIVE EDITOR'S NOTE

The narratives in this book are the result of extensive oral history interviews with thirty-one men and women from eleven countries, conducted over the course of more than three years. These recorded interviews—over two hundred hours of audio—were conducted by Corinne Goria and an international team of interviewers, and transcribed by a small corps of dedicated volunteers. Managing Editor Luke Gerwe and I helped the interview team shape and organize those raw transcripts into first-person narratives.

With every Voice of Witness narrative, we aim for a novelistic level of detail and a birth-to-now chronologized scope in order to portray narrators as individuals in all their complexity, rather than as case studies. With *Invisible Hands*, we did not set out to create a comprehensive history of human rights in the global economy. Rather, our goal was to compile a collection of voices and experiences that would offer an accessible, thought-provoking, and ultimately humanizing and intimate window on what can often seem like an abstract topic.

The sixteen narratives featured in this book are a collection of voices that offer revealing and moving accounts of lives closely affected by the global economy. Some of the narratives were chosen because they demonstrate gross violations of workers' rights. Others focus on forced displacement, environmental degradation, and civil war. We've also included narratives that are more "quiet," reflecting on the dehumanizing lack of dignity afforded to people working in menial or physical jobs.

The stories themselves remain faithful to the speakers' words (we seek final narrator approval before publishing their narratives), and have been edited for clarity, coherence, and length. They have been carefully fact-checked, and are supported by various appendices and a glossary included in the back of the book that provide context and some explanation of the history of industrial globalization. We have also included supplementary history "capsules" specific to each narrative.

We thank all the men and women who generously and patiently shared their experiences with us, including those whom we were unable to include in this book. We make available additional interviews, audio-visual materials, and news articles on the Voice of Witness website: voiceofwitness.org. and on the Voice of Witness Tumblr: voiceofwitness.tumblr.com.

We also thank all the frontline human rights defenders working to promote and protect the rights and dignity of these men and women, and without whose cooperation this book would not be possible.

mimi lok
Executive Director
& Executive Editor
Voice of Witness

MAP OF NARRATOR

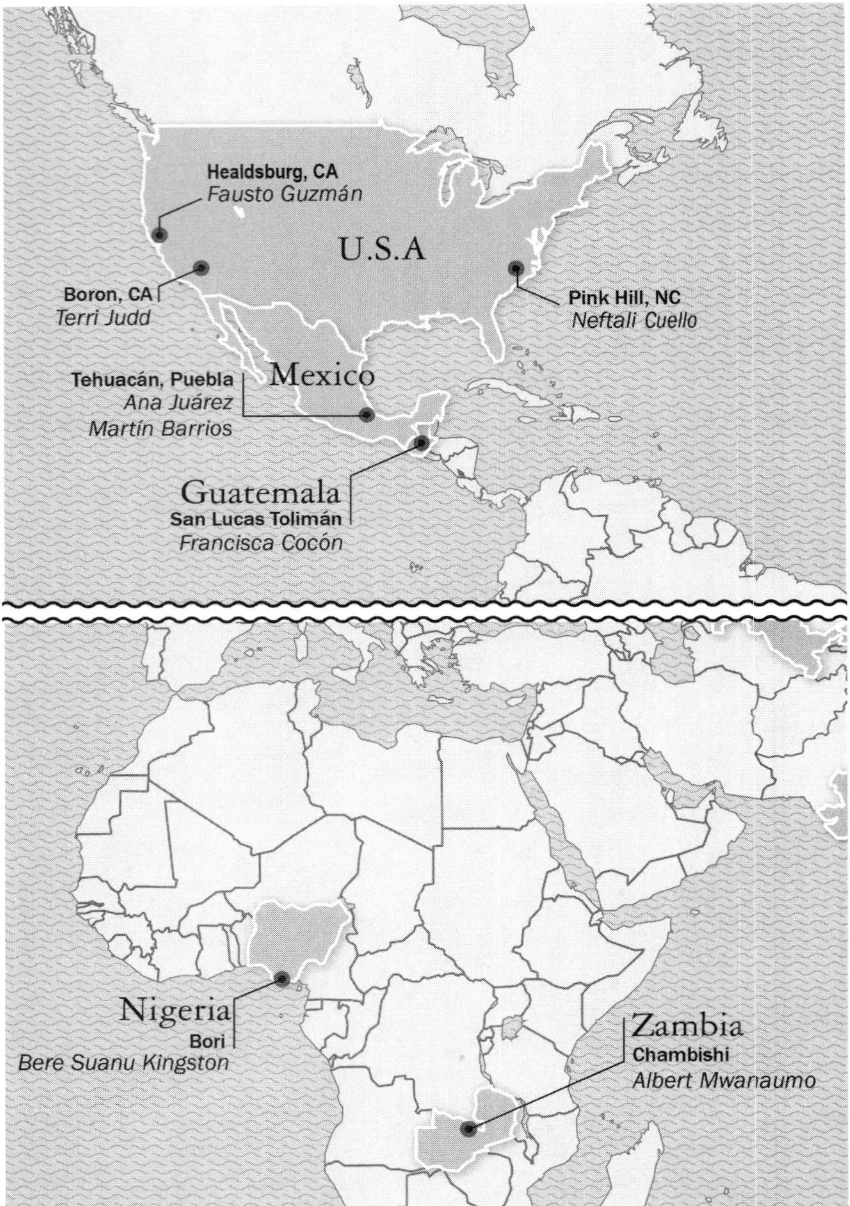

LOCATIONS IN THIS BOOK

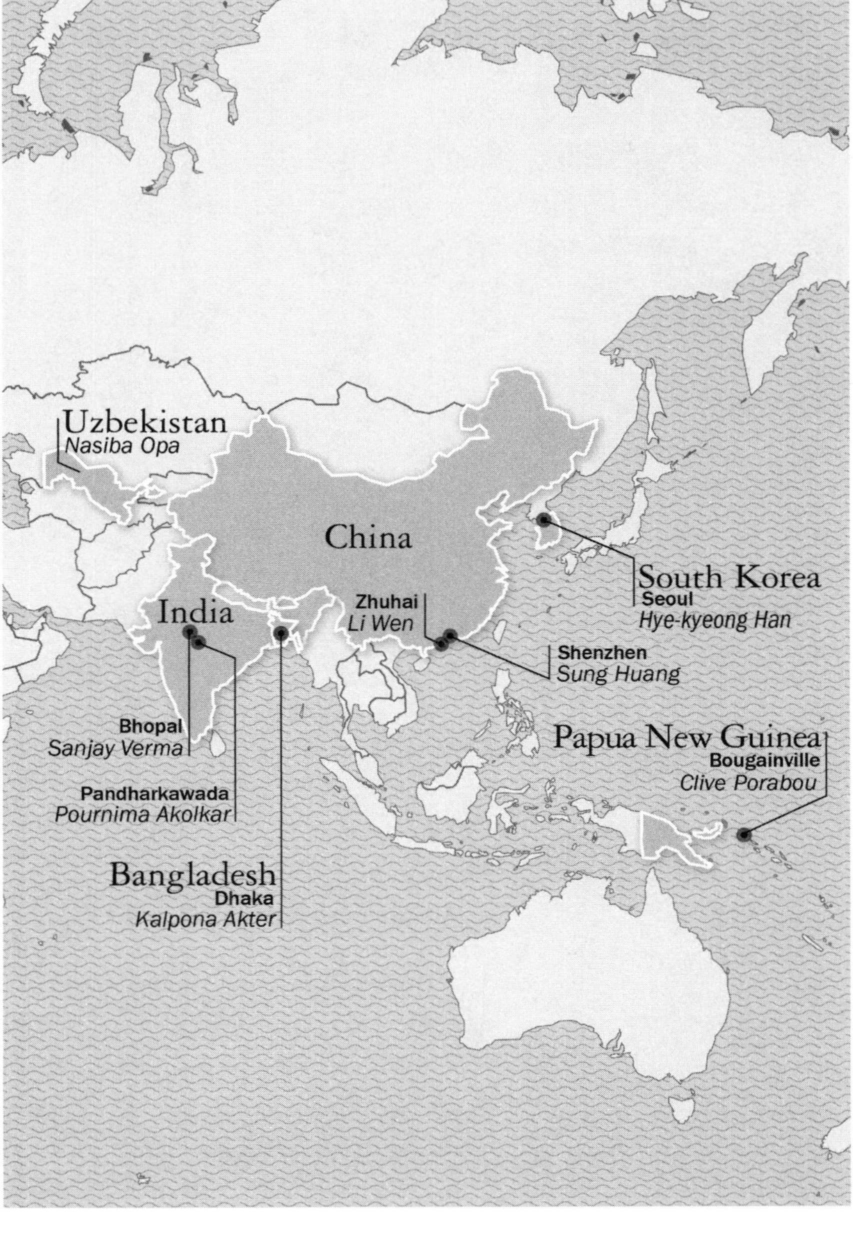

THE GARMENT INDUSTRY

A STRUGGLE FOR FAIR WAGES

The central question for textile manufacturers has always been how to make more product at lower cost. It's an ancient problem, first addressed by an ancient technology: the loom. Basic looms are as old as the Stone Age, and the desire to make them stronger, faster, and more productive has driven innovation for thousands of years. The basic technology of garment manufacture is so old that it's easy for most people to ignore, at least until some quiet new development leads to major societal change.

In 1589 an inventor named William Lee of Nottingham, England, demonstrated a fully mechanized knitting device, the stocking frame, for Queen Elizabeth I. He hoped to obtain a patent on his invention, but Queen Elizabeth refused to grant him one: she immediately sensed that while the invention might make Lee wealthy, it would devastate England's hand-knitting industry, leaving thousands unemployed.

Lee never found success, but his industrial heirs were undeterred. By the eighteenth century, English textile manufacturers had improved on Lee's design and added numerous other innovations capable of making textiles more efficiently as well as handling relatively inexpensive materials such as cotton. Textile innovation made Britain a global economic powerhouse and launched the Industrial Revolution. In the United States, textile production fueled the manufacturing economy of the North and the slave-based agriculture economy of the South; between U.S. independence and the Civil War, cotton was both the South's most important cash crop and the United States's leading export.

Just as textile manufacture has driven innovation, it's also driven the labor movement. The southern United States wasn't the first or last export region to use forced labor to keep prices competitive, and the emancipation of its slaves didn't end labor exploitation. At the start of the eighteenth century, in industrial centers like Manchester, England, children were plucked from orphanages and indentured to work in wool and cotton mills. In 1788, as many as two out of every three workers in Great Britain's cotton mills were children.

More than a hundred years later, conditions had improved only slightly. By the twentieth century, sweatshops featuring dangerous working conditions and wages that kept workers hungry and dependent on their employers were common throughout the industrialized world. The infamous 1911 fire at the Triangle Shirtwaist factory in New York City marked a turning point in workers' rights in the U.S. garment industry. After the high-profile accident at the Greenwich Village factory, in which 146 garment workers, some of them girls as young as fourteen, were burned or jumped to their deaths, the federal and state governments began to enact laws to protect worker safety and require better wages. Following these labor reforms, garment manufacturing moved, for the most part, from New York to the less regulated West Coast. When federal labor regulations passed throughout the twentieth century made production cheaper outside the United States, garment manufacturers moved again, this time to countries like Mexico and China.

Whenever laws or regulations are established to improve safety and stability for garment workers, the garment industry shifts quickly to less regulated, less protected labor pools. China remains the largest exporter of finished apparel to the United States. However, its prominence has been challenged whenever cheaper labor becomes available elsewhere.

In 1994, the United States and Mexico signed the North American Free Trade Agreement, cutting tariffs and making imports into the United States from neighboring Mexico incredibly inexpensive. Through the 1990s, Tehuacán, Mexico, quickly grew to become the world's largest denim producer. Between 1991 and 2001, the population of the town and surrounding suburbs more than doubled from a sleepy 150,000 to 360,000 as hundreds of garment- and textile-manufacturing plants, free from import and export taxes, sprung up rapidly. Throughout the decade, wages remained at poverty levels, with many workers earning less than US$50 a week. Aside from providing unsafe working conditions, the factories also caused devastating environmental damage when chemicals used to treat denim, such as acid wash, were leaked into the region's water supply. By 2001, Mexico had surged ahead of China as the leading apparel exporter to the United States.

As narrators Martín Barrios and Ana Juárez recount, efforts to organize workers to improve their conditions have been stifled or violently quashed by factory owners. Some vocal workers have found themselves blacklisted from factories; others have been beaten and imprisoned. Still, despite efforts to hold down worker wages and production costs, Mexico's prominence in the worldwide garment-manufacturing industry diminished when manufacturers had the opportunity to produce garments even more cheaply in Central America and Asia. By 2011, Mexico had dropped to fifth on the list of garment exporters to the United States while China reclaimed the lead spot. Bangladesh, meanwhile, had surged to the second spot.[1]

In Bangladesh, the landscape for workers' rights is bleak. The garment industry accounts for nearly 80 percent of Bangladesh's exports, with US$19.1 billion in exports between 2011 and 2012. At the same time, the country's wages remain the lowest in the world for garment manufacturers—now nearly US$40 a month, wages were as low as US$23 a month just over a decade ago. With labor costs for China's garment workers going up by as much as 40 percent in the past three years, Bangladesh became an increasingly attractive supplier for clothing retailers, at least until recently. In April 2013, the Rana Plaza industrial park in Dhaka, Bangladesh, collapsed, killing over 1,100 workers and injuring 2,500 more. The tragedy alerted the world to the abysmal working conditions in the Bangladeshi garment industry, though reform to workplace safety legislation in the country has been slow.

Workers' attempts to meaningfully participate in negotiations over workplace conditions in Bangladesh have been met with resistance. Efforts to organize and bargain collectively have been shut down, at times violently, by police, security forces, and hired thugs. Narrator Kalpona Akter, a child garment worker turned labor activist, notes that over 50 percent of the Bangladeshi Parliament is directly involved in the garment industry; many parliamentarians own factories themselves. She sees little hope of reform without intense international pressure. Kalpona has faced harassment and anonymous threats in response to her activism, leading to her wrongful arrest and torture in 2010 along with two of her colleagues, and then to the torture and murder of her colleague Aminul Islam in 2012. Though incidents such as the factory collapse and the murder of Aminul Islam have led to international action against Bangladesh

---

[1] For an analysis of changes in worldwide wage and production trends in the garment industry, see Appendix IV, page 366.

(the U.S. government suspended favorable trade agreements with Bangladesh in 2013), the future is still murky for Kalpona and her fellow garment workers.

If meaningful change is enacted in Bangladesh, clothing companies may start to look elsewhere for cheaper labor. U.S. apparel companies occasionally audit conditions in countries where they source their goods. Still, the bottom line seems to rule as countries willing to offer the cheapest labor pools and the lowest costs of production continue to find willing customers and billions of dollars in investments from companies in the United States and elsewhere. And for garment workers, the struggle for better pay and better rights will continue to be distorted by their political leaders into a choice between a high-risk, low-wage job and no job at all.

KALPONA AKTER

AGE: *38*

OCCUPATION: *Former garment worker, labor organizer*

BIRTHPLACE: *Chandpur, Bangladesh*

INTERVIEWED IN: *Los Angeles, California*

We first interview Kalpona Akter in Los Angeles after she speaks to the local branch of the AFL-CIO.[1] *At the panel discussion, workers from different points along the supply chain for a major U.S. apparel retailer—from the tailors who sew the clothes abroad to the warehouse workers who supply them to stores—compare stories of forced overtime, uncompensated injuries, and retaliation for bringing grievances to management. When it's Kalpona's turn to speak, she describes her evolution from twelve-year-old seamstress to activist to prisoner. She explains that in Bangladesh, garment workers often enter the factories as children, facing superhuman quotas for piecework, harassment and physical abuse from supervisors, and a minimum wage*

---

[1] The American Federation of Labor and Congress of Industrial Organizations is the largest federation of unions in the United States, made up of over fifty-six national and international unions from dozens of industries. In all, the AFL-CIO represents over twelve million workers both in the United States and abroad.

that comes out to about 20 cents per hour, by far the lowest of any significant garment-producing nation.[2] *Workers who try to organize face intimidation not only from their employers but also from politicians who opine that they should be grateful to have work at all, regardless of the toll on their bodies and spirits.*

Bangladesh has nearly half the population of the United States, yet geographically, it's smaller than the state of Florida. As densely populated as it is, the country still has a largely agricultural economy and, with a per capita income of under US$2,000 per year, is one of the poorest countries in Asia. Starting in the 1990s, however, garment production boomed as international clothing retailers began to take advantage of the country's inexpensive labor supply and the Bangladeshi government encouraged investment with tax incentives. Today, Bangladesh is second to China as a leading exporter of apparel. Around four million garment workers produce US$20 billion worth of clothing for export a year; this figure represents the vast majority of the country's total export earnings. Meanwhile, the garment workers themselves—mostly women—struggle to survive as wages decline compared to the cost of living, and abysmal working conditions lead to workplace disasters such as the Rana Plaza factory collapse in April 2013.[3] *For Kalpona and fellow labor activists, speaking out is not just a matter of achieving more favorable working conditions—it's a matter of life and death.*

AS A CHILD, I WAS SO NAUGHTY

When I was around six and in my second year of school, my family moved from Chandpur to Dhaka, which is the capital of Bangladesh.[4] My first memory of Dhaka is of waiting with my four-year-old brother for my dad

---

[2] This figure is based on the Bangladeshi minimum wage rate of 3,000 taka per month from November 2010 to October 2013.

[3] For more on the Rana Plaza collapse, see Appendix III, page 353.

[4] Chandpur is a city of 2.4 million located sixty miles southeast of Dhaka, the capital of Bangladesh. The Dhaka metropolitan area has a population of over fifteen million.

to come home from work in the evening. He worked as a construction contractor in the area around our home in Mohammadpur,[5] and he used to bring home treats after work. He might bring us sugarcane, or it could be cookies, chocolates, or some fruit. He would bring home something for us every night. Besides my brother, I had a sister as well at that time, but she was only a year old and still nursing.

As a child, I was so naughty. I used to talk back to my mom all the time, and I irritated her with a lot of questions. "Hey Mom—why is Dad late?" "Hey Mom—why is the sky blue?" "Hey Mom—why isn't it sunny? Why is it raining?" When she was cooking, I'd say, "I want to see."

My mother used to cook all the kinds of traditional food we have in Bangladesh: dahl, fish, she could do everything. I remember that we had an oven but we didn't have gas—it was a wood oven. We'd collect wood outside our house or buy it at market.

During that time our family had our own tin-roofed house, which is a common kind of house in Bangladesh. We had three bedrooms, two balconies. At the tin-roofed house, we had a backyard and front garden. We had guava and mango trees, and my mom also used to grow vegetables in the garden.

But we were forced to sell our house at a low price to a local politician. It was in a nice area of the city, and the politician put a lot of pressure on my dad to sell it. I don't know too many of the details. Later I tried to speak to my dad many times about the nice house, but he didn't want to talk about it. We bought a smaller house without as much outdoor space. My father changed parties and political views after that, though. He was really hurt and felt he'd been cheated.

I don't remember exactly when we lost our house, but I was still in

---

[5] Mohammadpur is a neighborhood in Dhaka that was first developed in the 1950s and experienced a construction boom in the eighties and nineties.

primary school. I loved school. There we learned Bangla, basic English, and math. Bangla is our native language. There was a small playground at this school where I would go and run around with my friends. Near the school playground, there was a bazaar, so sometimes my mom or dad would give me some money to have a snack or something cool to drink. I would buy fruits, ice cream, or some sour pickles—I was eating everything.

In Bangladesh we go to primary school until grade five, and then we go to high school. I passed the primary school and was put into grade six, at the high school. In high school up to the ninth grade, we studied Bangla, English, math, social science, and then science and religion. Religion was the last subject I studied. Every religion had its own class. So if you were Hindu, you'd study Hinduism. Muslims, they had Islam.[6] All the students had other classes together, but we would split up for religion classes. We didn't pray much at home, and at the time, girls and women were not allowed in the mosque. So religion class was where I'd learn about the life of the Prophet and how to pray. We didn't have any choice of which subjects we studied, but I can remember that my favorite subject was science. I believe that I was one of the best students in my high school.

WHATEVER MONEY MY MOM HAD, IT JUST RAN OUT WITHIN A MONTH

Many people were building houses in Dhaka in the late 1980s, and my dad was a successful general contractor, or middle man—people would hire him to build the house, and then he would subcontract or hire others

[6] The population of Bangladesh is nearly 90 percent Muslim and 9 percent Hindu. Though the country is predominantly Muslim, principles of secular government were written into the original constitution in 1972.

to complete the smaller jobs on the project. So he would often have a lot of money on him, because people would pay him the whole sum for the project and he would use that fund to pay other workers.

I have a cousin who was living with us and was also working with my dad. My dad started to entrust my cousin with the finances for the business. My dad would put the money in a bank account, and then my cousin could draw on it when he needed to pay subcontractors or other workers.

One day in 1988, just after I had turned twelve, my cousin took all the money my dad had entrusted him with and just disappeared. My family didn't hear anything from him for a couple of months—he was just gone. And then, one day, he showed up again. He didn't say he took the money, but he didn't deny it either. He just didn't take responsibility.

After the theft, my dad suffered. He had two strokes within two months of each other, starting about a week or two after my parents learned that the money had been stolen. One stroke after the other. The whole right side of my father's body was disabled after the strokes, and he couldn't speak for many years. He had to be admitted into the hospital, and my mom really had a very difficult time during his illness. She had to pay all the hospital bills because, as far as I remember, we really didn't have health-care insurance or a health-care system in Dhaka back then. In any case, my mother had to find a way to pay all the medical bills herself. My father was back and forth to the hospital for maybe six months.

Whatever money my mom had, it just ran out within a month after my father's strokes. So then she had to sell our house. We moved to a rental house. The rental house had about six rooms occupied by three families. We had two rooms to ourselves, but we had a shared kitchen and a shared toilet and shower. It was a disaster. There were maybe eighteen people total living in this small house. The house had a small balcony off of our rooms, and that is where my father stayed mostly while he was recovering.

He'd sleep on a bed out on the balcony. It was too hot inside, and we didn't even have a fan.

There was a lot of tension in our family at that time. My dad couldn't talk. He had lost use of one side of his body. He couldn't leave the bed, or even move. Within six months, we ran out of all the money we'd received from selling the house and all the other savings my parents had. We didn't have anything.

My mom decided to go to my father's other siblings to seek justice, or to have my cousin come and give us back the money he stole. But my cousin never came to our home at all. He refused to take responsibility. And it turned out that none of the other siblings wanted to help us. No one was helping us. There were six of us at home, or seven, after my littlest sister was born. We barely had enough food at home for my younger sisters and brother. And my dad needed to have his medicine.

My mom had never worked before—she had always been a housewife and we'd had a happy family. But because of everything that was happening, my mom decided she had to get a job. At the same time, Mom asked me whether I thought I should also work. I was twelve years old. And, because I saw what was going on in the family, I said, "Yeah, I want to work. But how I can get a job, Mom?" I didn't want to quit school since I was doing well. I was even class captain for many months, but I felt I had to help my mother and father if I could.

There were some garment workers who used to live next to our house whom we'd known for a long time. Mom spoke to some of them, and they said that they would speak to the midlevel management at their factory to see if I could get a job. About a week later, our neighbors came and told me that they could get me a job. So one day I went to school and the next day I went to the factory.

MY FRIENDS ARE AT SCHOOL, BUT I'M STUCK WORKING HERE

I didn't tell anyone that I'd left school. They began to worry after about two weeks, though. My teachers showed up at my house. They said that they wanted to give me some sort of scholarship to keep my studies going. But my mom said, "How can she go to school? There are still four other kids. They don't have any food. Kalpona has decided to work." My teachers kept insisting then that I should stay in school, that I should not work, but, you know, my mother had no other choice.

So I didn't go back to school. I went into the factory, and my mom did too. She got a job in a factory far from our house. It was about ten kilometers away from our home. But I got a job in a factory close to home, maybe one kilometer away. I could walk there.

The very first day I went to work in the factory—oh my gosh—it was a crazy experience. There was so much noise, more noise than I had ever heard before, and people were shouting all over the place. Midlevel supervisors were yelling at the workers all the time. We had two buildings in the factory and around 1,500 workers all together, and everything just seemed like chaos to me at first.

Every day, I'd walk to the factory along with my neighbors who had helped me get the factory job. The supervisors at the factory first gave me a job cutting the belt loops in pants. The loops were made of four or more layers of fabric. I had to scissor the four-layered fabric, and it was tough. When I cut the fabric layers, the scissors made my fingers and hands hurt. I must have cut more than a thousand a day. Except for a couple of breaks to eat, I'd be cutting nonstop for fourteen hours a day, from eight in the morning until ten at night.

After my first couple of days, it was like my skin had been rubbed away. When my hands started to bleed, I would bind them with some pieces of fabric from the production floor. It was unhygienic, but I had to protect my hands so I could keep working. You can see these black marks on my hands. The very first day I hurt these fingers. These scars I got from that scissoring. I stayed on the belt loops for four or five weeks, and then moved on to a different job with a different order of clothing.

It was painful for me to go to work because my factory and my old school were so close. We would often go to the rooftop of the factory to have our lunches, and from there I could see the playground in my school, and I could also see my friends playing. I mean, almost every day during the lunch hour I would cry, because I thought, *My friends are studying there at school, but I'm stuck working here.* But I also had a brother and sisters. And when I went home and saw them, saw their faces, it would remind me that I had responsibilities that I needed to take care of.

IT WAS A VERY SAD PART OF MY LIFE

When my mom and I started working at the factories, my mom would wake up early to cook something like rice, dahl, or vegetables for the whole family—that was food for the whole day. While we were at work, my brother, who was ten at the time, would take care of my youngest sister, who was a newborn baby, my other two sisters, and my dad, who was still sick from the stroke. Sometimes my mother and I used to take food with us to the factory; sometimes we wouldn't, because we didn't enough food to take with us. Sometimes we would work the whole day without any food. And sometimes when I came home from work, I would see there was no food at home either, so that meant that my mom and I wouldn't eat for two days.

It hurts sometimes, not having food. It makes you weak. But when you see that your younger siblings do not even have food, you don't have any choice. My brother would not even eat the food we left for all of them in the morning. He would save this food for the two youngest and for my dad, because the two youngest used to ask for food all the time, so my brother would save his portion for them. So he was like a dad and a mom to them—he was raising them all by himself. He was ten years old.

After five or six months working at the factory, my mom got sick. She was dehydrated, malnourished, and the doctor said there was something wrong with her kidneys. She was so dehydrated that she couldn't breastfeed my baby sister. She had a pain in her kidneys and it became impossible for her to work.

After she quit the job at the factory, she started feeling better. So we decided that instead of my mom, my brother would go to the factory with me. Around this time I also changed to another factory. The new factory was farther away, but I could make a little more money there. At the old factory, I could get maybe 240 taka in base salary per month, and maybe 400 to 450 taka per month after overtime.[7] At the new factory, I could make a base salary of 300 taka per month and up to 500 taka per month with overtime, because I used to do the night shift as well.[8] If I made 500 taka a month, I could pay for much of our rent——which was a little under 500 taka a month—but not for food. That is why we decided my brother should work at the factory as well. So I took my brother into this new factory and convinced my supervisor to give him a job. My brother got a job as a sewing-machine helper and started working in the building next to me.

There were other children working in the factories, too. The youngest child I saw in the new factory was a boy about eight years old. I think during that time I had been promoted to sewing-machine operator, and the eight-year-old was my helper. That eight-year-old boy used to cut the

---

[7] In 1994, 240 taka = approximately US$3.80. 400 to 450 taka = approximately US$7.

[8] In 1994, 300 taka = approximately US$4.75. 500 taka = approximately US$7.90.

threads and pile up the clothes that I sewed. And I can remember he used to come in the morning and say, "Oh sister, I'm so sleepy." He was a young kid, so you can imagine.

Our factory work used to start at eight, so my brother and I needed to get out from the house at something like six thirty or a quarter to seven. Then we'd walk about one kilometer to get the bus to the factory area, and then we'd walk about a half kilometer to get into the factory. And that is what we would do for three or four years, the same routine every week.

The factory is not far from where I live today. The site still exists and some of the buildings are still there. So I can see the factory every day, twice a day sometimes. When I see it now, sometimes I laugh. Sometimes it gives me pain. Sometimes it gives me lots of things to remember. It was in this second factory, too, that I met my future husband.[9]

It must have been around 1991 or '92. He was in the embroidery section and he was a relative of the factory owner—I think a cousin or second cousin—so he'd gotten the job in a very easy way. I don't remember how I met him, maybe when I was on the bus to the factory. Or while going into the factory or coming out, I saw him. I was seventeen years old when we got married in 1993 and I moved in with him and his family. I was so young.

If I want to, I can remember that part of my life, but it's really painful for me. It was a very sad part of my life when I met him. The marriage was troubled from the start, and the factory workers were just beginning our fight at the same time.

WE REALLY GOT ANGRY

I remember how the trouble started at the factory. Basically we were working sixteen days in a row during Ramadan in 1993, right before

---

[9] Kalpona has asked us not to name her husband or use a pseudonym.

Eid ul-Fitr, the breaking of the fast of Ramadan.[10] We were working day and night, and the Muslims in the factory were fasting for Ramadan. We would fast over the day and break the fast in the factory with little snacks, and we'd eat our dinner after sunset with the little money that the factory provided. And then working the whole night and getting food at around three a.m., before fasting again after sunrise.

When we worked overnight, we might work ten hours of overtime, and the custom was that the factory would give us an extra five hours of bonus pay. In 1993, after we'd already done sixteen days of overnight work, management announced they weren't giving out any bonus pay for overtime that year. They said they could not afford it.

And as I mentioned, it was before Eid, so when we were working those extra hours, we were planning to have the bonus money for the feast at the end of Ramadan. We really got angry. We didn't have much of an idea about labor law or our rights as workers, but some of the senior workers said to us, "We will not work ten hours overtime without the bonus. We will strike until they pay us the amount they owe us." I agreed with them.

I was one of the initiators of the strike. We had 1,500 workers in two units at the factory, so among the 1,500, it was 93 of us who called for a strike until the factory agreed to pay the bonus.

When I returned home the day we decided to strike, my husband had heard that I was involved, and he beat me. He was related to the factory owners, so he didn't support the idea of a strike. At the time, I was feeling very helpless. Very helpless. But the next day, the day of the strike, I told some of the other ninety-three who were protesting, and they said that

---

[10] For the month of Ramadan, observant Muslims fast from dawn until sunset every day. Eid ul-Fitr is a major feast marking the end of Ramadan and traditionally includes lavish meals and charitable giving. Depending on local tradition, the holiday may last from one to three days. In 1993, Ramadan began in February.

they understood and would always support me, that they wanted me to always stand with them, and that I was one of the courageous ones. We continued with the strike, and after a single day the management agreed to give us the bonus money. But they made it clear that they would not pay the same bonus in the future, and we agreed. At the time, we didn't have any idea about the law.

After the strike, we factory workers went on holiday for Eid. After holiday finished, when we came back, we learned that twenty of my co-workers who had demanded the bonus money had been fired. The twenty fired workers were the ones the factory considered the main instigators of the strike.

The organizers decided they would not give up, and they started to look for an organization that could help them. And they found Solidarity Center. Solidarity Center is an international wing of AFL-CIO, the big U.S. union. The full name is American Center for International Labor Solidarity, but during those days, the branch we worked with was known as AAFLI: Asian American Free Labor Institute.[11]

The Solidarity Center had already begun helping a group of workers to form an independent union for garment workers, the BIGUF, or Bangladesh Independent Garment Workers Union Federation. The new garment worker reps met with some of our leaders and said they would help us to sue the factory owner for retaliation. And at the same time, they said they had awareness classes where my co-workers could go and learn about labor law, and then they could better take on their management. So some of my senior colleagues, they went to the law classes and they

---

[11] The Solidarity Center, or American Center for International Labor Solidarity, was launched by the AFL-CIO in 1997. Its purpose was to help develop union representation for workers in developing economies, and it replaced earlier, regional AFL-CIO union-development organizations such as the Asian American Free Labor Institute (founded in 1968).

found it really interesting. They came to work and encouraged some of us interested in fighting back to go to the classes.

A SECOND BIRTH

It was around the end of 1993, and I was seventeen. I wasn't allowed to go anywhere without my husband, or I had to at least tell him where I was going. He was a very controlling man, so I didn't tell him the truth when I went to the labor classes at the Solidarity Center.

When I learned about labor law and rights, it was like a second birth for me. I thought, *Wow, we are working in hell.* So then I decided to commit to organizing. When I came home in the evening, my husband asked me where I had been. I told him the truth then, and he asked me, "Why have you been there? Did you get my permission?" I said, "No, I didn't," and so he beat me. But I was determined that I would not take a step backward.

So the next day, after realizing that there were all of these laws that were covering workers' rights in the factory, during the lunch break, I started telling my co-workers that I had gone to the Solidarity Center and had learned a lot. And I brought some of their booklets with me to the factory. It was risky, but I had to do it.

Some of us started to meet in a small room in a co-worker's house, which was close to my house. And we were also going to meetings sponsored by Solidarity Center for BIGUF. I had back-and-forth communication between BIGUF and the workers at my factory. The center was giving me guidelines for how I should organize. So I was really doing the organizing part and persuading our workers to sign the union application.

My husband was an anti-union guy. I didn't listen to him. But once he discovered the signed union forms that I had gathered from my colleagues, he tried to take them and give them to the factory owner. So then I went to some of the other union members working at the factory that day, some of the local people who were very close to my husband. I explained to them what happened. And they ran up behind him as he was taking the forms to the factory owner and got the documents from him and told him not to do that.

I was beaten by him because of my involvement with the union, because I was helping to organize workers in his cousin's factory. Also, when I tried to give some of my wages to my family, he beat me because he wanted me to give all my money to him, whatever I earned. So he kept me from helping my family, even though my family was so needy during that time. They needed my support, but I couldn't help.

My husband had control of my life. But I felt like I couldn't leave him because of cultural expectations. If I got divorced or left him, it would be bad for my younger sisters. I mean socially, it would look bad. The culture expects that if the eldest sister got divorced, then she must not be from a good family, and no one would want to marry any other sisters. So I had to tolerate my husband.

We were together for about nine months and then we had something like a settlement: a partial separation. We were staying in the same house, but in two separate bedrooms. I started sharing a room with his sister. And I was with him for a couple more years like that.

"IF YOU WANT TO FIRE ME, YOU HAVE TO TELL ME THE REASON"

I was eventually fired because of my work helping to form BIGUF. It happened in 1995. Some of my co-workers, I think they whispered about me, or maybe my husband told the factory bosses about my organizing. However they found out, they came to know that I was involved in forming a union. The bosses called me into the office several times to indirectly threaten me, and one time, I was suspended for twenty days without any reason.

Finally, one morning just after I had started my work for the day, a co-worker approached me and let me know I had been called to the office. I went to the office room and the bosses told me I was fired. But they weren't just sending me home. They were offering me a good amount of money to leave. I don't know how much it was, but it was a big bundle right there in the office. And they said, "You're fired, you can take this money and go." And I said, "I will not take any money. If you want to fire me, you have to tell me the reason." And they said that they could terminate my employment anytime they wanted. And I said, "I know that you have the right to fire me, but you have to tell me why I'm being terminated."

The company made a lot of drama. They wouldn't state officially why I'd been fired. I sued them in the labor court. My husband was angry. Many of our mutual co-workers supported me, though, so he was careful not to come out too strongly against me. But he let me know that he would not support me, and he would not spend any money to take the case to court, and he would not allow me to spend any of my money on the case. Instead, I got legal support through BIGUF.

During that time, my dad still couldn't walk much at all, but he got his voice back. So I explained to him, "I've lost my job and some difficult things are happening with my husband, and I need you to help me out." But my mom wouldn't agree with a separation or divorce because it would make it hard for my other sisters to marry. I hadn't told my mom that my husband was beating me, because I didn't want it to hurt her. So later I had to tell her that this was happening. I was like his slave, I told her. So then my dad said, "Okay. Move out."

So I moved to my parents' house. Six months after that, I divorced my husband. I lived with my parents and I would go out looking for work. I had trouble getting work in other factories, because I had been blacklisted. I found work in two other garment factories, but I was quickly fired from both of those jobs. The owners of the factory I was suing, they informed those factory owners who hired me that I had sued them in the labor court. The bosses at one factory, they told me that I could continue my job at that factory if I withdrew my case against my previous factory owner, and I said no. So they fired me.

The BIGUF gained official union status in 1997, around the time I was being blacklisted, and so I checked in at the new BIGUF union office. I told them what was happening to me, and that I couldn't get a job anywhere. So at first they appointed me as an intern organizer for three months. And then they appointed me as a full-timer with the union up to 1999. That's when my court case was dropped, and the judge ruled that the company that had fired me owed me only my severance pay.

When I was working full-time at BIGUF, my task was to organize workers door-to-door. In the mornings before factory shifts started and in the afternoons during the factories' lunch breaks, I used to go to the areas outside the factories to organize workers, to tell them there's an organization where they can come and learn the law and their rights. And in the evenings, I had to do house visits, to go to the workers' houses and speak to them there. And on Fridays there were awareness-raising classes. During those classes, I had to give a lecture about basic law and rights, what I had learned coming to BIGUF, and my life before I joined them. My task was to educate workers.

ACTIVISM WAS IN MY BLOOD. I COULDN'T HELP MYSELF.

In '99, I quit the BIGUF. The BIGUF would work only for garment workers; many other kinds of workers used to come to our union office to get support, but we couldn't help them. It was frustrating not to be able to help. So I quit, and I decided I wouldn't work for labor rights anymore.

I'd had a bad experience: I'd lost my court case, I couldn't find work, and I couldn't help a lot of people who needed help. So I thought I would do something else, like set up a small shop selling food or other little things close to my house. I thought, *I can survive with that.*

But you know, activism was in my blood. I couldn't help myself. Many workers knew my face, they had my contact info. The workers used to call me and ask for help, and I couldn't help them because I wasn't with a union anymore. Then, around the end of '99, one of my former union colleagues, Babul Akhter, contacted me. He said, "Let's do something ourselves!" So Babul and I started our own program that year through sponsorship of the international Solidarity Center, and we called it the Bangladesh Center for Worker Solidarity, or BCWS. The formal launch of the BCWS was in August 2000. I was about twenty-two years old.

We got funding from the AFL-CIO and organizations like the International Labor Rights Forum.[12] Our whole philosophy was that our organization was going to be a long-term commitment to all workers. And we were going to work in an innovative way. If you talked about unions in Bangladesh, the factory owners would say, "Oh, unions are evil! They destroy everything." We wanted to change those perceptions, so that not just the workers but everyone else would have respect for unions and for workers' rights. Our focus was on providing information, so we made posters and pamphlets and met with workers to inform them about their labor rights. We wanted to train female garment workers to form their own organizations, to speak out themselves about their rights. So that was the beginning of the BCWS. We were pretty successful for the next few years. I think the BCWS was doing a great job achieving our goal of raising workers' awareness about law and rights, helping them to handle

---

[12] The International Labor Rights Forum is an international non-profit coalition of human rights organizations, academics, and faith-based communities that seek to address labor rights concerns in the developing world. For more information, visit www.laborrights.org.

their grievances, giving them legal service, legal support. Helping them to grow their leadership capacity. Giving them educational programs, helping working mothers get educations. So that was really successful in the following years, after our formation.

We also wanted to form a kind of federation that could be a national voice for the workers, more of an actual union rather than just a source of information about unions and labor rights. So in 2003, we were able to do that. I helped found the Bangladesh Garment and Industrial Workers Federation, of which Babul is the president. The two organizations work out of the same office, but have different functions. BCWS is an NGO and our mission is educating workers about their rights, and BGIWF is a union federation that has the legal power to help workers negotiate with their employers and assist other unions.

During this time I was still living with my family. Luckily, even though I had been divorced, two of my little sisters got married. We remained very close after they moved out and started having children. My younger brother joined me in helping to grow BCWS as well; he's been a big source of support. My parents, too—my family has stuck by me through everything I've faced.

AT THE BCWS, WE DID NOT SUPPORT VIOLENCE

In 2006, there was a big uprising of workers across the country. The major issue, among other issues, was that there was a big gap between workers' wages and the cost of living in Bangladesh. The minimum wage of 950 taka per month was set in 1994. And factories weren't even complying with that standard.[13]

---

[13] In 1994, 950 taka = US$18.

At the BCWS, our position was to support the workers and help amplify their voices on issues like a new minimum wage. During the uprising, some property was vandalized and damaged across the country. There was a lot of violence between political parties leading up to national elections as well. At the BCWS, we did not support violence and damage to property. None of us had any prior idea about this movement, or this uprising. It wasn't planned, it just happened. But the uprising had an impact. Afterward, the minimum wage was raised and better enforced.[14]

But it was also after that 2006 uprising that Babul and I began to feel that the government had taken notice of the BCWS. They started to follow our work around that time. They would visit our offices, follow our activities, and seemed to be watching us closely.

Worker associations in Bangladesh such as Kalpona's BCWS and BGIWF made gains throughout the early 2000s, including the legalization of worker association groups within free trade export-processing zones and updates to minimum wage and worker safety laws.[15] *In 2006, a string of violent confrontations between political parties and a series of labor strikes effectively halted the nation's economy. President Iajuddin Ahmed declared a state of emergency and turned the government over to a military-run caretaker regime. The emergency resolution also suspended the right to assembly and granted police the power to arbitrarily detain citizens for any length of time. Though elections would be held again in 2008, abuses by police, including arbitrary detentions, continued.*

---

[14] In 2007, minimum wage in Bangladesh was set at 1,663 taka a month (approximately US$23 per month) and then raised again in July 2010 to nearly 3,000 taka a month (approximately US$43 per month at the time of the wage hike, but devalued to below US$40 per month by early 2014). For more information on wages in the garment industry, see Appendix IV, page 366.

[15] Export-processing zones are designated geographical areas without export tariffs or taxes. See glossary, page 348.

HIS TOES HAD BEEN BROKEN

In April 2010, we started hearing serious threats. Babul was approached by an NSI agent who told him that we needed to stop talking about labor rights with workers or the agency would take strong action against us.[16] Then, in June 2010, the Bangladeshi government decided to revoke BCWS's NGO status registration. This was a big deal, because if we wanted to have foreign funds to run our programs or activities such as educating workers, we had to have registration with Bangladesh's NGO Affairs Bureau. So all of the backing that we got from international organizations like the AFL-CIO was no longer legally available to us. The government stated that our registration had been revoked because we were doing antistate activity—which was not true. And they didn't give any proof or any evidence of that. We weren't sure what kind of work we were still legally allowed to do since our license was revoked, but we were meeting at the offices anyway. Now we no longer had any funding, and we were certain then that there was a campaign being waged against us.

And that's when we had our first confrontation with the NSI. It started when the chief inspector of factories with the Labor Ministry, someone we had worked with before to resolve worker conflicts, called us to come help settle a dispute between striking workers and their company, which was called Envoy. I reminded him of our registration issues and asked that he make sure we wouldn't have trouble with the government if we participated, and he agreed.

We sent one of our colleagues, Aminul Islam, to gather a group of Envoy workers as representatives to bring to the meeting at the Envoy offices. Aminul was an excellent negotiator and one of the most effective

---

[16] The NSI is the National Security Intelligence agency of Bangladesh.

members of our staff at BCWS and BGIWF. He'd been with us since 2006. He'd been a worker in a garment factory as well, just like me and Babul, and he had been quite successful organizing in some of the factories in Ashulia, a big industrial zone just outside Dhaka.

So Aminul was able to gather about eighteen workers and headed off to the meeting. Babul and I were trying to get there as well, though we were running a bit behind Aminul. We were on our way to the meeting when we got a call. Another one of our colleagues who had arrived at the meeting said that men had stormed in and blindfolded Aminul and taken him off just after they'd arrived. Our colleague who was telling us this had gotten away himself, but he said that there were men waiting for us and that we shouldn't come.

We were shocked. First we called the chief inspector and demanded to know what had happened. We were really yelling at him, but he wouldn't tell us about Aminul or promise to protect us. He wouldn't say anything, really. Then we called every police force and security agency contact we had, but nobody would tell us anything about Aminul.

Early the next morning, June 17, another BCWS colleague got a call. It was Aminul. He was crying, terrified. He said he'd been picked up by the NSI and driven north of the city where he was interrogated and beaten. The NSI officers had asked him things like: Why did you stop the work at the garment factories? Who ordered you to stop the work? Why? Tell us his name. Tell us if Babul asked you to stop the work at factories. The persons who told you to stop the work at factories should be punished. If you just say that Babul and Kalpona asked you to stop the work at the factories we will set you free. We will arrest them in a moment and take them here.

Aminul had managed to escape in the middle of the night when they'd let him out of their vehicle so he could pee. We were able to get Aminul to a safe place and get him medical attention, but he was badly wounded. His toes had been broken and he had a lot of internal hemorrhaging from being struck with a stick across his back and head. He told us the NSI had tried to get him to sign confessions and implicate me and Babul in all sorts of antistate activities like inciting riots. We knew we were being closely watched, but eventually we got Aminul back to his home so he could be with his family.

WHEN THEY ARRESTED ME, MY HEAD WAS BLANK

Then the next trouble started with a demonstration in Dhaka on July 30, 2010, in which there was vandalism and property damage. The issue at the time was that the government was set to raise the minimum wage again, and on July 30 it was announced that the minimum wage would be raised to 3,000 taka a month.[17] Many worker advocacy groups had advocated for much more than that, because inflation was making the cost of living much higher very rapidly. So there were demonstrations on July 30 protesting the new minimum, and some vandalism took place five kilometers away from our main office. But we at BCWS weren't involved. I was at a staff meeting thirty-five kilometers away, and I didn't know anything about the incident.

While I was at the staff meeting, I heard about the demonstration and vandalism through a U.S. embassy officer that I knew. He was on vacation in Malaysia, but he texted me, and he said that there was something on television about an uprising going around the factories in Dhaka. And he wanted to know whether we were safe or not. So I started checking in with some people, and I called one person I know in the Dhaka office. He said he and some other colleagues were in the office and had locked the doors,

---

[17] In 2010, 3,000 taka = US$43.

and that they were all safe.

After that, I went home. In the middle of the night, maybe around midnight, Babul called me and said that in the newspaper there was a story about the demonstration. The story mentioned that six criminal cases had been filed, and our names were there. The story claimed that our organization had helped start the unrest. And I said, "What's going on, it's crap! We weren't there." I was a target, Babul was a target, and so was Aminul, as well as a few organizers from other unions. They were charging us with things like inciting riots and using explosives. Very serious charges.

So the next day, a Saturday, we started calling my colleagues and our lawyers and informing them about what was happening. We also started to talk to those other federation leaders who had been accused in similar cases.

Soon the police started looking for me and began to bother my sisters and their husbands, threatening and harassing them to try to find where I was. That's when Babul and I went into hiding. We were able to stay in a safe place we'd set up in some unused BCWS offices until August 13, when the police finally found us. They stormed in early that morning. It was still dark. When they arrested me, my head was blank. I couldn't understand what was going on. I wasn't sure what to do. They shined flashlights in our faces, cuffed us, and took us to the police station.

Babul was sent to a cell. There was no cell for females so I was told to sit on the floor in a tiny, dirty office room. They forced me to sit squeezed behind a desk and a wall. The two-by-four-foot space was so small I couldn't even lie down. That's where they kept me sitting, cramped for seven days. I couldn't sleep the whole time. I would lean against the wall and maybe nod off at moments, but I could never fall asleep fully. The whole experience was so scary. During this time, the police would take me out of the space only for interrogation. They would interrogate me at any time of day for two, three hours. The longest session was something like eighteen hours in a row.

They would ask the same few questions over and over. Sometimes just to me or just to Babul, sometimes to both of us together. They would ask questions like: Who funded us? Was there any international organization or any specific country who was giving us funding to destroy the garment industry of Bangladesh? Who were the other organizations we worked with? Why did we start the recent unrest?

When we stated that we hadn't anything to do with the incident in July, they'd say, "Then tell us who is responsible, we have to bring them in." They wanted us to talk about our families, our international connections, basically tell them about everyone we knew or had ever worked with. There were maybe a dozen interrogators who would take turns asking Babul and me the same questions over and over, thousands of times.

After a week of interrogation, we were brought to the courthouse for our initial hearing. We were charged with vandalism, arson, and inciting riots. I faced seven charges and Babul faced eight. After that, I was sent to central jail for another three weeks.

The central jail was like something from a century ago, except there was electricity, but we actually couldn't turn the lights off at night. I was with about 130 other prisoners. We could take showers only rarely, and when we did it was in an open courtyard in full view of everyone, including male prisoners held in another part of the same facility.

A couple of days after I was sent to central jail, my sisters brought their children for a visit. By this time I had a nephew who was about twelve and my nieces were about nine and five. The prisoners were allowed visits from family once a week, and we all gathered in a big room that was separated in the middle by two nets a couple of feet apart. It was loud, and the only way we could hear each other was by shouting. I remember my nephew and nieces just crying, asking why I was in this place and why they couldn't touch me. I remember one of my nieces trying to reach me through the netting. I was just crying the whole time. I couldn't even talk, really.

While I was in central jail, Babul was taken to a police station in Ashulia, the industrial park where some of the vandalism and arson supposedly occurred. There he was severely beaten many times, usually with a stick against his back. It got so bad that Babul gave a fellow prisoner his wife's and lawyer's phone numbers and asked that he call them when he got out to let them know what had happened, because Babul didn't think he'd be leaving the prison alive. The worst was on August 30. He was assaulted by several non-uniformed persons who entered his holding cell, blindfolded him, and beat him with a thick wooden stick, inflicting injuries on his leg, hip, and groin. Babul's assailants also threatened him, telling him that he'd be taken from the police station and shot by police during a staged incident. The same threat that was made against Aminul when he was detained by the NSI on June 16.

After thirty days in jail, Kalpona and Babul were released on bail, along with their colleague Aminul, who had been arrested and sent to a different facility, where he had also been beaten. The three continued their regular worker training and organizing work while awaiting trial until April 4, 2012, when Aminul was kidnapped outside the BCWS offices, tortured, and killed. His body was discovered sixty miles north of the BCWS offices with broken toes and massive internal bleeding. Signs point to NSI involvement in the murder, but so far no perpetrators of the crime have been brought to justice. Lack of progress in the murder investigation quickly raised concerns of cover-ups to protect security forces. Meanwhile, labor leaders feared for their safety. Eventually, Aminul's death led to major international protests, including condemnation by U.S. Secretary of State Hillary Clinton on a trip to Bangladesh in May 2012.

I DON'T WANT TO BRING SOMEONE INTO THIS WORLD WITH THE STRESS THAT I'M FACING

I still live with my parents. They've been through so much stress. For years they were harassed by the police, security agents, anonymous calls. They've been through a lot, and I worry about their helth. My siblings have suffered harassment as well. Still, we are a close family. My younger brother has worked by my side at BCWS. He's had a difficult time as well, but he remains so strong. And I'm very close to my nephew and nieces. Very, very close. I mean, they call me "Mom." Yeah, sometimes my sisters get jealous!

My family has always been such a comfort for me. I have one strong memory of being picked up by the police in the courtyard just outside my house and put in a van to go to trial. My family was there, including my nephew. It was a very hot day, and I was sweating. After the van started to pull away, I heard my nephew running by the van, crying out to the police, "Where are you taking my Mom? I want to give this to her!" The police asked me if he was my son, and I told them he was. So the police stopped and took something from him and handed it back to me. It was a paper fan. I shouted through the window to my nephew that he should go back home. But I was very touched.

I'm just crazy about babies. I want babies myself, but I can't figure out how that would happen. I don't have time to think about being a mother. And of course you need an appropriate person. You cannot have a baby with an irresponsible person. So this is another reason. And sometimes I think if I really do want a baby, why don't I try in vitro fertilization? So then I need to figure out who could be the donor for this. And he has to have a good soul, at least. I just don't have a lot of time to think about it all. This is another problem with having babies myself: I am doing too much work, there are too many stresses, and I don't want to bring someone into this world with the stress that I'm facing.

In June 2013, two months after the Rana Plaza collapse captured the attention of the world, the United States announced that it was suspending certain tariff-reducing preferential trade benefits with Bangladesh because of serious labor rights violations. Part of the Bangladeshi government's response has included dropping most of the charges against Kalpona and Babul and formally reinstating BCWS as an NGO in August 2013. It remains to be seen whether the government of Bangladesh will carry out a full investigation of the torture and murder of Aminul Islam and bring those responsible for his death to justice.

ANA JUÁREZ

AGE: *31*

OCCUPATION: *Garment worker*

BIRTHPLACE: *Ecatepec, Mexico*

INTERVIEWED IN: *Mexico City, Mexico*

Tehuacán, Mexico, was one of the main garment manufacturing hubs for brands like Abercrombie & Fitch, American Eagle Outfitters, Express, Gap, Levi Strauss & Co., and Calvin Klein for nearly a decade after the signing of the North American Free Trade Agreement in 1994. Then, in the 2000s, transnational clothing manufacturers began sourcing their goods in countries where labor was even cheaper, including Honduras, Guatemala, Bangladesh, and Vietnam.[1] *The rapid arrival and departure of garment work in Tehuacán brought thousands to the region during the nineties and left thousands underemployed after the boom ended in the 2000s.*[2]

---

[1] For an analysis of garment industry wages and trends across the world between 2001 and 2011, see Appendix IV, page 366.

[2] For more on the history of the economic boom and bust cycle in Mexico after the North American Free Trade Agreement, see Appendix III, page 354.

We first talk to Ana Juárez in early 2011 while she is living in Mexico City and looking for work. At the time, Ana has worked almost half her life in the clothing industry in Tehuacán: she started her first job at the age of fifteen, as a sewing operator's assistant. In the years of garment work that followed, Ana experienced harassment, insults, mistreatment, poverty wages, unjustified layoffs, and poor work conditions.

In 2006, Ana was working at Vaqueros Navarra, a local contracting company of global brands like Levi Strauss & Co. That year, senior workers began to organize informally to demand across-the-board raises after two years without any increase in worker pay. Though they were able to win a 7 percent raise for all workers, the factory's management responded to the action with a chain of layoffs and counteractions and ultimately closed the factory the following year. Because Ana emerged as a leader of the workers' attempts to formally unionize, she found herself on a blacklist that kept her out of garment work in the region.

HOW CAN I NOT GO TO SCHOOL?

I'm originally from Ecatepec, near Mexico City.[3] There are twelve kids in our family. Antonio is the oldest, and there are two boys and ten girls. I'm one of the youngest. I have a twin sister named Maria, and there's only one younger sibling, our sister Lucero.

The story of my family is like that of many others who ended up in Tehuacán—my father struggled a lot before we went there.[4] My dad was a mechanic in Mexico City. He worked at Ruta 100 for fifteen years.[5] The

---

[3] Ecatepec is a large Mexico City suburb of over 1.5 million.

[4] Tehuacán is a city of over 250,000 inhabitants in the state of Puebla, 160 miles southeast of Mexico City.

[5] Ruta 100 was a federally operated bus transit line that ran throughout Mexico City and surrounding states. The route opened in 1981 and shut down in 1995, when it was replaced by private bus lines.

friends he had at Ruta 100 were like family. We would go out to dinners or parties with other workers' families, and my parents would be like, "This is your uncle," although they'd just be talking about some guy who worked with my dad. My dad's co-workers came to my house many times to drop him off after work, and my mom would ask them, "Have you eaten? No? Come in and have an egg at least, or beans, or tortillas with salsa." Childhood with my parents was very good until Ruta 100 shut down. Our lives quickly changed after that.

In early 1995, we heard that Ruta 100 was bankrupt and would close. The Thursday before Holy Week, a bunch of my dad's friends came over as usual for a few drinks at our house.[6] My mom started talking with one of them, and he told her that it was important for them to have fun—be with friends, have parties, because things were so stressful. My mom told them, no, what they really needed was to find new work, since they'd all be out of jobs soon. That weekend, maybe around two in the morning on Saturday, twelve of my dad's friends came looking for him. They came practically in their underwear and pajamas, and they told my dad, "The control center has just been taken.[7] Get your coat, let's go!"

When my dad and his co-workers got to the control center, the police had occupied the building. They were officially shutting down Ruta 100 for good. Many of the workers couldn't even get their clothes that were inside. They left with what they had in their hands. I remember that my dad said he left with only a piece of cheese he'd had in his locker.

After that, my dad couldn't find work, and unfortunately he fell into alcoholism. And soon my parents didn't have the money to send us to school. For me, it was very traumatic. Before the layoffs, money was tight,

---

[6] Spring break in Mexico lasts for two weeks surrounding Easter, including what is called Easter Week and Holy Week. During Holy Week, most workers and all students are on holiday.

[7] "Control center" was the term for Ruta 100's central offices.

and sometimes we had to go without new shoes or clothes. But now that my dad was without work, we couldn't afford even to go to school. My parents needed us to help support the family. I was only twelve, and I had it stuck in my mind that I would go back to school soon, after my dad got a new job and things returned to normal. I would think, *How can I not go school? I want to study.*

I remember times that we just didn't have anything to eat. So I had to go and collect leftover food from other families. It was my sister Azucena, who was two years older, me, my twin sister Maria, and Lucero, though Lucero was too embarrassed to go out collecting leftovers. My mom would start crying because she didn't have money to feed us, and she'd go to the neighbors' to wash their clothes or to do whatever work she could find. I started thinking, *I don't want to just wait around for someone to give me food.* And so my sisters and I started to look for any kind of work. While my mom washed clothes, we would go to the market to see what we could do. We might ask to help the man selling tortillas, for instance, and he'd give us tortillas as payment. I'd babysit neighbors' children, I'd wash clothes for people. It was all about looking around, getting ahead.

"YOUR MOM LEFT"

Since we couldn't afford to buy supplies for school, I started studying in a *telesecundaria* when I was around fourteen, in 1997.[8] I dreamed of being in a normal school, but I actually had a very good experience in the telesecundaria. My older brother Gerardo was in his twenties and was good at math, and he would help me out a lot. He'd say, "Maybe Dad doesn't scold you but I will. You have to show me your tests, show me your homework."

---

[8] A *telesecundaria* is a school with classes broadcast through a public-access television channel.

And he was the one who watched over me very carefully.

Unfortunately, the following year, in 1998, my mom decided to leave the house. She couldn't put up with my dad anymore. She didn't tell me she was leaving. She just left one day when all of us kids were at school. And when I got home that night, my dad said, "Sit down, I need to talk to you. Your mom left." I asked him where, and he said, "She went to Tehuacán, she's living with your grandfather, and she won't come back. You can go live with her or you can stay here." My sisters Maria and Azucena left to go live with her, but I stayed at first, because I wanted to continue studying and be around my older brother. I also went to work part-time in a clothing store. But then my dad became very violent with us kids. And then, a month after my mom left, her dad passed away. So I went to Tehuacán for my grandfather's funeral. I said to my mother then, "I want to be with you, not with Dad anymore." And so I went to live in Tehuacán.

"DO WHAT YOU'RE TOLD, AND DON'T TALK BACK TO YOUR BOSS"

I was fifteen when I moved into my grandfather's old house in Tehuacán at the end of 1998. I lived with my mother, my two aunts Juana and Rafaela, who were twenty-six and twenty-seven, and my sisters Maria and Azucena.

My aunts worked as sewing-machine operators in a jeans factory. My mother had always done things like wash clothes, iron, but she was older and did more work around the house—she didn't bring in much income. When I got to Tehuacán, it was clear that I needed to work to help support the household. I told one of my aunts, "I don't want to work in a factory; I know how to do other things, like sales." But my aunts convinced me, and they got me and my two sisters in to work at Vaqueros Navarra when it was called Calle Isabel la Católica.[9] The factory was growing fast at the time and they needed new workers to keep up with orders from companies like Abercrombie, Lee, and other big brands. This was in December of 1998, and I was fifteen, almost sixteen at the time.

I started working as a *manual*, or manual laborer, who helped the sewing-machine operators. Most days we'd get to work at eight a.m. and start assisting the sewing-machine operators right away. Where I first worked, they were sewing back pockets of jeans, and then it would be my job to gather up the pockets into bundles of fifty, tie them up, and send them off down the line where they'd be sewn onto the jeans.

I'd be helping two machine operators at the same time, and they had quotas. When they finished their work for the day, they could leave. For example, they might each have to sew fifteen hundred pockets that day, which meant that I had to make sure that the three thousand pockets they made between them got bundled. If there was a mistake with how they were made, I'd have to send them back or find another operator who could fix them before I was done.

I remember one of my first days there, one of the operators I was working with, called Blondie, said, "If you hurry up, we can leave early." But Blondie and the other operator were too fast for me at first. The pockets would pile up on me and then a supervisor would come by and yell at me, cursing at me and insulting me. I started crying in front of everyone, and then I went to the bathroom and cried there. Then I came back from the bathroom and tried to act as if nothing had happened, and Blondie whispered to me, "We're going to help you with the work, but don't tell the boss." I was naive when I started at the clothing factory, and I didn't know how to stand up for myself. I'd think, *I just have to put up*

---

[9] Vaqueros Navarra was a *maquila*—a factory set up in a free-trade zone immune from import and export taxes. Isabel la Católica is the street where the maquila was located. For more on maquilas, NAFTA, and free trade zones, see Appendix III, page 354.

with what the bosses say.

After a couple of weeks, I caught up with the pace and could go faster. Since my supervisor saw that I hurried, he'd say, "Go to the machine over there because a girl has fallen behind." So I would go help the other girl, but when I turned around my work had already piled up on me, and my supervisor would complain.

Even when I finished all of my work early and was supposed to go home, the line boss might tell me, "No, no, you can't leave, go over there to lift those bags." Basically they wanted me to work overtime when it was time for me to leave. Usually I was supposed to leave when I was done with my bundles, but many times I'd have to stay until seven thirty or even much later to finish, and I wasn't paid overtime.

At Navarra, my two sisters were working on line 6, and I was on line 7. At the time, I believe, there were thirteen assembly lines all together in three factory buildings at Navarra, with about 260 sewing-machine operators and bundlers in each line. The work there was really boring, especially because there were a lot of bundles to lift. I often had to stay very late. Sometimes I'd see that my older sister Azucena would leave earlier than me. "How is it that you leave early and I can't?" I asked her. And she said, "Well, I fight back with the supervisor." But I was afraid that I would get fired if I fought back. I'd complain to my aunts, "They always make me do more than I'm supposed to." And they'd say, "Well too bad, that's work. Just stay and do what you're told, and don't talk back to your boss."

My aunts were very nosy. We didn't have privacy in the house we shared. My aunts would come into the room where my mom and sisters and I were staying whenever they pleased. They'd even sleep there with us sometimes. My sisters and I would hesitate to talk about work in front of them. Even though they were the ones who had helped us get in the company, they were also always telling us what to do and what not to do, how to behave. My aunts had the mentality that if a boss tells them to work longer hours than they're supposed to, then they work for him for free. But I understand how they could get that way. At first when I started working at the factory, I was grateful to have a job at all. I got to the point of thinking that the boss was very good, that it was only because he employed me that I could eat.

The work wasn't just boring, it was dangerous. One Friday about a month or so after we started working, my sister Maria came home with her waist hurting a lot. She'd been given a bundle of about a hundred finished jeans to carry—it was bigger than it was supposed to be—and she'd strained her back. By Sunday morning, she couldn't get out of bed, and she screamed because she couldn't feel her legs. At the time we didn't know if she was paralyzed. We took her to the regional hospital, where they told us we should apply for workers' compensation.[10] But my sister was too young to work legally and she wasn't qualified for social security benefits, so we just had to wait out her injury until she could work again.

It took two months for my sister to walk again. We lost my sister's income, so during that time, my mom would take food to work for me, my aunts, and Azucena to save money on expenses. Maria would stay at home alone. We were still at our grandfather's home at that time, and Maria told us that she heard his ghost walking around sometimes. One day after a couple of months, my mom came home after bringing us food at the factory, and to her surprise, she found my sister standing. My sister said, "All my pain is gone." Later, Maria told me, "I heard Grandpa walk up to the door and say, 'Stand up, you lazy girl. Your mom needs you to help her. Your mom doesn't want to see you at home. Stand up.'" And three days later Maria went back to work.

---

[10] For more on workers' compensation insurance, see glossary, page 348.

WE JUST HAD OUR CLOTHES AND THAT WAS IT

So, by the time I was sixteen, I was living the life of an adult and going to the factory every day. But after we were working at Navarra for a few months, my aunts began to argue a lot with my mom. They wanted my grandfather's house to themselves. Finally, in the spring of '99, they just kicked us out of the house. We didn't have any furniture. We didn't have much of anything. We just had our clothes and that was it.

We rented an apartment near the factory. At first, we had to sleep on cardboard because we didn't have a mattress. The good thing was that it was warm during the summer, and during the fall each of us had a sweater, and we'd cover ourselves with our sweaters at night. We sat on empty vegetable boxes and we cooked with a portable stove and a pan. My sisters and I took care of the expenses of the house, even though my salary was not much, just 261 pesos a week.[11]

It was hard. I would say, "In our house with Dad, we didn't live like this. I had a bed, I had a TV to watch, I had a radio to listen to." I remember that I sometimes dreamed of returning to live near Mexico City with my dad. I used to think, *I hope my dad calls today to say, "Come home."* It was the hope that my dad might repent and that we'd return to school, that I could finally have real opportunities in life.

Sometimes my sisters and I would talk about the things we were missing. "Well, we can't do all of that with what we earn," we would tell each other. Because we had to pay for food and rent and utilities and we had to somehow help my mom, because she was fifty-two years old at that point, and she was not well. She had breathing problems. In Tehuacán, there was a lot of smoke from wood fires used for cooking as well as

---

[11] At the time, 261 pesos = approximately US$26.

smoke from the factories, and after we moved out from my grandfather's house, my mom got pneumonia. She was really ill, and there were nights that I was scared that she'd die and leave us there in Tehuacán, without anything, without stability.

I admit, I was angry with my life. I'd think, *Why did I have to go through this? I could have had a normal life.* As much as I wanted things to be the way they were before my dad lost his job, I started to realize that wouldn't ever happen. I'd think, *The problem is, Dad didn't step up to the plate.* And then with time, I began thinking that we were in Tehuacán for a reason. To realize that not all things come easy—you have to keep going and learn to overcome all the bad things that happen to you.

THE NEW SUPERVISORS FORCED ME TO STAND UP FOR MYSELF

I decided to leave Vaqueros Navarra in the fall of 1999. I hadn't even been there for a full year, but I didn't like the way I was treated, or the way that my sister was treated. I told my mom, "I don't want this anymore. I can't stand it. I'm going to look for another job." My sister Maria left too, but Azucena stayed at Navarra—she was old enough to be employed there legally, and she was treated a little better.

I found a job at a small jeans maquila in town called Choco. When I started, the supervisor asked me, "What can you do?" I told him, "Well, I'm manual labor." Luckily, the supervisor wasn't a creep, and he told me, "I'm going to teach you to sew. Sit down, you're going to learn. Do you know what a bobbin is?" I said I had more or less of an idea because we had a machine at my grandpa's house, but I didn't know how to sew on it. He told me, "Well, I'm going to teach you. Step on the sewing-machine pedal just a little, otherwise you'll get your fingers caught by the needle. It can move fast." Choco was a very small shop, but I got paid a little better, around 380 pesos a week since I was doing needlework.[12] I worked there for a couple of months, but it was hard: it was far from where we were living, and the hours were long.

Then one of our neighbors told us about openings at a bigger maquila called Industrias Georgia that did jeans for brands like Polo. The factory was only three blocks from our apartment, so I decided to apply. The supervisor who interviewed me asked what I could do, and I said that I could sew pockets—the fastest, easiest part of the jeans to sew. They tried me out and saw that I knew a little, but not a lot. Still, they took a chance on me and taught me how to sew more, as well as assemble parts into a finished pair of jeans, how to fold and pack the jeans—basically all the jobs that go into garment production.

At Industrias Georgia, they paid me a little more, maybe 450 pesos a week before overtime pay.[13] But they also treated me with respect, and that was more important to me. They didn't insult me or my family, I didn't have to stay late if I didn't want to, and if I did stay late, they would pay me overtime.

In my first year at Industrias Georgia, I became very skilled as a needleworker. After a year or so, my sisters joined me there as well, and we were all important employees. Every once in a while, a representative from a brand like Polo would come and request that we produce samples for new jeans they wanted to manufacture, and my sisters and I were usually chosen to help produce the samples. The representative would watch us work on the samples, and the size of the order they placed would depend on how fast and how well we could produce the jeans. When the brand representative came, he was very good toward me and my sisters. He'd say, "You're very good at sewing, you don't leave behind anything that needs

---

[12] At the time, 380 pesos = approximately US$28.50.

[13] At the time, 450 pesos = approximately US$33.50.

corrections or any extra mending, you're fast." I came to like sewing jeans. It was something I was good at.

But after the first year at Industrias Georgia, things began to change. I think it all happened after Vicente Fox was elected in 2000.[14] Not long after he came into office he signed the Puebla-Panama Plan. It was like a trade agreement, and the idea was to make it easier to do business with countries south of Mexico like Panama.[15] For Tehuacán, this meant that brands that made pants in town started looking toward Central America, because labor was cheaper there. In fact, some factory owners here would take a few Tehuacán workers with them to places like Panama to teach new workers how to sew.

Suddenly, there was more pressure to hold on to clients at places like Industrias Georgia. After 2001, a lot of new supervisors were hired who were very rude. They wouldn't say *please*, they would say, "I don't give a damn, you do it, and do it faster!"

If you don't treat me with respect, then I'll treat you the same way. The new supervisors forced me to stand up for myself. It was there that I became very vulgar.

IF I DIED, HOW WOULD THEY PAY FOR THE BURIAL?

My sisters and I worked very hard back then. Sometimes I'd work for fourteen hours straight, but I'd tell myself, *I can handle it, I can handle it.*

---

[14] Vicente Fox was the president of Mexico from 2000–2006.

[15] The Puebla-Panama Plan was an economic development plan signed into law by President Vicente Fox in 2001. Its purpose was to enhance economic and industrial links between southern Mexican states and all of Central America and Columbia. Other than eliminating tariffs and other trade barriers, the agreement also funded industrial infrastructure such as roads and telecommunications integration.

But when we finished working it was midnight, and we were very tired. Our backs ached. It was nasty. Unbearably painful.

Then around the spring of 2002, I got sick. We had a lot of orders to fill, and I was working quite a few extra late shifts, working a lot of overtime. I'd think, *I can do it, I can do it.* I didn't have the luxury of going home to rest, because I knew that there were expenses coming. I had to pay the rent, pay the electricity, pay for food. I started on Monday, and all night into Tuesday morning I had a fever. I slept a little and then Tuesday morning I went to work with the fever lingering. By Wednesday, I was getting worse and having stomach problems. And I worked like that until four in the morning on Thursday. I slept a little again and went in Thursday morning, but I wasn't feeling well enough to work. I told my supervisor, "Give me a pass so I can go to the doctor. I'm very sick and I've had a fever for over three days, and it's not going away." He told me, "If you sacrifice a little and work tonight, I'll give you the pass tomorrow." That's when I woke up. I said, "I've already sacrificed for you, and now being sick is what I get for trying to help you meet these orders. Go to hell."

When I got home, I was at the point of severe dehydration. I remember I was crying, and I told my sister Maria, "Take me to the hospital, because I can't make it."

When we got to the hospital, the doctor who saw me told Maria, "If you hadn't brought her right this minute, your sister might have died from her fever." I got scared then because I thought, *If I died, how would they pay for the burial?*

I remember that we got there at nine, ten at night and they let me go at four in the morning. We got home walking because we didn't have money for a taxi. I woke up the next day around eight and I still had a fever. But I told my mom, "I'm going to work." And I was walking toward the door when I passed out. After taking some antibiotics for a few days,

I started to feel better, so I went back to work. I couldn't really afford to take much time off.

Then, six months after I got sick, the company shut down. It happened on October 2, 2002.[16] It was very ironic. I remember that day well. We were all keeping up to date with the marches and protests that occur on that day. Then our supervisors told us there was no longer any work and that the severance papers were being filed. As they say, "Never forget the second of October." I definitely won't.

I began to cry, because that's when I understood my dad's experience when Ruta 100 fired him. I thought, *Where am I going to work if I don't know how to do other kinds of work?* I was already used to it there; it was my job for almost three years and I was established there.

There was another problem: the owners claimed they had no money to pay us the back pay they owed us. I had weeks' worth of overtime and unused vacation time, thousands of pesos' worth, and we were told by our bosses that we might not get it. We were also told we might not get any severance pay, that we hadn't worked there long enough yet. At home, our mom heard me and my sisters talking about our predicament, and she encouraged us to talk to a lawyer whom one of our cousins knew. She told us to make sure never to just give our work away. So we ended up suing for back pay and severance.

The company lawyer tried to negotiate with us when we met. He told me that only I would be able to get my money, but neither Maria nor Azucena would get anything, because they had been there less than a year. It was going to be given to me because of the amount of time I'd put in. In the end I was able to get 8,000 pesos by negotiating with the company

[16] October 2 commemorates the Tlatelolco Massacre of 1968, in which dozens of students and activists were killed by the Mexican army during a protest.

lawyers.[17] I think the other workers resented me, though—they'd say, "Why are you suing the boss? He's a nice guy." Nice or not, the bosses will always win. We'll never win, unless we demand what we're owed.

WORKING IN A FACTORY, EVERYTHING SLIPS AWAY FROM YOU

After I was laid off from Industrias Georgia, I moved to Mexico City to look for work. I had heard rumors of blacklists for workers who sued, and I didn't want any more conflict. Actually, the boss liked me enough that he offered to set me up at a maquila in a neighboring town even though I had sued him! It didn't seem like an appealing place to work though, so I tried Mexico City. There I stayed with my dad in Ecatepec and made shopping bags at a small shop in La Merced, but I actually missed the work I had been doing.[18]

When I first started working in a factory as a teenager, I'd think, *I don't want to end up like my aunts, chained to sewing work, dealing with the insults*. Because yes, life slips away. Working in a factory, everything slips away from you. Your lungs wear out, your life runs out.

But then I thought, *No, working is a way to move beyond the problems you have*. The clothing factory becomes your home. For me it was about learning to be responsible and to have ambitions. That's how I came to see the clothing factory. I also wanted to continue studying, I wanted to study medicine, and to do that I needed to work to save money.

So in May 2003, when I was twenty, I went back to Tehuacán and began working again at Vaqueros Navarra, the first company I'd worked for. My older sister Azucena was already back at Navarra, ever since

---

[17] At the time, 8,000 pesos = US$600.

[18] La Merced is a neighborhood of Mexico City with a large open-air market.

Industrias Georgia closed. Maria worked elsewhere in town, but she'd eventually join us as well.

So for years I worked with Vaqueros Navarra as a needleworker, assembling completed pants. For me, there was beauty there at work. I began to enjoy myself in the clothing factory. There in the factory you get to know people. You get to know their lives, how they started out. And you begin to talk. You become part of the family. More than anything, I enjoyed making samples, models for pants. Because it made me proud to say, "I made that pair of pants." The pants are not only a piece of clothing and nothing more. There are the workers' experiences and life that they give each day to the clothes they sew. Tears go into it. Laughter goes into it. Dreams go into it. Many memories go into it.

WE WANTED TO KEEP OUR JOBS

I worked at Navarra again for years with everything normal. My pay was about the same as at Industrias Georgia, but at Navarra our contracts also included profit sharing, so we would usually see another 2,000 pesos once a year in May.[19]

Navarra was able to survive where other maquilas failed around that time because they were big. They formed an association with some other maquilas called the Navarro Group, and because of scale they could afford to offer better prices to companies like Levi's and Gap. But they also got contracts because Navarra workers did good work, and the representatives and auditors from big brands who would come and see us work appreciated our care and speed.

The only thing I didn't like about Navarra during the first years of my return was that I was asked to work as a *comodín*, or "wildcard" employee,

---

[19] At the time, 2,000 pesos = approximately US$150.

who covered a lot of different assignments instead of just working at one sewing station. I'd make samples, make pieces like pockets or zippers, whatever was needed at the time. I made more money that way, but the hours were longer than if I had a set quota like I would have as a sewing-machine operator. But this way I also got to meet a lot of other workers, see what was going on around the factory.

In early 2006, maybe January, I first started hearing about workers organizing. We hadn't been given a raise in two years, and some of the senior employees formed an informal commission and proposed a 20 percent raise to the bosses. I think the senior organizers never expected to win that much, but it was a place to start—maybe we'd end up with 10 percent. The workers agreed to strike, thousands of us, without any formal support from outside unions. Then one day in January four men showed up and met with company owners, and then called all the workers together during break time. They said they were representatives from CROC, and that they'd negotiated a 3 percent raise for all of us.[20] But none of us in the factory knew who CROC was, and none of us had signed any contract with them. We were like, "Who are these guys?" We didn't accept the deal and carried out a work slowdown. We were making thousands fewer pieces a day than normal, and the company was losing money. Finally, after a few days, we got a 7 percent raise. We figured that was the best we could do.

As a wildcard employee, I knew the factory pretty well. Soon after our raise, I began to notice that certain people I was used to seeing weren't around anymore. When I asked about them, I was told by supervisors that they'd been given new positions. Meanwhile, the bosses kept setting our daily quotas higher and higher, asking for faster work. Then I remember

[20] CROC is the Confederación Revolucionaria de Obreros y Campesinos, or Revolutionary Confederation of Workers and Farmers, a national coalition of unions in Mexico.

one day in April when a supervisor asked me to cover for a girl who didn't show up that day. I was confused, since I remembered seeing her that morning. I ran into her later outside the factory, and she told me she'd been laid off that day. I started to worry.

My sisters and I did work on the side as party planners, fixing up birthday parties and videotaping them, things like that. Around that time we did a birthday party for the daughter of a man who worked in human resources at Navarra. At the party, he told us that Navarra was firing people who had been there only a few months, and also those who had been there many years. The company didn't want to have to pay the pensions of older employees nearing retirement age, and the newer employees hadn't been there long enough to be given a severance. He told us Maria would probably be fired, since she'd been at Navarra less than six months. And she was. Maria was laid off a few weeks later in May, along with twelve others the same day. Nobody knew what was coming next.

We were also accustomed to receiving profit share every year around May, somewhere between 1,500 and 2,000 pesos.[21] That year we received virtually nothing. That month my envelope had only 125 pesos in profit sharing, when I was used to seeing thousands of pesos of profit share every year.[22] The thing was, we were working more than ever. We didn't believe we were getting less because of fewer orders. And we didn't believe it was because of our 7 percent raises. What was happening was that the company was subcontracting some work to smaller maquilas in the area, small shops where brand auditors wouldn't see what was happening and the company could make jeans without the same high standards we had in the main factory. We'd make samples and models in the main factory, but a lot of the manufacturing was shifting elsewhere.

---

[21] At the time, 1,500 to 2,000 pesos = US$115 to US$150.

[22] At the time, 125 pesos = US$9.34.

One day in early summer of 2006, just a couple of weeks after my sister Maria had been fired, a labor rights organizer named Martín Barrios and a couple of his associates from the local Commission for Human and Labor Rights came by the factory to hand out flyers.[23] The flyer invited workers to a meeting at the house of one of his associates who lived nearby. My sisters and I and some other workers began to attend meetings with Martín regularly. When we first started talking about organizing, we just wanted the layoffs to stop, and we wanted people who were laid off to get fair severance pay. Martín explained that under federal law, anyone terminated without cause was entitled to ninety days of severance, and twelve days of pay for every year served. This was important to learn about, but mostly, we wanted to keep our jobs.

We didn't have a formal union that really represented us, but from Martín we got the idea that we could organize a collective bargaining agreement so that we could negotiate our contracts with the bosses.[24] We wanted to figure out how to negotiate contract terms directly with the bosses. There were hundreds of us participating in making a collective bargaining agreement, and we elected eleven leaders, a commission, at a meeting away from the factory. The next day, ten of those eleven workers were fired. Someone had told the boss. The factory manager distributed flyers to all us workers explaining that those who were fired were rotten apples and that the company wouldn't employ people like that. I guess he only wanted apples that were ready to be eaten.

The next day we elected a second commission, eight workers including my older sister Azucena. They lasted only two or three days before they were fired—all but my sister. I'm not sure why she was spared; it might

[23] Martín Barrios is the director of the Commission for Human and Labor Rights, founded in Tehuacán in 1995. To read his story, see page 87.

[24] For more on collective bargaining agreements, see glossary, page 348.

have been because she denied being part of the commission.

The layoffs stopped for a few weeks, but started up again. In August, Martín said to me, "There is going to be a meeting. Can you attend?" I told him, "I don't want to lose my job right now because we're not in the position to lose it." Because of what I'd seen my dad go through, I said, "I'm not going to go to marches, I'm not going to go to meetings anymore. I'm not going to expose myself." But the more I thought about what happened with my dad, the more I realized I needed to stand up for myself or I could lose everything. So I went to a meeting one Sunday and helped form a third commission. Azucena was in that one, too. We tried to be quiet about it, and our job was to report about what was going on in the factory. Martín's group was in contact with transnational brands as well, and some of their representatives secretly interviewed us away from the factory to learn about what was going on. We told the brand reps that the bosses claimed that orders weren't coming in and that's why they had to lay off workers. But the reps showed us the contracts they had with Navarra—they had orders placed for years' worth of production!

WE WEREN'T ABLE TO KEEP THE FACTORY OPEN

In September 2006 we sought the support of formal union backing. There were big national unions like CROC, but many of us workers thought that they were too big and too friendly with ownership to really represent our interests. We didn't think they'd push for enough. We learned of a smaller union called the 19th of September, and it was made up entirely of seamstresses like us—it was named in memory of the 1985 earthquake where hundreds of seamstresses died, and thousands were left without jobs. By this time there were less than five hundred workers left at the Navarra factory, where once there were thousands. We had a vote about which union should represent us as part of collective bargaining, the 19th of September, CROC, or one other national union, and 19th of September got the majority of votes.

Unfortunately, we weren't able to keep the factory open. In December, Navarra announced that there was no work at the moment and they sent us on early holiday vacation on December 8. When we returned on January 3, 2007, much of the machinery had been sold. By January 20, we were all laid off. The union stayed in negotiations with Navarra the whole time. It turned out the bosses would rather close the factory and push orders on to other maquilas than negotiate with unionized workers. Even though Navarra was at one point the biggest, best known maquila in town, the group that owned Navarra was just as happy to send work to other maquilas that they operated. The 260 of us who remained to the end were able to fight for our full severance, though. We got 90 percent of it in February, and then the remaining 10 percent was paid in old sewing machines after the factory was taken apart the next fall.

I DIDN'T EVEN KNOW WHAT A BLACKLIST WAS

After Navarra, I started working at another small maquila in town. The first day, it was noon and I was almost done with my work. The line boss came to me and said, "I need to talk to you." I said, "Sure, what is it?" But I kept sewing. He said, "There's no work for you because you're from Vaqueros Navarra. You're part of the 19th of September committee, so there's no work for you. I don't want to have any problems. I'll pay your day. I'll even pay you more." He gave me 200 pesos, and then he said, "Leave your bundle, don't finish it."[25] So I left, crying.

---

[25] At the time, 200 pesos = US$15.

Then I was hired in a second shop, and I lasted for only half an hour. I had just started, and a supervisor came up to me and said, "You know what, honey? Give me the work back. I think you already know why. I recognize you. You were in the newspaper."

When I first started organizing, I didn't even know what a blacklist was. But now I realized how it worked. Every factory in town knew my story. Factory owners had been sharing names of individual workers affiliated with the 19th of September union—not only in clothing factories but in the shoe factories, department stores, agricultural suppliers, and in the pork business too. I thought, *It can't be. Even the little shops are kicking me out.*

With no garment work, I dedicated myself fully to the struggle, and I had a little income through work with Martín's organization. I'd visit workers and help organize meetings. I took charge of the attendance sheets. Martín became my friend—when he saw me, he'd ask me, "Have you eaten?"

In early 2008, when I still couldn't find work, I came to Mexico City. I had a nephew there who had a small business. He told me he could give me work. But in the end I didn't want to work for his business since he couldn't offer health benefits. Large expenses were coming our way because my mom was having breathing problems again, getting sicker each day. Also, after working so long in Tehuacán, I started getting sick too. I was having breathing problems like my mother and I practically lost my sight in one eye. So to obtain the medical benefits, I went to Pino Suárez, where there are clothing factories that aren't that big.[26] But in every factory I went to, human resources would tell me that they knew about me already, that I was on a blacklist.

I think it's not fair that one is denied work for fighting for one's rights. If owners see it that way, I hope they never have the same needs as I do,

---

[26] Pino Suárez is a neighborhood near the center of Mexico City.

and that they're never in my shoes. But I haven't lost hope of going back to work at a clothing factory. I want to continue working.

My sister Maria has said, "It was wrong of you to get involved because, as you see, they won't give you work. What did you learn from all this? Did you learn anything good?" It was as if she were telling me, *Did you learn to not get into trouble?* And I told her, "I did learn something. I have rights, and it was my job, and I knew that the company should not act like this. I would do it again." You can't win if you're afraid. To win you have to be brave, not remain ignorant. Everyone has dignity. That's something that nobody will be able to change, and that's what is most important: the dignity that one has as a person, as a worker.

My message for all the workers is to never think that you're less than the boss. Just the opposite—you're worth more than they are. Because thanks to your work and your efforts, they have their car, they can eat better than we can. The work we're doing is very worthy. If one works in a factory, whether it's making televisions or a pair of pants, whatever we're making we feel proud of. Every time I see a pair of pants I say to myself, "How proud I am that I made those pants. It was my work. It was my effort. It was my night shifts when I didn't sleep." My youngest sister Lucero is a fashion designer now, and I tell her, "It's worthy to design something, but it's more worthy to sew it together."

er

MARTÍN BARRIOS

AGE: *42*

OCCUPATION: *Labor organizer*

BIRTHPLACE: *Tehuacán, Mexico*

INTERVIEWED IN: *Tehuacán, Mexico*

Martín Barrios was raised in a family of activists in Tehuacán. He has spent over twenty years working as a human rights advocate in the Mexican state of Puebla, and he has defended labor rights for over twelve years. According to Martín, the fight for rights among indigenous Mexicans shares a close affinity to the struggle for labor rights in Tehuacán's numerous maquilas.[1] *For Martín, the power dynamic of the maquila echoes the centuries-old relationship between European colonizers and the native population of Mexico.*

Martín keeps busy between his activism and a rock band he's led for years,

---

[1] In the 1960s, Mexico established free trade economic zones to encourage foreign investment, primarily from the United States. When the North American Free Trade Agreement (NAFTA) became law in 1994, the presence of maquilas expanded rapidly throughout Mexico as U.S. manufacturers sought out inexpensive labor. For more information, see Appendix III, page 354.

and he can be hard to pin down. Still, we manage to reach him for a series of interviews between 2011 and 2013. Today, Martín is the director of the Commission for Human and Labor Rights in Tehuacán Valley, and he has opened up his house as a meeting space ever since the commission's office closed down due to financial difficulties. A victim of violence, death threats, and wrongful imprisonment—as well as the beneficiary of protective measures by international agencies—Martín says that his work defending human rights comes from the positive examples of his parents.

IT WAS A PEACEFUL LIFE

I've lived here in Tehuacán, Puebla, since I was born in 1972. When I was a kid, Tehuacán was a lot smaller than it is now—the downtown area was only four or five blocks long. There was less infrastructure, and the housing built for workers at the maquilas was just starting to pop up.[2] From where I lived, you could walk for ten or fifteen minutes and reach the fields. At that time there were trees, gardens outside. You could play soccer all day. The streets were safe, and I spent a lot of time playing in the street—playing soccer, shooting marbles, flying kites. Something else we did as kids was go to the matinee on Sundays to watch movies of all those *luchadores*, like Santo.[3] It was a peaceful life.

I also spent a lot of time swimming. There are many natural springs and pools here in Tehuacán, and back then there were a number of soda factories in town that used the springs as a water source. There were a few garment factories as well, but they were small and served only local brands. The soda factories were a larger source of employment in the

---

[2] After NAFTA was signed in 1994, Tehuacán and surrounding suburbs more than doubled in size from about 150,000 residents to nearly 400,000 over a ten-year period.

[3] Rodolfo Guzmán Huerta, or El Santo ("The Saint"), was a legendary *luchador*, or masked wrestler. He acted in over fifty *lucha libre* films (movies starring masked wrestlers) from 1952 until his death in 1984.

region. A few of those soda factories would have swimming pools on site that the public could use for a small fee. Then there was a big economic crisis in Mexico in 1982, and many of those soda factories went broke and shut down.

When I was a child, my parents taught classes at the university in Puebla. My father taught philosophy, and my mother anthropology. My parents were also activists. There was a first generation of activists from the era of the sixties and seventies who fought against the Dirty War in Mexico, and my parents were among them.[4]

In the eighties in Tehuacán my parents participated in many protest marches. I remember them explaining that we lived in a very oppressive climate, because the control exerted by the PRI and local businessmen was vast.[5] The PRI had so much power then—the radio was censored as well as the newspapers, which toed the party line. Tehuacán was a very conservative city, and very Catholic. The concept of human rights didn't even exist in our part of Mexico, and my parents helped carve out a space for protest and resistance.

In the early eighties, my mother left the university to focus on activism, and she went to work at INI[6] in Chiapas.[7] My mom spent many

---

[4] The Dirty War *(la Guerra Sucia)* was a conflict between loosely affiliated leftist movements and student groups on one side, and the Mexican government on the other. The conflict culminated in the Tlatelolco Massacre of 1968, in which dozens of students were killed and thousands arrested during a protest.

[5] The PRI is the Partido Revolucionario Institucional, or Institutional Revolutionary Party.

[6] The INI was the Instituto Nacional Indígenista, which was replaced in 2003 by the Comisión Nacional para el Desarrollo de los Pueblos Indígenas, or National Commission for the Development of Indigenous Peoples. The INI was an agency of the Mexican government established to promote the welfare of indigenous peoples. Indigenous ethnic groups, many of whom speak pre-Columbian languages such as Nahuatl, Maya, and Zapotec, comprise nearly 15 percent of the Mexican population.

[7] Chiapas is a state in the southwest corner of Mexico. A mountainous region, it is home to a number of indigenous populations.

years in the mountains. She supported the legal defense of political prisoners, and people fighting for land rights and land ownership.

From my earliest years we had many activists at the house, so often that I didn't even notice most of the time. My parents were also active in organizing with the PSUM.[8] It was normal for me to have political activists in the house, but when I was young, I didn't want to participate myself. When I saw these gatherings at home, I'd get the sudden urge to go outside and play soccer with my friends.

The garment maquilas also started in the 1980s, and that's when my parents started their work with the maquila workers. There were always meetings at my house, so I got to know some of the workers even when I was still a kid. So seeing the struggle of workers is something that influenced me, even if I didn't choose to participate.

My dad was always an activist, but his focus was teaching. His main influence on me was inspiring me to love literature. There were always many books at my house, fiction and poetry. Ray Bradbury was big. I remember Lovecraft as well. Many Latin American writers as well—Cortázar, Borges, José Agustín. The whole Onda literature.[9] José Agustín even wrote about Rockdrigo.[10] I didn't learn about activism by joining my parents, or by having them explain their work to me. I learned by watching what they were doing, and by reading and figuring things out for myself.

---

[8] PSUM is the Partido Socialista Unificado de México, or Unified Socialist Party of Mexico. PSUM, which descended from the Communist Party of Mexico, existed from 1981 to 1987.

[9] La Onda was a Mexican literary and artistic movement of the latter half of the sixties that dealt with counterculture topics such as drugs, rock and roll, and sex.

[10] Rodrigo "Rockdrigo" González was an influential singer-songwriter whose work dealt with the everyday life of urban culture in Mexico.

I WAS A BAD INFLUENCE

By the time I was in high school, I was really into liberation theology.[11] I myself am an atheist, but I have close relationships with many priests who fight for the rights of workers and indigenous Mexicans. I've known a priest named Father Anastacio Hidalgo since I was a little boy. Father Hidalgo, whom we call Father Tacho, used to work with my aunt Marta with tuberculosis patients from indigenous populations in the Sierra Negra area.[12] He's a man who has helped me find the path I'm on. My aunt Marta was a medic, and Father Tacho would bring tuberculosis patients to see her at our house, where aunt Marta would treat them. Sometimes I'd visit the Sierra Negra with my aunt. And here in Tehuacán during the eighties there existed the Regional Seminary of the Southeast, a Catholic seminary formed by all these priests like Father Tacho who fought for the rights of the indigenous and the poor. When Norberto Rivera Carrera became bishop of Tehuacán in 1985—the man who later became archbishop of Mexico—he closed the seminary. He said the seminary was communist, the typical slander.

When I got to high school, I wanted to play music. Sometime around 1989, when I was around seventeen, I started a band with my friends. We tried to make our own songs. It was tough, because whenever we played at bars, people only asked for covers of popular songs. We wanted to play our own material. It wasn't really political material we were writing, but back then even playing rock music at all was an act of protest, since the culture

---

[11] Liberation theology is a Catholic religious and political movement started primarily in Latin America in the sixties that seeks to address economic, social, and political inequality. The movement flourished in the sixties and seventies, but its influence diminished in the eighties after its leaders were accused of promoting Marxist ideology and admonished by the Vatican for overt political actions.

[12] Sierra Negra is one of the highest mountain peaks in Mexico, located an hour north of Tehuacán.

was so conservative. Now you have all sorts of urban expression like punks and goths, but back then, twenty years ago, the police would come down on you for having long hair. You could be beaten. And we had to make our own spaces to play in. I remember when the city wouldn't allow a rock festival, so some bands got together and we organized it ourselves. Of course, when the festival was a success, the city took the credit.

I had a lot of trouble in high school because the people in charge there were aligned with the PRI. It was the local custom to coerce students to attend rallies in favor of the PRI, march for the PRI, celebrate patriotic holidays with the PRI, and any number of other idiocies that the mayor came up with. We students were forced to participate or else our grades would suffer.

I wasn't able to finish high school because the school administration disappeared my documents. They held a grudge against me. They once asked me and my band to play patriotic music at events for the PRI and I refused to go, so they found a way to fail me. We had to take exams to graduate, and they kept losing my exams—that happened three times. I decided then that they must really not want me in school. The education system here in Puebla is horrid anyway; I couldn't learn anything from them.

I was eighteen when I left school. I worked at a sombrero factory for a few months afterward. My job was to put MADE IN MEXICO labels on the sombreros. They were exaggerated palm leaf sombreros that were sent to the United States for Cinco de Mayo. They celebrate Cinco de Mayo over there, not September 16 for some reason.[13] I'd slap the MADE IN MEXICO

[13] September 16 is Mexican Independence Day and marks the beginning of revolt against Spanish rule in 1810. Cinco de Mayo commemorates a major military victory over an invading French force in Puebla on May 5, 1861. Cinco de Mayo is celebrated primarily by Mexican emigrant communities and is a far less significant holiday inside Mexico than September 16.

tag over and over again on so many sombreros—they love those extremely exaggerated sombreros in the United States.

I worked at the sombrero factory for maybe six months, but the work bored me. The manager, not even a manager really, just a foreman, he treated us badly. And the factory would cheat on our pay. The factory would pay something like 80 pesos for one week of work.[14] It was a laughable salary; you couldn't even afford to go to the movies on the weekly wages. I was a bit more informed, so I'd explain to my fellow workers that we were supposed to be paid double for overtime. I told them the same applied to holidays, and we're not obligated to work on holidays. The foreman would hear me and he'd send me to work by myself in the warehouse, away from the other workers. I was a bad influence.

THE SPRINGS AND RIVERS TURNED BLUE

I never went to university. After I left school, I played with my band for a few years. Then, when I was in my early twenties, I really started to get involved in activism myself. Father Tacho was building an alliance of different social justice organizations in the area, an association of human rights activists called the Human Rights Commission of the Tehuacán Valley, and I got involved that way.

In 1993, I got together with a few other young people and activists in the area, including some others from the liberation theology school of thought, and we formed a working commission on indigenous rights called Cetirizchicahualistli. *Cetirizchicahualistli* is a Nahuatl word that means "to make one single force."[15] We worked with indigenous groups

---

[14] At the time, 80 pesos = approximately US$5.

[15] Nahuatl is an indigenous Mexican language and was spoken by the Aztecs before the Spanish colonial period in Mexico.

around the Sierra Negra on issues like land ownership. And in town, we also worked for indigenous civil rights. We'd defend the indigenous women who came to Tehuacán to sell their goods. The police would crack down on them for selling without permits. And we'd defend the boys who did work in the streets like cleaning windshields.

We established an office, and starting around 1995, it was my job to run it. I'd scrounge funds to pay the rent. In those years we had a government subsidy from the INI, the same governmental organization my mother worked for. And we found funding from NGOs in Canada and the United States. Probably 90 percent of the work we did was in promoting the rights of indigenous people in Puebla, but we also began to take a look at labor rights, especially after the maquilas began to move in.

Garment factories had existed in town when I was a kid, but they were small and served local markets only. Then in the nineties, especially after NAFTA was signed, there was a boom of maquilas in town that served transnational corporations. Just after NAFTA, the mayor of Tehuacán traveled extensively to the United States to bring foreign investment. From '95 up until '99 or 2000, new maquilas were popping up everywhere. Tehuacán didn't sleep. Workers were moving here from all over the valley, from all over Puebla. The movement of people was impressive. There were dozens of factories that needed two thousand workers or more each, and the demand for labor far exceeded the working population of Tehuacán. More than a hundred residential districts grew in the city's urban area, and migration into the areas around the city was rapid. Foreign retail stores like Woolworth and others appeared. Meanwhile, farmland outside the city disappeared. The metropolitan areas turned into blocks of dense residential development, while suburban neighborhoods, which were not planned well, became immersed in absolute instability.

The new factories served a number of well-known brands. Guess, Levi's, Calvin Klein, and Dockers have all been supplied by the maquilas of Tehuacán. Some of the factories themselves were relatively small, but many of the maquilas in town were run by a couple of big consortiums—the Tarrant Apparel Group and the Navarro Group—which ultimately employed around ten thousand and twenty thousand garment workers respectively, and were formed from alliances between U.S. business interests and local wealthy families.

These new companies moved into the old soda factories that had been shut down in the eighties. The maquilas were finding this infrastructure already set up for their needs, which made the area even more attractive. The natural springs the soda companies had used for their mineral water were now used to wash jeans. The old soda companies had been an important part of the community—they had made their pools available for recreation, and they had even supplied fresh water for free to locals who wanted to fill up gallon jugs at outdoor spigots. All the new maquilas were using the same springs, but they were terrible for the health of the community. The springs and rivers turned blue. The fields that were watered from local springs began to turn blue as well, all from the dye runoff from jeans production.

And these waters are toxic. Last year there was a study done by Greenpeace on the waters of Tehuacán, and they found cancer-causing chemicals. Even with the process the maquilas use now to give the water a clean, translucent appearance, it was found that the cancer-producing chemicals were not eliminated.

Tehuacán and the whole region are becoming waste areas, debilitated by the runoff from their own maquilas. Here in Tehuacán we have at least twenty industrial laundry facilities. These have always existed at the maquilas, and they serve to wash the clothing after it's made. The pollution is worsened by certain kinds of jeans fashions. In the nineties brands started to use acid wash or stone wash, which meant using pumice stone or special chemicals to wash out the jeans and give them a distinct look. The "stone bleach" style that became popular for a while involved eliminating the indigo dye from the jeans with enormous quantities of bleach. Finally, there's the "sand blast," which entails submitting garments to silica sand baths to give them a worn appearance. The use of these materials harms workers' respiratory tracts. Some even get sick with silicosis, which is an illness that otherwise only affects miners.

Our organization began investigating all these issues in the mid-nineties, because our city was transforming rapidly, and every other human rights issue was suddenly tied to the impact the clothing factories were having on the community. As early as 1995, we were involved in helping some international labor organizations report on the conditions of workers employed by the Navarro Group, and out of that collaboration, my current work grew. Our job was to help find workers to interview for international labor groups and unions such as UNITE, and through our work we learned of many cases of underage labor, unfair firings, and wages withheld arbitrarily. We knew the workers at these companies must live under incredible fear, since we were threatened by anonymous calls and by the local police because of our help on the ground with that report.[16] Finally, in 2002, a handful of my colleagues and I formed the Commission for Human and Labor Rights in Tehuacán Valley, and we really started to fight directly to protect the rights of garment workers in the area.

THEY GAVE ME A SERIOUS BEATING

In 2003, a year after I'd helped form the new labor commission, I had my first big conflict with the Tarrant Apparel Group. It was the first time we were right in the middle of the fire. I'd been speaking to workers about

---

[16] The report, *Cross Border Blues: A Call for Justice for Maquiladora Workers in Tehuacán*, was released in 1998 by the National Interfaith Committee for Worker Justice. The document was presented by UNITE, a U.S. union to U.S. companies such as Guess.

their rights under Mexican labor law for a few years, but our conflict with Tarrant was my first big fight.

That year there had been many layoffs at Tarrant. The workers didn't know what to do. They were being fired, but they didn't know how to organize. We were able to make a workers' coalition of about two thousand to resist further layoffs and a possible shutdown of Tarrant Apparel, a company that employed more than ten thousand in Tehuacán and nearby towns. The problem was that Tarrant had found an even less expensive source of labor in Central America, and wanted to leave Tehuacán altogether. When the shutdown was inevitable, we wanted to make sure that the company didn't flee without paying the workers a fair severance.

Had we not informed the workers of their right to severance pay, they would have been robbed of it. We were able to win 10 or 12 million pesos to distribute to the workers.[17] I don't remember the exact amount, but it definitely affected the company—I started receiving anonymous threats.

Then, on the morning of December 29, 2003, just a month after we won the severance pay, I was heading to our commission's office when two guys jumped me by the door of my house. I heard a voice just behind me mutter something, and when I turned I was struck with a brick in the temple. I didn't even have time to put my hands up. I fell to the ground, and then I felt the two men kicking me and hitting me on the back with the brick while I was down. Then they started turning me over, pulling me up by the hair so they could get at my face with the brick. I managed to block the brick with my arm as it swung at my nose. The guy dropped the brick, and he started kicking me in the ribs with his steel-toed boots. I was able to pull away, and when I did, the two guys started to run. I grabbed a pipe in the road and started to chase them—I had no idea how badly I'd been hurt, but I was drenched in blood. I chased them thinking I could

---

[17] 10 to 12 million pesos = approximately US$1 million.

grab one of them, or maybe the police would come by. I just wanted them to be interrogated, to find out who sent them. I caught up to them on a street corner, and one of them said, "Come on, come on, if you think you can do anything to us." I didn't dare go up to them. Then a taxi came by, and *phoom*, they were gone.

They gave me a serious beating. I ended up in the hospital that day. I was in bed for a week not able to move. I reported the incident, but the police didn't do anything. The two attackers were never found.

THEY BEGAN TO FIGHT BACK HARD

In 2005, the maquila owners were fed up with our commission's labor rights campaign, and they began to fight back hard. That year, the governor of Puebla, Mario Marín, had just started his term in office and he began working closely with the factory owners to keep workers from organizing. One of the governor's first measures was to remove the Tehuacán arbitration board's power.[18] What this meant was that the workers from the Tehuacán area had to go to the city of Puebla, over eighty miles away, to bring their labor lawsuits to trial.[19] So the intention of this was really just to discourage their complaints.

Because of my leadership among labor activists in the area, I always knew that the bosses wanted to teach me a lesson. Sometime in 2005, a worker at a factory managed by the Navarro Group told me he heard that the companies were planning something against me. And soon I was receiving death threats by telephone.

On December 28, 2005, I was walking along the street on my way

---

[18] An arbitration board is an impartial committee assigned to resolve labor disputes. For more information, see glossary, page 348.

[19] The city of Puebla is the capital city of the state of Puebla. It is a city of over 1.5 million, eighty miles northeast of Tehuacán.

to my house to pick up a cell phone. A group of men tackled me, asking my name. They said they were police, though they were in plainclothes. They had me at gunpoint and hoisted me into a car.

At first they didn't tell me their motive. I thought they wanted to intimidate me. But I got worried when I realized that they were taking me all the way to the city of Puebla. At that point I thought that the accusation could be more serious, since they were taking it to the state capital.

The police then showed me a warrant and explained the charges, that a maquila owner named Lucío Gil was accusing me of blackmailing him. Then things took an unexpected turn when they next took me to Gil's house. Gil was a sort of midlevel guy, a factory owner who worked closely with the Navarro Group but wasn't really one of the more powerful owners in the city. I'd helped some workers in his factory in the past, but I'd never spoken with him or dealt with him directly. At first I thought, *Why are the police bringing me to a private home? They're going to torture me.*

Then some of the police went to Gil's door to bring him out and identify me. When he came out, Gil was angry; I could see him outside cursing and telling them that he didn't have anything to do with me and asking why they had brought me there. When the police returned, they told me that the man had lost his nerve, and that he wasn't pressing charges against me anymore, that he didn't have anything against me.

"Well, that does it," I said. "So let me go home."

One of the police responded, "How are we going to let you go when we've already let everyone in Puebla know that we've arrested you? We can't do that."I couldn't believe it. Gil had said that he didn't have any charges to press against me, and in spite of this, the police proceeded with the arrest, and we drove into Puebla where I was booked.

"YOU COULD GET OUT IN A DAY, OR IN A YEAR"

I was put in prison in Puebla, and when my lawyer got there, he said to me, "You're basically a political prisoner, Martín—you could get out in a day, or in a year." I wasn't sure what to think. I was still confused about why they were holding me even though Gil had renounced the charges right in front of me.

The first days were really tough, a total psychological war. I couldn't sleep. The first night, the tiny cell was crowded with fourteen of us, and I had to sleep on the toilet. Then the next day they wanted to put me to work at four in the morning—hard to believe, but there was a secret maquila in the prison using prison labor. And they had me serving food in the violent offender ward of the prison, with murderers, rapists, and assorted psychopaths.

On January 4, 2006, after I'd already been in prison for a few days, the criminal court announced the formal charges of blackmail against me and denied bail. According to the accusation, I had demanded $150,000 from Gil and threatened to mobilize workers against him if he didn't pay up.

The maquila owners made the most of the days that followed my arrest. They published spreads in the local daily newspapers saying, "This time the governor has come through for us by putting that saboteur behind bars." With that, we could be certain that the maquila owners had played in the arrest and confirm that everything that was happening was related to my work in defense of labor rights. They published the spreads in the *Puebla Sun* and the *World of Tehuacán* among many other newspapers.

Whoever it was who had me arrested thought that I'd have less support if they moved me from Tehuacán to Puebla, but they were mistaken. In fact the case became high profile very quickly. The local media and later the national media picked it up, and immediately human rights organizations organized a campaign. There was broad solidarity among workers from many sectors, academics, NGOs, unions, and so on, and a very strong international campaign started. All of them were pressing for my release.

My defense consisted of presenting evidence regarding my participation in an event that was twenty-four miles away from Tehuacán at the moment I supposedly blackmailed Gil. There were at least 150 workers at that event who were witnesses to my attendance, so there wasn't the slightest doubt. I could not have blackmailed that man. Gil himself never testified in court, and I think he was still trying to disassociate himself from the case. I believe he'd been pressured to press charges by more powerful interests, but he knew the whole thing was a farce.

By the second week I was in prison, the political climate wasn't favorable for the governor, who was facing a lot of national and international pressure to release me. In the end, the pressure was so strong that the governor himself was sending lawyers to defend me. His lawyers told me that the offense had changed. They said, "Agree that you only threatened Lucío Gil, you didn't try to blackmail him, and we'll arrange bond so that you can go free." But I was willing to stay for several months if I had to. I didn't want to plead guilty to any charges.

I REFUSED TO SIGN THE PAPERS

Sometime in mid-January 2006, I was asked to take a call at the prison office. It was the secretariat of governance, saying, "We have forced Gil to grant you forgiveness, so you are free. Good afternoon."[20] They were offering a sort of pardon: getting Gil to say he forgave me for my

---

[20] The secretariat of governance is the head of the governance department in the state of Puebla.

supposed blackmail, but not drop the original accusation. I didn't accept it. "Forgiveness for what? I haven't done anything."

I refused to sign the papers acknowledging Gil's supposed act of forgiveness, and because that was my letter of release, I couldn't leave the prison. Instead I asked to speak with my lawyer. But the prison officials tried to deceive me by telling me, "Your lawyer already knows all of this. He's asked you to sign." I refused again.

The situation got out of control because by order of the government of Puebla they had to release me, but because of a signature that seemed like a formality, I couldn't get out of jail. The director of the prison finally arrived, saw me, and yelled, "Please Martín, go already! If you stay we'll be accused of illegal detention."

So I was free, but it was all a very important experience to me. I met commendable people in the prison. Some were really supportive, including young people who initially wanted to give me a hard time and later became my protectors. There were many indigenous people in the prison, many political prisoners, and even groups that had organized to denounce the prison conditions they had found themselves in.

DENIM ITSELF ISN'T THE CULPRIT

After I was released, I went back to work fighting against the worst abuses of the maquilas. In 2007, we fought to support a campaign against Vaqueros Navarra, one of the major factories under the Navarro Group. Vaqueros Navarra, like Tarrant, was trying to squeeze out workers while looking to move operations to countries where it was even less expensive to operate. Under the contracts in place, workers were supposed to receive a share of profits, but the bosses were cheating them. We began to counsel the workers, and we sought a just payment of their profit share. We weren't fighting for the U.S. brands to stop contracting with Navarra.

We didn't want the factories to close—we just wanted the workers to be treated fairly. But when Navarra saw that losing control to organized labor was a possibility, they no longer sought new contracts.[21] They closed up most of Navarra to teach us a lesson, but other factories under the Navarro Group remain in the city. Thousands of workers lost their jobs, and many of those went to the United States to look for work.

The transnational garment industry has left the valley. There are still large numbers of maquilas in Tehuacán, but the difference is that the focus is now on the Mexican market only. And the working conditions have actually worsened. Work hours are longer, and salaries are lower. Sexual harassment is common, as well as daily layoffs. Maquilas are still everywhere in Tehuacán, but the difference is scale. Homes have turned into maquilas. In order to get away with not paying for many benefits they have dispersed into all the neighborhoods. You see signs at many different houses soliciting needleworkers.

In Mexico there are a lot of fights over the defense of labor rights, from the south up through the north, in the smallest cities and in the biggest cities, along the northern border as well as the southern border. The challenges we have as labor rights defenders in Mexico are many, but most important is to influence consumers of these products to pressure the companies and brands to address the inadequate labor standards in their maquilas.

One problem is that many consumers aren't concerned with knowing where the products they're using come from. And for those consumers here in Mexico who know what's going on, they don't have as much power to change things as consumers in other countries. For instance, in Mexico, the act of boycotting some products isn't as effective as it would be in the United States.

---

[21] For more on the labor battle between Vaqueros Navarra and labor organizers, see Ana Juárez's narrative, page 63.

It's a difficult goal: we're seeking conscientious consumers, consumers who know how to research, who know how to examine a whole production chain, who know how to follow up on the brands, who demand information from companies, and so on. Denim itself isn't the culprit; the way the companies handle manufacturing and the workplace is the problem.

CITIES IN MEXICO ARE BECOMING AMERICANIZED

I remember that before NAFTA was passed you'd rarely see people with electronics like Walkmans or other new gadgets of the time, because you couldn't bring them in. If you did, it was usually contraband, but now it seems you see electronic devices everywhere. Everybody has the newest devices like iPads and tablets. With the passing of NAFTA I've seen how all the medium-sized cities of Mexico are becoming more and more Americanized. Cities are beginning to lose their identity. Walmarts, Burger Kings, and malls are everywhere.

One aspiration I have is to create a cultural center that's also a union headquarters, with an office and everything. We want to build a place where workers feel at ease, where they can gather to defend their rights and those of other workers. We want them to be able to inform themselves, have access to the Internet, read the newspaper, and analyze what's going on in this country. We want the cultural center to be a space for conferences about labor rights.

I work on reaching people through art, too. About four years ago I bought a drum kit and formed a band called Mixtitlan. Now I have a band called Necromancer. We play thrash metal but we have blues and stoner rock influences. We sing in Spanish because that was the idea, to play our own music in our own language and touch on social topics. The people who follow us work in the maquilas.

I don't know what the future holds for Tehuacán. It's increasingly polluted and congested. The living standards are low. If the government doesn't find another form of investment here, then Tehuacán will remain the same: a city with work but poorly paid workers. The children of the maquila workers from the boom in the 1990s are now the ones looking for work, and their exploitation is worse than it was for their parents. But we'll keep fighting for the rights of workers as long as our bodies hold up.

AGRICULTURE

THE ORIGINAL GLOBAL ECONOMY

More than ten thousand years ago, humans first sowed seeds from foraged plants and harvested the resulting crops to supplement food yields from hunting and gathering. The transition to early plant agriculture (and the domestication of animals) happened independently in regions of China, India, the Middle East, Africa, the Americas, and numerous other locations around the globe, and accelerated with innovations in irrigation—the management of the water supply to cultivate crops. Agriculture allowed people to live in one location year round rather than follow game herds, and agriculture surpluses allowed for economic specialization, the development of towns and cities, and the rise of complex societies.

Until the Industrial Revolution in the late eighteenth and early nineteenth centuries,[1] the vast majority of people around the globe labored as farmers, tied to the land. New farming techniques such as mechanical harvesting allowed for more intensive food production and the growth of a nonagricultural labor pool. Then, after millennia of farming fueled largely

---

[1] For more on the Industrial Revolution, see Appendix I, page 343.

by natural elements, human cultivation of land took a dramatic shift in the twentieth century when scientists learned to chemically synthesize nitrates—the essential component in fertilizer.[1]

Nitrates were also essential to the manufacture of explosives. Nitrate factories were dedicated to the production of ammunition through World War I and World War II, and after World War II, the United States had a near monopoly on nitrate production due to the flattening of ammunition plants in Europe and Asia during wartime. Other U.S. wartime manufacturing centers were repurposed to agricultural production—modern pesticides were developed from nerve-gas research, for instance. With a global food shortage in the wake of the war, the U.S. government began subsidizing the production of commodity crops to feed hungry populations in Europe and elsewhere. Farmers who had once cultivated diverse crops to increase nutritional components in the soil moved to the mono-cropping of rice, corn, soybeans, and wheat to exploit economies of scale and to take advantage of these government subsidies.[2]

Starting in the 1950s, high-yield agricultural methods developed in the United States were quickly disseminated around the world, at first by philanthropic organizations that hoped to feed a booming global population. This was the beginning of the Green Revolution, a global shift in agriculture that emphasized farming as a commercial practice rather than a subsistence practice.[3] Between the early sixties and the mid-eighties, global production of grains such as wheat, rice, and maize increased by 100 percent, a rate of growth that allowed for a doubling of the world's population between 1960 and 2000.

---

[1] Michael Pollan, "Farmer in Chief," *New York Times*, October 9, 2008.

[2] For more on commodity crops, mono-cropping, and economies of scale, see glossary, page 348.

[3] For more on the Green Revolution, see Appendix I, page 343.

In many ways, the price of industrialized, globalized agriculture has been steep, with environmental costs such as increased soil erosion, surface and groundwater contamination, and pest resistance, as well as the release of greenhouse gases and the loss of biodiversity. Then there are the humanitarian costs. Farmers who do not own enough land to take advantage of globalized mono-cropping, or enough capital to invest in the latest high-yield seeds or fertilizers and pesticides, have found a way of life passed down through centuries suddenly threatened. Many farmers have been forced into the migrant labor pool, often traveling hundreds or thousands of miles from their homes in search of living wages.[4] Ironically, modern agricultural production has returned many workers to the nomadic subsistence that traditional agriculture supplanted thousands of years ago.

In developing nations, globalization has hastened the transition from subsistence and small-scale farming to wage work for many farming families. Pournima Akolkar, a cotton farmer in India, lost her husband to suicide in the midst of spiraling financial pressures resulting from a convergence of factors: the cost of new strains of genetically modified seeds, paltry harvests, and mounting debt to seed and loan brokers. Though she grew up on a family-owned farm that met most of her family's subsistence needs, Pournima now lives in a small rural town and works as a cook and field hand so she can feed her children.

Retaining ownership of family farms is a priority for subsistence farmers around the globe, but it often proves impossible. Many farmers cannot afford the capital investment needed to take advantage of the most profitable agricultural technologies, leaving them unable to compete in the open market with large commercial producers. As a result, families operating small farms end up selling their land to large producers and working for them as low-wage field hands instead of cultivating their own land.

---

[4] For more on living wages, see glossary, page 348.

In the mountains of Guatemala, for example, this kind of economic desperation spurs families to bring their children, some as young as three, to work alongside them cultivating coffee in the *fincas*.[5] As Francisca Cocón—a Guatemalan woman who labored as a child in fincas—explains, wages are often delayed, reduced, or withheld, and workers are left without recourse other than to move to other plantations. Wages are so low (Francisca remembers wages of less than a dollar a day in the eighties) that, even when paid on time and in full, families struggle.

For itinerant farmworkers, the United States is a comparatively attractive destination, even if many who do the actual work of planting and harvesting crops earn less than a living wage, are subjected to dangerous working conditions, and are excluded from full legal protection. Of the 1.4 million farmworkers estimated to be currently in the United States, roughly on quarter to one half are undocumented men, women, and children. Often, newly arrived immigrant workers are more concerned with keeping their jobs and keeping under the radar of immigration authorities than asserting their rights to fair wages and safe working conditions.

Fausto Guzmán, an undocumented worker from Oaxaca, Mexico, lives in California wine country. He works the cultivation, harvesting, and processing of grapes at a winery in Sonoma County—a job that led to a near-fatal accident and heart failure several years ago due to faulty machinery and poor ventilation in the winery's warehouse. Having received a nominal settlement, Fausto continues working at the same winery, chancing another heart failure and the persistent threat of deportation for the relatively high wage of $12 an hour.

Neftali Cuello, a teenager whose parents are from Mexico and the Dominican Republic, has worked tobacco fields in North Carolina since the age of twelve. Though U.S. labor laws prohibit child labor in most

---

[5] *Fincas* are plantations. For more information on fincas, see glossary, page 348.

sectors of the economy, laws are much looser regarding child labor on farms—a standard designed to allow children of independent farmers to help their parents starting at a young age. Large commercial growers are able to take advantage of the legal loophole by hiring children such as Neftali to work long hours for minimum wage.

Still, Neftali gets paid a regular wage for her labor in the summers and she can attend school starting in the fall. Nasiba Opa's daughter is not as fortunate. In Uzbekistan where Nasiba's family lives, the government forces many of its citizens, including children, to set aside other tasks and pick cotton every harvest season, paying them nominal wages for months of forced labor. Uzbekistan is the third-largest exporter of cotton after the United States and India, though its population is just thirty million—one-tenth that of the United States and one-fortieth that of India. This incredible level of productivity is possible because of substantial savings on field labor costs.

POURNIMA AKOLKAR

AGE: *37*

OCCUPATION: *Former cotton farmer, day laborer, cook*

BIRTHPLACE: *Kolai, Maharashtra, India*

INTERVIEWED IN: *Pandharkawada, Maharashtra, India*

According to the Center for Human Rights and Global Justice, in 2009 alone, 17,638 Indian farmers committed suicide, or one farmer every thirty minutes. They estimate that more than a quarter of a million Indian farmers have committed suicide in the last sixteen years. In 2011–12, the number of suicides was particularly severe among cotton farmers.[1] *Numerous surveys and reports link farmer suicides to debt and the pressures of repaying loans with steep interest rates. Increasingly, cotton farmers will borrow money in order to buy seeds, fertilizers, and pesticides, and the cost of these investments has risen dramatically, even as the market has kept the price at which farmers can sell their cotton relatively flat.*

We meet Pournima Akolkar at a banquet in honor of over two hundred widows of cotton farmers in Vidarbha, a region with one of the highest rates of

---

[1] India is the world's second largest producer of cotton, and the top exporter of cotton to the U.S.

farmer suicide in India. Pournima agrees to talk to us about her husband Hanshal, who committed suicide two years ago by drinking pesticides. She later invites us to her house, where we sit and talk in the middle bedroom. This is where Pournima has been spending most of her time since she broke her hip nearly a year ago. On the wall behind us hangs a photograph of Pournima and her husband.

We share food and laugh together as we exchange photos of our families. Then Pournima tells us about how she works hard to provide for her two children. She speaks with determination to share her story, though her voice wavers when the subject turns to her husband.

Names have been changed at the request of the narrator.

MY FATHER IS A GOOD PERSON, A HAPPY PERSON

I was born in Kolai, in Vidarbha.[2] My family is big, and we were happy growing up. We are four sisters and two brothers, and I am the youngest daughter. My father is a farmer—there are lots of farmers in Kolai—and he owns six acres of land. My father is a good person, a happy person. He loves us.

When I was little, I used to work on the farm along with my parents and siblings. I stopped going to school when I was eleven years old. There was no school after elementary school in Kolai, and my grandmother didn't allow me to go to the nearest town, Pandharkawada, for higher studies.[3] She was afraid for me. There was no bus at that time, and I would have had to walk over three miles to get there. She didn't think it was safe

---

[2] Pournima was born in a village in Vidarbha, an eastern region of the central Indian state of Maharashtra. The exact name of her village has been changed (here, to Kolai) to protect her identity. Vidarbha is rural and poor compared to much of the rest of relatively prosperous Maharashtra.

[3] Pandharkawada is a town of nearly thirty thousand in Vidarbha.

for young girls to make the trip by foot.

For kids in the village, even if we didn't do any work, we had to go to the farm with our families to learn about the work that was done there. The farmland surrounded the village, and most of the village families owned fields beside each other, so we'd all work in the fields together. Usually the men and women went separately and did different sorts of work. Sowing seeds, spreading fertilizers, weeding—these were the sorts of things my mother and other women taught me to do to help out. I used to enjoy that sort of work. It was done with love and nurturing and care, and there was a sense of community. I remember being on the farm with other girls and women. Most neighbors worked on their own plots of land, but everyone in the community would help each other out when our own work was done, and we'd socialize as well. We used to take our own tiffins with us.[4] I enjoyed the environment.

Saturday and Sunday, they used to be days off. On those days, my siblings and I would still go to the farm, but only to play there with our friends through the day. We would take our kitchen sets and all our toys, and we'd use ropes and vines to make swings in the trees. We'd do whatever we wanted. There was a lake near the farm, so we would go there, have a bath, then wash our clothes and utensils, and horse around.

My family hardly had to buy any food because we got most of what we ate from the farm. Of our six acres, four were dedicated to crops we could sell, like cotton and *jowar*.[5] The other two acres were used to grow vegetables—eggplant, onions, chilies, lentils, okra. Whatever crop we grew on the farm was used as food at home, and we'd sell our extra vegetables. We had oiling machines, so even the oil that was used at home came from

---

[4] A *tiffin* is a packed lunch or a light meal. It often consists of rice, lentils, chapati, and a vegetable curry.

[5] *Jowar* is a variety of sorghum, a grain.

the sesame and peanuts that we grew.

As for investments to make the farm grow, my father never took out bank loans. When I was a child, there were no bank loans for farms or anything else, really. There was just an informal society that would lend money, so every year my father would borrow as much as he needed to begin the planting season, and then every year he'd repay whatever he owed after we sold our cotton. Of course, we needed money for other things besides just the operation of the farm, and Father borrowed some money to pay our dowries as well.[6] The dowry was very high in our community, around 1 to 2 *lakhs*. The grand total for my dowry was 2 lakhs, and 75,000 rupees of that was in cash.[7] And then there were all the other household things.

It was very hard for someone who had only six acres of land to find husbands for four daughters, but he married all of us off. We are thankful to him for that.

My brothers Amol and Sudhir helped out with household expenses and with our dowries as well. My two brothers studied through high school and then started working. Both brothers had their businesses that provided income, and a lot of that income would go into farm expenses. Amol had a *paan* shop.[8] It was a good job. Besides investing in the farm, Amol used the money that he earned from the paan shop to pay for dowries for me and my sisters, as well as other big family expenses. The daily household expenses were with Sudhir, who sold milk. His business was as good as Amol's.

Amol and Sudhir each got a dowry from their wives' families when

---

[6] For more on the dowry system, see glossary, page 348.

[7] A *lakh* is an Indian unit of measure = 100,000. One lakh is 100,000 rupees, the basic unit of currency in India. 1 lakh rupees = approximately US$1,600. 75,000 rupees = US$1,200.

[8] *Paan* is a kind of snuff or chewing tobacco that also contains ground betel nut (another stimulant) and spices.

they got married. In our community, almost everything is given in dowry—from basic kitchen utensils to the beds. Amol got 2 lakh rupees; Sudhir got 1.5 lakh rupees.

I was eighteen years old when I got married. It was around 1995. My father arranged it all, but he chose my husband Hanshal because he had a reputation in the community as a good, kind man. At the time, I was scared. I had also heard good things about Hanshal, that he was liked and respected, he was known to be very hospitable and treat friends like family, but I had never met him before. I didn't know much about him or his family.

AT MY IN-LAWS' PLACE, I HAD A LOT OF RESPONSIBILITIES ON MY SHOULDERS

After my wedding I went to my husband's village, Andavi.[9] Andavi is a few miles from where I grew up, on the other side of Pandharkawada.

Many decades ago the government gave three acres of land to my father-in-law through a program called *Bhoodan*.[10] Its English meaning would be something like *land donation*. My father-in-law held the title to the farm, and my husband and his brothers used to work with their parents during the growing season. After their marriages, Hanshal's brothers did other work since the property was small and they could make more money

---

[9] Andavi is not the real name of the village. The name has been changed to protect the identity of the narrator.

[10] *Bhoodan* was a program instituted a few years after India gained independence from Great Britain in 1948. The movement evolved into a series of land reform acts passed state by state in the 1950s and 1960s. The Maharashtra Agricultural Lands (Ceiling on Holdings) Act of 1961 limited the number of arable acres that a family could own. Surplus land was donated to landless poor on the condition that the land had to be used for agriculture and could not be resold. Over four million acres were donated throughout India, though rarely would landowners part with their most fertile property. Land acquired through Bhoodan and the agriculture land ceiling acts was often rocky, barren, or otherwise difficult to farm.

with other jobs. His elder brother worked as a laborer on other people's farms. His younger brother was a driver.

My in-laws cultivated mostly cotton for sale at market, and some jowar and lentils. The routine was familiar in many ways, but there were differences between my new home and the community where I'd grown up. Just as in Kolai, all the villagers in Andavi would head to the fields together in the mornings. But in Andavi, the land was dry and it wasn't irrigated like it was near Kolai, so there were more limitations on what crops we could grow and what times of year we could grow them. Our growing season was only six months in Andavi. Also, we had to purchase food in Andavi that we'd grown for ourselves in Kolai, things like wheat, nuts, beans, chilies, chickpeas, which required irrigation to grow.

For me, there were other differences between life in Andavi and in Kolai. The main difference was that back home, I was with my mother, and at my mother's place I was nurtured and cared for, and my work in the fields and at home was done with love and care. But at my in-laws' place I had responsibilities on my shoulders. There, I'd work hard because I had a constant sort of a fear—*If I don't do the work properly will my mother-in-law say something to me? If I don't get up early enough, will my father-in-law say something to me?*

Each day during the growing season from June to November, I would go with my in-laws and neighbors to the fields to weed, spread fertilizer, tend to the crops. Then I would come home early with my mother-in-law, and we'd prepare food, do the housework along with my two sisters-in-law. My father-in-law and my husband used to come home a bit later, after feeding the cattle. They would be at the farm until eight or nine at night. Before my husband came home I would serve food to my in-laws, my husband's brothers, and their children. Then after Hanshal came home, he used to wash, freshen up, have food, and then rest.

When my husband and I first got married there was not a very heavy workload on the farm. We had time to talk about future plans—work that needed to be done on the farm later on to improve it, and raising money for the education of our future children. We were really happy.

Then in 1997, when I was about twenty, I had my son Sachin. In our community it's traditional to return to your childhood home when you're five months pregnant and stay there for one complete year after the child is born. So I lived with my parents for a little over a year starting in 1997, and then I had my daughter Indumati three years later, in 2000, and again I went home for a little over a year. During those times, my husband would come to Kolai and stay for eight or nine days at a time with me. My husband was very nice to the kids. He would bring gifts for them and nurture them, look after them. All the care and love for me was now mainly concentrated on the children. My husband was very happy having a son and a daughter; it was like a complete family.

MY HUSBAND WOULD BUY THE SEEDS. MY HUSBAND WAS EDUCATED.

There's been a lot of change in the cost of farming over the years. I remember when I was around twelve years old, the price we got for our cotton used to be 400, 500 rupees per quintal.[11] We'd grow eighteen to twenty quintals of cotton on three acres, and so in a good year we'd be able to make about 10,000 rupees off of our cotton crop.[12]

The rates have risen, but the expenses have also gone up. Around the time of my marriage, the rate of cotton per quintal was approximately

---

[11] A quintal is 100 kilograms, or about 220 pounds. At the time, 500 rupees = approximately US$30.

[12] At the time, 10,000 rupees = approximately US$590.

1,800 to 2,000 rupees. The best quality would get 2,000 rupees.[13] But at the same time, the costs have increased for seeds, fertilizers, and pesticides. Since the early 2000s everyone uses Bt seeds, which can grow a lot more per acre.[14] There are different strains—one called Mallika costs about 500, 550 rupees per bag, and one that grows a little better called Brahma costs 700, 750 rupees per bag.[15] And the big difference is that we have to buy new seeds every year.

Before Bt seeds arrived, farmers in the area would plant seeds that were reusable. After harvest, farmers would pick cotton from the buds, separate the seed from the actual fibers of cotton, and then soak the seeds in water mixed with cow dung as a kind of fertilizer. Then after the seeds were dry, they'd be ready to plant. Nobody bought seeds every year like they do now.

There's been a significant change in the way we grow cotton since Bt was introduced around 2002. My husband started planting the seeds around that time. With our old strains of cotton, we had to spray the crops with pesticides four times through the growing season. With Bt, we had to spray only two times. We also needed less fertilizer with Bt cotton.

The Bt seeds, I don't know what they're coated with or what is applied to them. They germinate almost as soon as they are sown. After they germinate, the cattle won't eat them, so it's not a problem. If the cattle eat them, their stomachs swell. Bt has no problems once it's germinated. With our old cotton crops, in one spot we used to put down two seeds—if one doesn't germinate, the other will. With Bt, it's not that way. In one

---

[13] At the time, 2,000 rupees = approximately US$80.

[14] Bt crops have been genetically modified to produce a substance naturally found in the bacterium *Bacillus thuringiensis* that is toxic to insects but not to humans. For more information on the introduction of genetically modified crops to India, see Appendix III, page 355.

[15] 500 to 750 rupees = approximately US$8 to US$12.

spot you put only one seed and it is guaranteed that it will germinate. So there are advantages, but it costs a lot more to plant the crop every year, and you must have a good crop to justify the costs.

When it was time to plant, Hanshal would go back to Adilabad to buy seeds for the farm.[16] My husband was educated, so the neighbors would say things like, "You're going to Adilabad? Get fertilizers and pesticides for me." They would contribute money, help pay to rent a truck, and then he'd get the fertilizers and pesticides in bulk amounts. Every year, the merchants in Adilabad would have different strains of seeds to sell and advice about which was best. Fertilizers and pesticides, too—my husband bought them from the same place where he bought his seeds; it was called a *krishi kendra*, or farming center. Every year the merchants would have new advice, and nowadays they sell only Bt seeds.

When the harvest was ready, my husband would rent a truck to take his cotton to sell in Adilabad. The merchants there are employed by the ginning mills. First the farmer goes to the merchant and then the merchant goes to the mill with the cotton, even if it's bad quality. The merchant says to the farmer, "I'll fix a good price with the owner of the ginning mill even if the cotton is bad. But then you have to pay me some extra commission for it." The mechant would usually charge a commission of around 500 to 1,000 rupees.[17]

THE RAINS BETRAYED US

Our first year with Bt seeds was good, and in 2003 or 2004 my husband and his father used 1.5 lakh[18] they'd saved up to buy a house in the town

---

[16] Adilabad is a town of nearly 125,000, located thirty miles south of Pandharkawada.

[17] 500 to 1,000 rupees = approximately US$8 to US$16.

[18] 1.5 lakh = approximately US$2,400.

of Pandharkawada so that we could have a place to stay when we went into town.

Then in 2007, my father-in-law gave the farm to my husband. At the time, he didn't explain how he'd managed the farm's finances—how he'd taken out loans each planting season, how he'd managed savings. He just handed over the fields to Hanshal. So my husband started to take out loans every year, for pesticides and fertilizers and seeds, just figuring it out on his own.

That first year he was in charge of the farm, Hanshal took out a loan of around 1 lakh from a private bank. The interest rate on his loan was 3 percent. There was another bank loan with the farm as collateral; that was less. No bank would give a big loan for a farm.[19] With the farm as an asset we couldn't get a loan of more than 10,000 rupees.[20]

Then, from 2007 through 2010, the rains betrayed us. For two years it didn't rain, and the other two years it rained so much the seeds were washed away.

Because bank loans were small, my husband started to take out loans from other farmers or private moneylenders, and he wouldn't tell me exactly what the interest rate for these were. He would just say, "Why are you worried about the interest rate? I'm taking a loan, that's it. You don't bother about it." My husband had to make multiple payments, like paying the moneylender's interest, then taking up a loan, then paying off the bank's interest, then keeping the principal amount aside and paying off all the interest rates.

---

[19] Many farmers initially take a loan anywhere from 5,000 to 15,000 rupees from a bank as well as additional loans (usually for greater amounts) from moneylenders. The consequences of not paying the loan from the bank are minimal; if the loan from the bank remains unpaid then the farmer usually cannot take out additional loans. Interest rates on loans from private moneylenders are generally much higher than interest rates on bank loans.

[20] 10,000 rupees = approximately US$180.

Starting in 2007, my husband wasn't able to pay back much of anything on the loans. He wouldn't tell the rest of the family much about what was happening with the banks. He actually kept the gold chain he'd given me as a wedding present as collateral in the bank, and he took a loan on that.[21] I didn't know it; he didn't tell me he had taken it. One day I saw a notice from the bank about the loan and learned they had my wedding chain. So he deposited 30,000 rupees and released the chain and gave it back to me.[22]

We made around 80,000 to 90,000 rupees from cotton after the 2007 season.[23] We were just able to pay back the interest. After that the bank and moneylenders started talking. They said, "If you don't repay the loan, your house will get confiscated. This'll happen. That'll happen." My husband was experiencing a lot of stress. He said to me, "Everything I earned is all gone now. What will happen?"

In 2009, my husband couldn't pay back any money at all, since our crop was washed away. I told him, "Sell the house in Pandharkawada. Pay back the money." But he said, "I've taken a bank loan on the Pandharkawada house already. It's an asset, so I cannot sell it."

For business with the banks, my husband used to go to Bori.[24] When he came home, he didn't talk to me. He wouldn't talk to the children either, and they were nine and eleven years old, old enough to sense that something was wrong. If I asked him, "Why are you not talking? Why are you so low?" he'd say, "I have a headache. Don't disturb me."

Hanshal changed a lot after 2009. Sometimes he would behave very

---

[21] Similar to a wedding ring, these gold chains are the symbol of marriage for women in this region.

[22] 30,000 rupees = approximately US$480.

[23] 90,000 rupees = approximately US$1,440.

[24] Bori, or Butibori, is a fast-growing industrial suburb of Nagpur, a city of nearly 2.5 million. Bori is located seventy-five miles north of Pandharkawada.

normally, very nicely. Otherwise, he would just shout at me, use foul language. My father-in-law would say, "Why don't you go back to your home and stay for four or five days till he cools off and gets normal?" So I would go back to Kolai and stay for one month, two months. Then when I went back to my husband, the situation would be the same. He would be very quiet and keep to himself, not talk much, and then suddenly lose his temper. I think he actually went kind of mad because of the loans.

He lost interest in the farm and wouldn't show up until four or five in the evening, and he'd just walk around the fields a little, talk to our neighbors. Then at night he would go to Bori. Once he went to Bori, he didn't come back till midnight sometimes. I don't really know what he used to do in Bori. If I asked him, he'd hit me. By 2010, he was almost gone. He would keep to himself, quiet, lost in his own thoughts.

I SEARCHED THE WHOLE HOUSE FOR THE POISON

Sometimes my husband talked about killing himself. He'd say things like, "I will leave. I will do something bad to myself if you continue to ask me questions." I used to say, "Why are you saying such things? We have a son. We have a daughter. If we lose anything, it'll be our home in Pandharkawada. We can survive." He would say, "I've lost my respectability. I'm going to lose the house." I don't know what got into his head.

My father-in-law would tell me, "Don't say anything to him. Don't cause more stress. I am there to make up for his part of the work." So our family didn't say anything to him. We were afraid he would actually commit suicide.

He'd stay at home for two or three days at a time. The children would tell me, "Mom, Dad was at home the whole day." I was still going to the farm and working, and so was Hanshal's father. During the last phase of cotton picking in 2010, I'd leave for the farm every morning and pick about five kilograms, ten kilograms of cotton. In the evening, I'd come home and he'd be asleep. I'd say, "Wake up, let's have food. Why don't you come with us to the farm tomorrow?" He'd ignore me.

One day in November 2010 he said to me, "Today I got some poison. I'm going to drink it."

I searched the whole house for the poison. Even my mother-in-law searched with me. When I found where he kept it, I showed it to my neighbors. I was desperate for help. I told the neighbors, "Here. He's got poison. Talk to him. Why is he behaving like this?" When the neighbors came, he lied. He said it was just pesticide for a crop of chilies.

He was honest with one of his brothers, though. Hanshal told him, "I want to commit suicide. I want to drink it. I have a lot of debt weighing on me." So my brother-in-law overturned the bottle and threw away all the poison.

Two or three days after my brother-in-law threw out the first bottle of pesticide, my husband got another bottle. I was home the whole day and he didn't show me, didn't tell me about it. He came home from the market where he'd bought the poison, we ate our lunch, and then at two o'clock he went to the outdoor toilets. When he came back he was sweating a lot and he seemed a little afraid. He told me, "Pournima, I have taken poison." Then he fainted.

My brother-in-law borrowed a car and we took my husband to Bori. There they kept him in the hospital for hours. The doctors said, "We can't save him." So we took him back to Pandharkawada. From Pandharkawada we took him to Yavatmal,[25] looking for a hospital that could save him.

---

[25] Yavatmal, a town of 120,000, is located about forty-five miles northwest of Pandharkawada.

We ended up in Sevagram.[26] He was at Sevagram for eight days. We couldn't talk to him. There was a mask over his face.

My husband died in late November. The postmortem was carried out at Sevagram, and then we brought him to Pandharkawada. There was a gathering of relatives, neighbors. The atmosphere was full of grief. We burned the body.

YOU HAVEN'T GOT ANY BEAUTY LEFT

After his death, I stayed a few months in my in-laws' house in Andavi. But in every corner, there was a memory of my husband. He used to sleep here; he used to eat food there; he used to sit down there. The grief at that time—it's hard to describe. When I saw other families that had a man in the house, it was hard to bear. The children had lost their father; my mother-in-law had lost her son. For about a month and a half, all I did was cry.

So I moved permanently to our house in Pandharkawada in 2011, four months after Hanshal died. I came here for my children's education, and to escape my grief.

It's still hard, though. On days when my children remember their father and miss him, they feel so sad they don't even eat. When we see families that are complete, we feel sad. When we're talking and I mention Hanshal, my son asks me, "Why do you talk about Father? It's painful to remember him."

But I have no complaints against my children. They don't ask for things. They behave sensibly. They eat whatever is cooked; they don't ask me for money, new books, or new clothes. They just go to school, study,

---

[26] Sevagram is about fifty miles northeast of Yavatmal and is home to the Mahatma Gandhi Institute of Medical Sciences, a research institute that also serves the region's rural community.

and help me. I am very proud of them. They're the only ones I can be proud of.

At my son's school, there are children whose fathers are big businessmen or servicemen. Even among them, he was first in his class this year. He's studying really well. Other people say, "Even though he's from a small village and has come to a big school, your son is one of the first in his class." I called his teacher and I asked her, "I'm not able to look after his studies, so what can you tell me about him?" The teacher told me, "He's a really sweet boy, answers all the questions, gives proper answers. He behaves nicely, and he studies well." I was overjoyed. It was like he'd got a job somewhere.

Here in Pandharkawada, it's just work, eat, live. Widows can't put on the *bindi*.[27] You can't wear earrings, or the necklace around your neck. You can't put flowers in your hair or wear rings on your toes. You haven't got any beauty left, the way you naturally are.

When I came to Pandharkawada, as soon as I put down my luggage, I started looking for work. I had to do something for my children. Earning 100 rupees per day, I had 3,000 rupees as an income per month.[28] For the first few months of 2011, the conditions looked good, looked promising. I didn't require any help from my in-laws' side or my parents' side.

I got work preparing tiffins for four DEd students.[29] I prepare rice, dahl, vegetables, chapati. Then I walk to the homes and deliver the meals. Even though preparing the tiffins is not very profitable, it is more

---

[27] A *bindi* is a cosmetic dot worn between the eyebrows. In Hindu tradition, the bindi may symbolize wisdom and introspection. Bindis are popular across various religions and cultures in South Asia, however. In rural India, wearing a red bindi generally signifies that a woman is married.

[28] 3,000 rupees = approximately US$50.

[29] DEd stands for diploma in education, the degree needed to teach in schools in India. It is equivalent to a teaching certificate in the United States.

profitable than farming.

Then I broke my hip. This was early in the harvesting season in 2011, and it was when I was going to pick cotton as a laborer on other people's farms. After preparing the tiffins, I would go to the fields. It was a Sunday and I had taken both my kids. On our way home, near the temple, there was a puddle of water. I slipped in the water and fell and broke my hip.

Almost a thousand people from my husband's village came to see me. Everybody was here, asking, "How did this happen? When did this happen?" My husband was a good person at heart; he used to help anybody. That was the way he behaved with everyone. So people came to see me.

After my hip got fractured, my mother was here for three months. Then I told her, "Why are you here? You go back to your place; all the farmwork is left behind. There are no laborers for work." Since the time my mother left, my daughter is doing all kinds of work: making tea, food, helping me out. It's just my daughter who is helping me and doing all the work.

I HAD TO LISTEN TO MY BROTHERS' COMPLAINTS. THAT WAS INTOLERABLE FOR ME.

My husband had taken a loan of 3 lakh on this house in Pandharkawada.[30] The loan on the house was not waived off by the government so the bank told me that I had to pay it off. A lot of bank officials from the private bank were troubling me and my children. They were warning us, "We will seal this house. You cannot touch anything." They were troubling me, so I told my parents.

My parents and brothers helped me pay off the loan and this house is

---

[30] 3 lakh = approximately US$4,900, or twice the original cost of the property.

now okay. The production of cotton that just finished and the cotton that we sold right now, from that money each brother gave me 1.5 lakh. My parents had told my brothers, "She has a right to part of the farm, so what do you want? Should we give her a part of the farm? Or do you want to pay her loan off?"

My brothers also have their own families, their kids to look after. They paid off the loan, but then I had to listen to their complaints about the cost. That was intolerable for me. Sometimes I felt I wanted to commit suicide. One day I went to sleep at eleven o'clock at night and woke up at four in the afternoon. Sometimes I'd go to my relatives' home and just watch TV, talk to them. It took a lot of courage to build myself back up after my husband committed suicide. But right from when my hip got fractured and they put this rod in my hip, I started to lose what hope I had left. Now I cannot work; I have to sit.

IF ANYONE READS MY KUNDALI, THEY TELL ME, "YOU'RE VERY LUCKY"

I'm the main breadwinner and now I cannot work, so I really feel sad. With the help of the Niradhar Scheme,[31] I get 1,200 rupees per month, and then my parents send some help, so I just depend on that. My children go to a government school so the fees are not that much. Till the seventh grade my son got books from the school itself. From the eighth grade onward we have to buy uniforms and books ourselves, so the expenses have increased. My son has major exams coming up next year and what

[31] The Sanjay Gandhi Niradhar Anudan Scheme is a government program that provides monthly financial assistance to the destitute, the blind, the disabled, orphaned children, persons suffering from major illnesses, divorced women, abandoned women, women freed from prostitution, and others living below poverty level.

can I do?[32] I am crippled at home. What can be done sitting at a place? I haven't asked anyone to help me. But even if anybody helps, to what extent can they help?

There are problems in my life due to Shani causing troubles—the loans, then my husband's suicide, then coming here.[33] For the last month, I haven't been happy at all. It's all tension and I'm not feeling good.

I just stay at my place, don't go anywhere, just lock up the main doors. I feel my husband is still here with me and I remember him always. It's like I'm not a widow, like I'm still married. I still feel the same way that I felt before. My husband always used to say, "Never go on the wrong path. Always do good deeds." So I always tell my son to do the same.

If anyone reads my *kundali*,[34] they tell me, "You're very lucky." I tell them, "How can I be lucky? I have so much trouble in my life." Then they say that I always have help whenever I'm in trouble. So yes, I'm lucky. My son is there to make my faith glow, make me more lucky. I am completely dependent on him. He says, "I will go to America and sell tea there because here, in India, it's too cheap, but in America, it's costly. So I'll go there and make money by selling tea." I say to him, "Do whatever your heart says. Let's see what happens." With my children, it depends on their hearts, what they wish and what they want to do in the future.

I just want to educate my children, for them to get a job, make their father's name proud. If they get a good education, then they'll get a good job and get a respectable place in the community. If my son studies well, he'll grow up and join the civil service, get a government job. Then people will say, "See how he is just like his father was."

---

[32] In India at the end of the tenth grade, there is an exam called the Board Exam that students must pass to continue their educations. A small fee is required to take the test.

[33] *Shani* is the planet Saturn in Hindu astrology.

[34] A *kundali* is a horoscope.

NASIBA OPA

AGE: *37*
OCCUPATION: *Seamstress*
BIRTHPLACE: *Unknown*
INTERVIEWED IN: *Uzbekistan*

Uzbekistan is a landlocked country of nearly thirty million in Central Asia and was formerly part of the Soviet Union. Today, the country is one of the world's largest cotton exporters along with the United States, China, India, Australia, and Brazil.

Every year, up to one million Uzbek adults and children are coerced into participating in cotton harvests. Cotton fields are only partially privatized, with landowners required to meet specific production quotas set by the national government and also required to sell at a set price. In rural regions, schoolchildren as young as seven (though most are high school age) are required to pick as much as one hundred pounds of raw cotton each day, seven days a week, from September through November. Public employees such as teachers, hospital workers, and police are required to help supervise the harvests, and private employers are expected to provide financial support or employee labor as well.

Children who are unwilling to participate or who fall short of quotas face expulsion from school, and their parents face reprisals such as having welfare benefits cut off. Adults who fail to participate can lose pensions or other benefits, depending on their work.

Although children are forced to work through the harvest season, they are paid a small wage—just enough to supplement the meager food rations they are given. The actual amount of pay is difficult to determine but at peak season may hover around US$2.50 a day, depending on the quantity of cotton the children are able to pick. Nordibek, a seven-year-old we speak with, tells us that with the wages he was given working six-hour days, he was able to save enough to attend a carnival with his father once after the harvesting season was over.

In December 2010, we are able to talk briefly with a few men, women, and children about their experiences with the annual harvest. The Uzbek-German Forum for Human Rights helps set up the interviews and translate. One volunteer, Nasiba Opa, describes for us the forced labor imposed on her family each year during the cotton-harvesting season. In the short time we have with her, she's able to eloquently detail the annual disruption of her family's life that the harvest represents. Nasiba's name and town and the names of her children's schools have been changed or withheld to protect her identity.

WHAT KIND OF FUTURE WILL WE HAVE IN UZBEKISTAN?

I live in a small town in a rural district of Uzbekistan. My husband teaches physical education in elementary school. I have a son and a daughter. My son, Amirkul, is nine years old. He is in second grade. My daughter's name is Ziola. She's in high school, and she's fifteen.

During the cotton season, it often seems the whole of Uzbekistan goes to the field—even soldiers, doctors, and other farmers who don't grow cotton are sent to the cotton fields. Everyone is encouraged to go, whether you're a child or a grown-up—everyone except those who can pay a bribe.

This season, my husband went to the cotton field with the other teachers to oversee the work of the students from his school. My daughter Ziola also went separately to the fields with her high school. She left September 15. In her school, it was eighth through ninth grades that went to the fields this year. College students went as well. My son and I didn't go this year—he's still a little too young and I'm home taking care of him. But at the end of September, some elementary school students went, too. When the weather turned cold and there was no more cotton in the fields, they came back, in late November.

While working the harvest, the students stayed in their school, which was right by the fields, as if it were a hotel. Those who had folding beds brought them from home. The rest slept on the floor of the school, and there was no way to wash your face or to take a shower.

My husband and I would walk a couple of miles to visit Ziola. It's about a thirty-minute walk. When I was visiting the fields, I asked Ziola about food and water, and she complained about the food. The students ate thin soup with a few noodles. The teachers and the school director ate separately—they had better food. Ziola said that the students would leave for the fields after breakfast, around seven a.m., and would come back around five thirty p.m. There were no days off. They were working on Sundays and holidays as well.

In order to pick quality cotton for sale, machines are not used. Mostly, cotton is picked by hand. We used to use machines to pick a lot of cotton quickly. Back when Uzbekistan was part of the Soviet Union, we were told that with technological progress the machines would replace physical labor. Now we have gone back to picking by hand, like during feudalism, because machines can damage the fibers of the cotton.

In the field, the students are under the teachers' and school director's supervision. Also, government officials, policemen, and inspectors go to the field to watch. Most everyone was in the fields, but my daughter told me that some students were exempt from picking cotton. There are thirty students in her class. Six students didn't go. Two were sick. Three obtained letters from a doctor excusing them because of other health conditions. And one more student, whose father is a director of an oil site, didn't go. It was said that the director bribed someone. But after we finished with the cotton and school started again, those students who didn't go were not allowed to take classes unless they paid 100,000 som.[1]

There was no contract with us or with our daughter. No one ever asked our permission to take her. If we were to decide, do you think we would agree to send her? She is the only daughter we have. But we can't do anything about it. If we don't send our daughter to the fields, the school cannot punish her officially, but we've heard that those who didn't go to the fields were expelled from school.

The school districts can fire school directors if their schools don't meet harvesting requirements. Uzbeks have a saying: "The government official who is threatened from above in turn threatens the school director below. The director threatens the teachers, and the teachers threaten the students." And what should the students do? Everything is taken out on the children. Teachers threaten students and sometimes beat them, saying, "If you don't cooperate, you'll be kicked out of school."

And what kind of education are the children getting at school? Children say that there is a computer in the school. But one or two computers, what is that for thousands of kids? In my opinion, if there is no computer at home, kids cannot learn to use the computer. And though they have a computer at school, kids are not allowed to use the Internet. Every day there are lectures about "spirituality" and how harmful the

---

[1] 100,000 som = US$45. The per capita annual income in Uzbekistan is less than US$700.

Internet is.[2] But the main problem in the schools, like where my kids are, is kids missing classes. If children are not going, it's because there is nothing to do at school once they're there. And then students spend two, two and a half months in the field, so almost one quarter of the school year is gone. When the students return, the teachers skip certain topics or cover everything briefly. If the state leaves schools without classes for almost three months—sending children to pick cotton, to weed, to dig—what kind of future will we have in Uzbekistan?

Following the breakup of the Soviet Union in 1991, Uzbekistan adopted a constitution and began holding national and local elections at the end of that year. Islam Karimov, the former Soviet governor of Uzbekistan, was elected the country's first president in 1991 and has held power ever since. Though Uzbekistan is nominally a democracy, there are no real opposition parties to challenge Karimov's twenty-three year rule.

Human rights organizations consider Uzbekistan an authoritarian state, and numerous human rights abuses have been documented in Uzbekistan since the country gained independence. Aside from forced labor, watchdog groups have decried Uzbekistan's unfair elections, suppression of free speech and opposition politics, and extralegal detention of citizenry.

---

[2] Uzbekistan is approximately 90 percent Muslim, and the Uzbek government maintains strict control over Internet access.

FRANCISCA COCÓN

AGE: *45*
OCCUPATION: *Farmer*
BIRTHPLACE: *Chimaltenango, Guatemala*
INTERVIEWED IN: *San Lucas Tolimán, Guatemala*

Francisca Cocón grew up on numerous Guatemalan fincas*—coffee plantations with origins in colonial serfdom. On traditional Guatemalan fincas, workers are compensated for their labor with inadequate food and housing on the plantation itself as well as with a small wage—often less than a dollar a day.*

During a childhood spent moving from finca to finca with her family in search of subsistence wages, Francisca survived malnutrition, the early deaths of her parents, and the Guatemalan Civil War. Today, Francisca owns her own plot of land. She also works with Ijatz, a women's organization that runs training programs, sells produce, and is a member of a cooperative association of small-scale coffee farms, most not more than a few acres in size. In the Mayan Kaqchikel language, ijatz *means "seed."*

We speak to Francisca in 2011 through a translator in San Lucas Tolimán, Guatemala, where Francisca lives and works. Our interview takes place on a sunny

August day in the gazebo at the main office of Ijatz. We enjoy fresh strawberry pie, jarred peaches, and lemonade, which the women of Ijatz produce and sell as part of a catering business that supports the work of the cooperative. Francisca struggles through memories of her earliest years, and the deaths of her parents still weigh heavily on her. But when she speaks of her current work and her future, she seems cheerful and confident.

I HAD TO BE THE RESPONSIBLE ONE

My name is Francisca Ajcibinac Cocón. I was born on the tenth of October, 1968, in a finca called San Bernardino. It's near Pochuta in the province of Chimaltenango in Guatemala.[1]

My mother is Juana Valeriana Cocón, and my dad's name is Doloteo Ajcibinac. We came from a very, very, very poor family. We grew up speaking Kaqchikel—I didn't learn any Spanish until I was a little older.[2] We are from an indigenous people that have been without land for a long time, and my family has been working on fincas for generations.

I grew up in the fincas, helping my parents—working, cutting coffee. We'd live in one of the worker houses set up in a row right on the plantation. The houses were little and had no electricity or plumbing, just a roof to cover our heads. The only electric light on the farm was near the center complex, the administrative center of the plantation. In our houses, we had to use a gas-powered lantern. There would be dozens of other families living in the other houses and working next to us cutting coffee, some of them our relatives.

---

[1] Chimaltenango is a rural, mountainous department, or state, in the southwest of Guatemala. The population is near five hundred thousand in an area approximately 1,200 square miles.

[2] Kaqchikel is a Mayan language spoken in the highlands of Guatemala. Today it has approximately four hundred thousand speakers.

When I started working as a child, I helped my parents and my two older brothers because, in the finca, the whole family has to work together in order to earn enough. Eventually there were seven of us kids all together—I had two older brothers, two younger brothers, and two younger sisters. And we all worked. This was the way fincas operated then, and we still work as entire families today on our farms.

When you're a kid, everything just looks so fun—I was happy to be accompanying my parents or brothers, and to learn how to harvest coffee. We'd set off early in the morning into the hills where the coffee trees were planted, and we'd work all day. As little kids, as soon as we were old enough to walk, our job was to pick the beans up on the ground. We'd follow the adults who were harvesting from trees and gather up anything they dropped. We'd give the beans we found to our parents, and they'd bring all we collected for the day to the boss. The tasks on the finca weren't just coffee harvesting. There was also keeping the coffee fields clean and free from weeds, gathering the mushrooms on the hill. We always had more to do on top of the coffee harvesting work.

We also helped in the fields because there was no education. We were very far away from any school. Sometimes a teacher would show up at the finca and say, "Kids have to study." But they didn't come often, and there were no real opportunities for education.

Then my mom died when I was only ten years old. She was just-thirty-nine, and it happened suddenly. We don't know what caused her to die. It was a surprise. I was the oldest girl, so after she died I had to be the person responsible for making the food for my brothers, for taking care of my sisters. We didn't have much—there were mostly only tortillas. And that's why we learned to eat chilies, spicy foods, which Mother had never prepared for us. Or we ate tortillas with lime or herbs along with beans. Sometimes a little bit of rice. That's what was available at the finca.

It was so, so hard for me to make the food because there was not enough time for one person to do it all. I used to wake up very early to prepare the food for my dad, for my brothers, because they would leave at four thirty or five in the morning to go to work. If workers were late getting to the fields, they might lose money. There was one person who was watching the entry time and the exit time, and to make sure the task was well done. If workers didn't produce enough in the field then they wouldn't get paid their salary. Field workers were always heavily pressured by the boss to produce more and more.

There were a lot of times I saw my father waiting for his salary on payday. When workers were paid, they received the payment every fifteen days. But many times the boss didn't arrive on time and the men simply waited for their payment until eleven, twelve at night because they were told to wait for the boss, who was supposedly on his way. But many times the boss wouldn't come. There really wasn't anything we could do if they decided not to pay us. There were many problems, and we suffered a lot on the fincas when I was a child. But we were survivors, and as time goes on God gives all of us some purpose.

And then came the violence.

WE WOULD SLEEP IN THE HOMES OF OTHER FAMILIES

When the guerrillas started appearing on the fincas, I knew they were fighting for the poor people, because they would always stop by and ask how the bosses and the overseers treated us. Sometimes we talked about it, and sometimes we didn't because we were afraid of what might happen.[3] Then in 1982, when the violence started, one of my brothers was kidnapped by soldiers. They took him away.

I was fourteen years old when my brother was taken, and he must have been around eighteen. I saw the army kidnap him. I remember it was around seven thirty in the morning. I got up and I saw that soldiers had arrived at our home. The only thing they said to him was that he shouldn't be afraid, because he was going to return home later. We waited that night for him to return, but he didn't. Sometime in the evening we heard gunshots in the distance. My dad said, "They've killed my son." We tried to calm him down, but we were panicked ourselves.

The next day, we woke up and went to meet with our cousins who lived on another finca to tell them what had happened. When we arrived at our cousins' place, they were crying and they told us that their parents—my uncle and aunt—had also been taken. All together there were six men and my aunt who had been taken, including two of my cousins' husbands and one man who wasn't from our family. He was the only one who returned, but we don't know why or how. My cousin was trying to get the truth out of him, but he never said anything. He just said that he and the others were tortured and that he had stayed down and pretended to be dead. But we didn't know what had really happened.

---

[3] The Guatemalan Civil War was long and bloody, spanning over three decades of Guatemalan history. Violence was commonplace during Francisca's childhood in the 1970s, when leftist guerrilla movements conducted strikes against the oppressive military-run national government, and the government responded by killing tens of thousands, including innocent civilians. In 1982, a nominal civilian government was overthrown in a coup led by General Efraín Ríos Montt, who waged a notorious campaign for control throughout Guatemala, employing death squads to murder and torture civilians who weren't able to prove loyalty to his military junta. Montt targeted indigenous Mayan groups such as Francisca's Kaqchikel people, believing that they were more likely to be on the side of the guerrillas. While Montt was in power from 1982 to 1983, as many as three thousand civilians were killed or disappeared every month. Montt was himself overthrown in 1983 by an opposing general, but the war continued on for another thirteen years, until 1996.

That was a difficult situation because my cousin was four months pregnant when her husband was kidnapped. She was pregnant and so was our neighbor, whose husband was one of the six men taken. Six months later they also took someone else—another of my uncles. He was too stubborn about staying at the finca, saying, "I'm not going to go anywhere with them, I don't owe them anything, so they can't harm me." The soldiers persuaded him, saying they just needed him to direct them to a road they didn't know. So he left with them, but never returned to his house.

After my brother's kidnapping, and that of my uncles, we realized that we could no longer live in peace. Now we knew that the soldiers might return again and attack us or attack our relatives at any time. Sometimes we would leave the fincas and sleep in the homes of other families up in the mountains, so that we wouldn't be sought on those nights when soldiers were nearby. But on the finca, we were exposed. There was no place to hide.

THE SICKNESS TOOK ITS TOLL ON HIM

Because of the kidnappings, my family and other families decided to abandon the San Bernardino finca. We packed up our things, including a few chickens we kept, and headed to another nearby finca, looking for a place that might be safer and pay better wages. We moved from finca to finca, a few miles at a time, but it was the same situation everywhere we went: there was work, but the wages weren't enough. Also, when someone is born in one place and comes to another place it's completely different—you don't know the people. I was very, very sad. We were asking ourselves, *Why? Why did all this happen to us?*

Eventually, we arrived at a finca called Costa Rica, also near Pochuta and not all that far from San Bernardino. It was even worse! There was work, but my brother said they paid 3.20 quetzales per day.[4] It still wasn't enough to live on, but we tried. And then, when I was sixteen, my dad started to get seriously ill.

He always had bad health, problems with arthritis and swelling. Sometimes when he worked he felt pain, and he would be hospitalized. So I knew he was a bit sick, but he always worked, always worked. He was already feeling very ill when we got to the Costa Rica finca. I think that what affected him most was the sadness he felt over my oldest brother. He was always remembering my brother and I saw that his health got worse and worse. He died sometime in 1984. He was around forty-five or fifty, I don't know. He wasn't that old, but the sickness took its toll on him.

LITTLE BY LITTLE A BIT OF CONFIDENCE

My father's death was that much harder for me to take because my remaining older brother already had his own family by then. The workload was very hard for him because he was the oldest, and he was responsible for so many of us. He couldn't also support his five younger siblings. And then one day he said that in the parish of San Lucas there was a house available through a priest we knew named Father Juan Goggin.[5] He is the one in charge of the project for children, CFCA.[6] We got to know him because he would always come to celebrate mass with us and he always valued the

---

[4] At the time, 3.20 quetzales = approximately US$0.40 per day.

[5] San Lucas Tolimán is a town of about twenty thousand about an hour's drive through the mountains from Pochuta. The San Lucas Mission was built around 1584. Today, its stated purpose is to address poverty in the area by helping indigenous Guatemalans access housing, healthcare, and land. According to the mission's website, it has purchased nearby lands and distributed them in two- or three-acre plots to over four thousand indigenous families.

[6] CFCA is the Christian Foundation for Children and Aging. For more information, see www.unbound.org.

farmworkers. He recognized the suffering in the fincas. So my brother talked to him about helping us find better opportunities. Father Juan told him that he would talk to the parish about having our family move to San Lucas. And, thank God! He was able to arrange it so that my sisters and I could move there. The letter from Father Juan said, "Yes, you can come here and we can help take care of you." So I moved to the mission with my two younger sisters while my younger brothers stayed and worked.

All of this happened when I was sixteen, just after the death of my father. I was still so young, but I had already spent ten years working, and I was exhausted. I was ready for someone else to take care of me. At first, the adjustment to life in the mission was difficult, because there was already another family in the house that we moved into. There were a lot of problems, just fights over space. And I was thinking, *Why did we move here?* For me it was a sad change to leave what I knew, and I was so weak—malnourished—that the move was very draining.

Not long after I arrived, I met a woman named Juanita, who worked in the mission's free clinic. She had a little boy, and she asked me, "Do you want to look after my son sometimes?" I said I did. It was an opportunity to have a little more food for myself, so I said, "I'll take care of the boy."

Apart from my new job, the mission also helped us with living expenses. They gave us 12 quetzales a day, enough to buy a little food, a little medicine.[7] It was a big help for us. I had my two sisters. So the three of us were together and could help each other, give each other support, but one of my sisters had a lot of health problems. Sometimes I was filled with despair because life seemed so hard, but I wanted to look after the boy, I wanted to stay in the parish. I started to feel more confidence, and I began to trust the people who were working there.

---

[7] At the time, 12 quetzales = US$1.53.

I LEARNED A LOT IN THE PARISH

Now I can approach people. But before, growing up, I was always very afraid, because I could not speak much Spanish, and I was too bashful. My mother could speak well in Spanish, which she'd learned mostly from listening to the radio, but none of the rest of us had ever picked up very much. Just communicating in San Lucas was a big challenge at first.

Father Gregorio, the head of the church here in San Lucas, told me, "If you want to learn to read and write, you can start to study from first grade to sixth grade. If you're interested."

I told him, "Yes, Father! I want to read!"

But it was very hard for me because it was difficult to be studying with children. I felt bad to be on the same level as seven-year-olds. They were all kids and I was an adult. But they never said anything; in fact, they gave me confidence and so I was able to be cheerful. I felt like I was important because I was so tall and they were all small. Sometimes I would play basketball with them during breaks. I was there for the five years it took me to finish all six grades. I finished sixth grade in '89, when I was around twenty-one.

Over the next few years I learned a lot in the parish. How to cook, how to clean the house. It was a huge change for me, and I felt valued. I felt animated with everything that I was learning and the relationships I had with people. This was healthy for me, to have friendships with people.

Then in 1992, I had an opportunity to travel to Minnesota. I knew a friend, Anna, who was like a role model for me. I had met Anna around the mission—she is from San Lucas, but she lives right now with her family in the States. I visited for eight months with her family in 1992. It was like a dream. And Anna's family spoke Kaqchikel. They fixed the papers for me to travel, and so it was a little easier for me to obtain the visa.

During one of our little trips we'd take, in July or August, we went camping on the Canadian border for a week. That was a great experience for me. At the end of the trip, there was a storm with rain and wind, and the lake near our campsite became very dangerous and choppy. But we went out on the lake anyway, and I was a little afraid that the canoe would tip over, but we were okay. I had a lot of other great experiences in the States, too. When I returned to the parish after eight months, I came back to continue studying some more, and I was able to finish middle school in '93. And then I met a man named Adolfo, and I fell in love.

THERE'S A MOMENT WHERE ONE NEEDS TO HAVE A VOICE

In 1994, Adolfo and I got married in San Lucas. I was twenty-six years old. The mission donated to us two *cuerdas* of land in the mountain—they provided land donations to a number of families in the area.[8] We cleaned it and planted coffee, and that first year we had a son. Eventually we had four children together—three boys and one girl. Pablo, the oldest, is now sixteen years old; David is fifteen; Lourdes is thirteen. And the smallest one, Josue, is ten.

I found out that the life of a woman is so hard. When a woman has her husband, it's not easy to go out and participate in the world. It has been a long process. According to the husband, it's not good that the woman is out elsewhere, involved in the community. What they want is that we be there tending, tending, tending the home. It's true that a woman has her responsibility in her home—cleaning, making food—but there's a moment where one needs to have a voice, interact with people. Because one learns

---

[8] *Cuerda*, when translated, means "rope." However, in the context used, it means approximately one acre of land.

many things out in the world and has many experiences that are important.

A little after my last child was born, around 2000, I learned about a women's group called Ijatz. The coordinator of Ijatz at the time approached me at the mission and asked me what possibilities there were to teach other women to prepare food, to teach them some of the skills I'd learned at the mission.

I had heard of Ijatz from other women in the mission and was curious. And I thought, *Now, this is my opportunity to go see what they're up to.* So I said, "Sure, I'll teach them." I felt embarrassed at first, because I was very shy. But I helped do the food-preparation training they'd asked me about, and when I finished the work, I wanted to stay with the group.

When I joined Ijatz, my husband didn't like it. He said, "I don't want you to go, because you have food to prepare in your own home. I am giving you money for the food. So why are you going to these people?" He said, "I make the money, so you take care of me and the house." But I wanted to have experiences out of the house, so I stayed on with Ijatz.

Then around 2005 we had an opportunity to travel to the capital and work with an organization called MuJER.[9] There we also had the opportunity to get certificates as workshop facilitators. It was a little hard for me because my children were small still. I had to take them with me for two days to the capital to attend the talks about women's rights, self-esteem, gender equality. I was in class with people who had titles. There were doctors, secretaries, students from the university. Those of us from Ijatz didn't have that level of education—but they all said, "No, we're all equal. You have to talk about your experiences, it really helps a lot." I was there with a woman who was a widow. The army had killed her husband.

---

[9] MuJER is Mujeres por la Justicia, Educación y el Reconocimiento (Women for Justice, Education, and Awareness). The organization's stated mission is to educate and provide resources for sex workers in Guatemala City, the nation's capital, and elsewhere throughout Guatemala.

We both went and supported each other until we finished the course. It was change, little by little. I gained the confidence to share.

WE COME TO KEEP IT ALIVE

My husband and I separated not long after my trip to the capital. The problem was infidelity. I couldn't live with a husband who did not respect me. So I had to make my decision. It would mean living alone, but also no problems or issues of mistrust between a husband and a wife. My husband's family said it was my fault, that I wasn't at home, that I wasn't taking care of my children. They said I was the guilty one. But I knew in my conscience that it wasn't so. So he moved out.

Not all women want to work. But I did it because I also wanted to learn interesting things, particularly about women. I don't know if you've read books or have experience in other countries where women are always subservient to men—but the point is that a woman shouldn't feel like that. Women have a lot of value and self-worth. And that is what a lot of men don't want to understand. The culture here is like that; a woman gets married and has to stay at home taking care of the children, feeding her husband. That's it. It's considered weird for a woman to want to go out and work. I see now that there are wives who still have that problem—they are afraid to go out for fear of their husbands. They are always afraid, silent, not speaking the truth.

Ijatz in past years had the support of international organizations. But in 2009, the funds ran out. So right now Ijatz is alone; it doesn't have support. It's a little bit hard. Because when there was the financing from outside, we would all have a stipend of about 300 quetzales per month.[10] Now we are sustaining ourselves. There are a few of us women in the

---

[10] 300 quetzales = approximately US$38.

San Lucas area who have sales on the side of the road to let people know what we do. Customers like the *dobladas*.[11] We make dobladas with masa, vegetables, salsa, and cabbage or onions on top, along with some cheese. We sell each one for only 1.50 quetzales, just a few cents. And we sell refreshments such as fresh juices as well.

Sometimes there are days we sell very little. But with this program we are sustaining ourselves. We don't pay ourselves a salary; all of our individual income comes from what we can sell of our own goods. We can each earn 50 quetzales per day when we have stable work.[12] The week that just went by, we were working Tuesday through Saturday. We were very tired because it was a lot of work, but it was very happy.

I HAVE CARRIED IT WITH ME EVER SINCE THE FINCAS

I haven't got by just on work with Ijatz. I also cultivate a little of my own coffee. This was something my family did ever since we were given land by the mission. After years of maintaining and growing two cuerdas of coffee, I was able to buy another four cuerdas after I separated from my husband. That means I now have six cuerdas devoted to coffee. I work with a local group that helps sell the coffee of small farmers like me to big markets. I also have a few beans, and a little squash, and some avocados. And a little maize—about half a cuerda, maybe about the equivalent of two blocks' worth.

I am doing this so that my children don't lose that knowledge, the value of planting, of knowing where our food comes from, who makes it. They have to have an understanding because they're studying right now.

---

[11] A *doblada* is a type of turnover, stuffed with vegetables or meat.

[12] 50 quetzales = approximately US$7.50.

Pablo and David are in *basico*.[13] But they are very helpful on the farm. They go with me to fertilize, to harvest the coffee. They can carry fifty to seventy-five pounds on their backs. And also my brothers and my nephews are always with me to help with the duties on our farm.

Cultivating the land is a knowledge I have carried with me ever since the fincas. We saw how to fertilize, how to cut, how to clean. Sometimes I wonder why we have our land now when in the past we were always slaves, under the orders of the people who had the power.

I remind my kids how situations were back then on the finca: twelve people in the house, but the house was deteriorating. And people lived in these houses out of necessity; they wanted to live in a better house but there was nothing to do about it. So I ask my kids to give thanks to God because now we have a solid roof over our heads.

It's a great advancement for me, a great blessing. All the accomplishments that I have had, I feel very grateful toward God, to the parish, especially to Father Gregorio for encouraging me to have new knowledge, new ideas. In Ijatz I have learned many things, like how to work with people, value people—the women, know about their problems, and how to find a solution, and to be an example as well. My sons are learning humility, to share, to help in the house. Many, many things. That one has to struggle, to fight. It's a constant struggle.

ONE PERSON ALONE CAN'T DO IT

For my family, my ultimate hope would be that my sons keep studying, and that they keep fighting for a career, and that they don't forget our origin and to value nature more than anything else. That they don't lose the knowledge of how to harvest corn and beans. And that they keep in

[13] *Basico* is the equivalent of junior high school.

mind that it's necessary to cultivate to be able to eat and live. That is what I want for them as well. So my sacrifice now is so that they can, in the future, have a better life. That is my goal.

For the group of women here, I hope that they realize that they have to fight in order to succeed. And they have to keep in mind that work is important in order to have an income. Because if you don't work, you won't have anything. They have to widen their minds, see the reality that we're living in. All of the workshops that we're having here are to improve the conditions for our families.

Our dream in Ijatz is to have a little restaurant. To be able to serve people. We recently had the opportunity to have a group of Canadians here who are doing volunteer work nearby. They came here for three nights, and we served them their meals. And always at the end we have a small chat, like we are having right now. Talking, telling the story of our lives.

What we want is for this to grow more and for all of us with Ijatz to have jobs. And we hope that in this way our sons and daughters will have more opportunity to study, to have better nutrition. And that the women will feel better, encouraged, so they forget their problems. We want to accomplish more things. We want to know more, discover more. That's what I want. But we have to be in groups because one person alone can't do it. So then all the people who are in need of advancement—we all have to be united.

It has been very difficult, since I was very little, my childhood. There was a lot of suffering, a lot of mistreatment. And it's regrettable because I think now if my dad were alive, in the conditions we have today, which are a bit better, perhaps I would have been able to give him what he needed. He never had the opportunity even to eat well. He was always very sick. Sometimes I remember him and others I have lost, and I start to cry and wonder, *Where are they? Where are they?* But thanks to them, because of all the suffering, we're a little bit better off now. Because now we have a roof.

We have a bed when we never had a bed before. We have a little better health, when before we didn't have that. We have a bit of property, the parcels. And there's confidence to move forward—one can do many things.

FAUSTO GUZMÁN

AGE: *45*

OCCUPATION: *Vineyard worker, Amway salesman*

BIRTHPLACE: *Paso de Aguila, Oaxaca, Mexico*

INTERVIEWED IN: *Healdsburg, California*

Fausto Guzmán has been working in the Sonoma Valley vineyards for nearly two decades. Our first interview takes place in Fausto's apartment at his kitchen table, where he serves an all-natural grape energy drink and bags of vegetable chips. Fausto lives with his wife and six children in Healdsburg, a picturesque commercial center in the heart of California wine country. His three youngest girls play in the living room as he speaks in Spanish, his second language after his mother tongue, Trique, a language spoken by indigenous people in his home state of Oaxaca, Mexico. Occasionally he pauses to search for the right words.

In a later conversation, while driving his van through Healdsburg, Fausto points out the seemingly endless vineyards that stretch out from both sides of the road into the hills. He contrasts the scenery with that of his hometown, Paso de Aguila, and he speaks quietly of his oldest son, who died in a car crash while crossing the border into the United States.

Although Fausto has found some measure of stability after years spent working in the fields and warehouses, his story highlights the perils faced by many undocumented workers in the U.S. wine industry. Here he explains how he survived years of homelessness, dangerous working conditions, a near fatal warehouse accident, and a lack of clear legal protections—all for the sake of earning a wage higher than anything he was likely to make back in Oaxaca.

I DON'T EVEN KNOW MY FATHER'S NAME

I'm originally from Paso de Aguila in Oaxaca, Mexico.[1] I think I was born around 1969. I speak the tongue of Trique.[2] I was raised in what was basically a ranch nestled in a hill. There weren't many people in Paso de Aguila, ten houses at the most. I didn't grow up with a dad because he died when I was two. I don't even know his name. I also had a brother, Sergio, about five years older than me. When my dad died, we left Paso de Aguila to go live with some of my grandma's relatives closer to the town of Putla.[3]

When I was living on my grandma's relatives' land we had goats, horses, cows—but they were my grandma's. I remember being about eight or nine and chopping firewood that my mom and grandma would carry to sell at the plaza in Putla on Sundays. There were people in the central square who baked bread, and they would buy some of our wood for their

[1] Oaxaca is a large, rural state of nearly four million in southern Mexico. The state hosts numerous native communities—many the descendents of Mayans—and has a mostly agricultural economy.

[2] Trique is a native Mexican language spoken by a little over twenty-five thousand people, mostly in the mountainous regions of Oaxaca. Southern states such as Oaxaca and Chiapas host many of Mexico's remaining indigenous languages.

[3] Putla Villa de Guerrero (or simply Putla) is a town of just over ten thousand in west Oaxaca.

ovens. We used the money from selling firewood to buy maize or different things to eat. That's what I did as a kid.

We returned to my dad's land when I was about ten. Our family still had some land there, but it wasn't my dad's anymore. After he died my uncle Carmelo took over. There I would work the land, take care of the crops. We planted bananas, maize, coffee, and sugarcane.

Then I met my wife Ricarla in Paso de Aguila when I was fifteen. She was also fifteen. She was a neighbor from Paso de Aguila and I knew her family. We got married very young—we were still teenagers. I've always worked; I never went to school or anything. My wife didn't go to school either. I did only one year of primary school in Paso de Aguila. I didn't continue going to school because I needed to work to buy food.

I THOUGHT PEOPLE WORKING IN THE UNITED STATES EARNED A LOT OF MONEY

At first my wife and I lived in a wooden house. It was made of sticks all around. There was only one room and it had nothing inside. The walls were wood and the roof was grass. In Oaxaca there's a grass that grows in the hills that you can tear out to use for your roof and it lasts a long time. Those houses, if you know how to make the grass stick to the roof, will last twenty or thirty years. I was able to weave the grass for the roof of my house—it was so good that when it rained we didn't get wet at all and it made no noise.

Later on I made another house. This one was made of adobe. I also got tiles for the roof, but one has to pay for these, it's not free like the grass. For the adobe you dig out dirt that's loose and fine, almost dustlike, then mix that with horse dung or donkey dung. You have to put it on the ground and step on it while adding water.

In Oaxaca, my wife would cook beans, chilies, or maize. She would make tortillas. We had a *comal*[4] and she would make them on there. They were made by hand, unlike in the United States, where machines make them.

From the family farm I took over a plot of about two hectares.[5] Half of it was sugarcane. Aside from working my own land, I was also harvesting cinnamon for a *patron*[6] who had a *trapiche*.[7] The trapiche is what the rich people who have a lot of cane use. I would plant the cane and then around October or November, when it was ready, I'd cut it down. I would take it to the trapiche to grind it and get *panela*, a type of sugar. It's like the kind you can buy at the store here that's shaped like a long cone, but ours was shaped like a big plate.

About two or three years after my wife and I married, my first son Nicéforo was born. Then later my sons Daniel and Virgilio were born. They were all born in Oaxaca, a few years apart. In Oaxaca my children would spend their time playing, and they went to primary school for a bit in Mexico. The teachers spoke Trique at times but also gave lessons that were in Spanish. They would speak both languages to the children, which was very important for their educations.

We were able to support ourselves in Oaxaca, but nothing beyond the necessities. I was about twenty when I first made the decision to come to the United States. I made my choice because I thought people working in the United States earned a lot of money. I would see people who came back from working in California, from the north, and they'd have good shoes, good shirts, they could afford to buy things. I saw a lot of people

---

[4] A *comal* is a large metallic or ceramic pan or dish used to make tortillas.

[5] A hectare is one thousand square meters, or about two and a half acres.

[6] A *patron* is a boss or landowner.

[7] A *trapiche* is a press or mill used to extract juice from certain fruits.

with good houses over in Putla. Even though I'd already built two houses, I started to want to build a new house, one with plumbing and electricity. I wanted to have new clothes for my family. I wanted to live well. If I had stayed on my ranch I couldn't have made much money. Just work to feed myself and my family.

There were also a lot of complicated politics in Oaxaca. For instance, I remember that the state government sent out money to poor farmers around 1985. I think the idea was to subsidize each of the *campesinos* who were living out in the fields so that they could work their land and plant traditional crops like maize, bananas, coffee, tomatoes, or beans.[8] But the politicians in Putla who were supposed to distribute the money to farmers put it all in the bank instead. They told us that they'd give us a certain amount each year. But you had to be politically aligned with them to get your money.

That's another reason why I didn't like being in my town: there was too much politics. I didn't like what was happening, so I left.

RENT WAS TOO EXPENSIVE BUT THE RIVER WAS FREE

I left my home and made my way toward the U.S. I'm not exactly sure when this was, but it was probably around '92 when I was in my early twenties. This was before anybody else in my family had gone to the States. None of us knew what to expect, so I volunteered to be the first to go, though my Uncle Carmelo was in northern Mexico, also thinking about crossing. My wife would stay behind and take care of the kids, help on the ranch while I made money.

First, after leaving Oaxaca I ended up in Ensenada, in Baja California,

---

[8] *Campesinos* refers to small-scale farmers or farm laborers.

where my uncle Carmelo was working.[9] I was picking tomatoes in a town near Ensenada called Maneadero. I met a coyote there after three or four months and he told me, "Let's go to the other side, you'll make good money."[10]

Uncle Carmelo told me, "You go first. And if you get through, you call me to tell me how it is, and then I'll follow." I paid the coyote $800 to get me across. He brought me and some friends through Tijuana and we ended up in Madera, California, and for the first time I lived in the U.S.[11]

It was in Madera that I first worked in the grape harvest. I worked for about two weeks shortly after I arrived, but the job was only temporary. I kept looking for work with my other friends who had come with me. We found some work one Monday and were heading back home after work. We didn't know Madera too well and my friend ended up driving by an immigration checkpoint where we were stopped. As soon as they saw we had no papers, the immigration agents said, "Out." They took my friend's car and we were thrown out of the country.

I was back at Maneadero after having been deported. I worked for a few months there and then returned to the ranch in Oaxaca. There I met with my brother Sergio. We immediately thought of getting back into the States. First we stayed a season to cultivate the farm. We harvested and sold our maize, and then we used the money to make our way back north, around '93. This time we were taken across by a coyote from Putla, and we crossed through the Sonoran Desert, a very harsh place.

We made it to California, and found out from acquaintances that my uncle Carmelo was living by the banks of the Russian River.

---

[9] Ensenada is a city of around seven hundred thousand on the Baja Peninsula, approximately eighty miles south of San Diego and the U.S. border.

[10] A coyote is an agent who helps smuggle Mexican citizens into the United States.

[11] Madera is a town of sixty thousand in central California, near Fresno.

When we got to where my uncle and his friend were, they were sleeping. They'd set up a tent by the river's edge, not far from the town of Geyserville.[12] They'd been living for a while next to the river and were hidden beneath some wild cane. A lot of it grows there, cane as thick as a finger. You couldn't easily see them or their tent if you walked past, and they were pretty safe.[13]

My uncle told me that the same coyote who'd brought me to Madera had returned to Ensenada to get him. With the help of the coyote, my uncle made it into California. He heard of a friend who was living by the Russian River in Sonoma County, so that is how he ended up living in the camp. My uncle had more luck than me and was able to find regular work in a vineyard in Sonoma, and he was able to avoid deportation by hiding near the river.

My brother and I joined my uncle and his friend on the riverbank and lived there for a long while. During the daytime we would go find work in the vineyards—harvesting, spraying, pruning. The work changed depending on the season. Soon I started working for a vineyard called Rivermark near Healdsburg, and the work became a regular job.[14]

There was also a lot of work to do to maintain our camp by the river. In dry weather we'd go out to look for firewood to cook with. During the cold season, we would heat up some water in a pot to clean ourselves with, but during the warmer season we'd bathe in the river. Everybody slept in tents at first, but once I had enough money I bought a car, and then I started sleeping inside my car. I didn't have a license, but I needed the car to get to work.

---

[12] Geyserville is a town in the Sonoma Valley, seventy-five miles north of San Francisco.

[13] The men were in hiding because they were undocumented workers. For more on farm work and undocumented workers in the U.S., see Appendix III, page 356.

[14] Healdsburg is a town of about eleven thousand on the Russian River in Sonoma County.

Perhaps one might live more comfortably in a room but we all lived there together by the river, as many as five at a time. It was always the same people. My uncle was the oldest; the rest of us were young, in our twenties. Nobody ever brought up the idea of moving. Rent was expensive but the river was free. I was there nearly five years.

While I was living by the river, in the late nineties, something very sad happened. My eldest son Nicéforo attended school in Paso, and when he finished at around age twelve he wanted to come over to the United States to work. I told him it was a good idea. He and about twenty others were traveling with the same coyote from Putla who had taken me and Sergio across. They were about two hours outside of Los Angeles when their van flipped over. That's as far as my son got. He died along with some of the others in the van. The coyote was okay, though.

Even after that tragedy, my wife and I still planned to have the rest of the family come to the United States so we could live together. I needed to find a home first—I didn't want my wife and children living in the river camp. First I moved into a trailer that Rivermark set up. It was only for vineyard workers, and there were several of us. The trailer could fit four people. We were charged $50 a month. I spent about two or three years in the Rivermark trailer. But then I was making enough money, about $9 an hour, to rent an apartment so my wife crossed over with my two remaining sons, Daniel and Virgilio, in the early 2000s. We moved into an apartment in Healdsburg.

Since my wife joined me in California, we've had four daughters: Patty is the oldest. There's my twin girls, María Guzmán and María Guadalupe Guzmán. The youngest girl is Esmeralda. They were all born in the United States, and they've never been to Oaxaca.

My brother Sergio still lives nearby, but my uncle Carmelo no longer lives here. He was here for many years and twice went back to Oaxaca. The second time he didn't come back—he was murdered in Putla. He'd become an influential figure in Paso de Aguila and was advocating for a return of land from large landowners to the campesinos for farming. He was shot one day at a small shop where he had gone to buy some soda.

I USED TO BE SENT WITH THE BACKPACK ON TO SPRAY THE GRAPES

I've been working at Rivermark now for over seventeen years.

The routine changes a little season to season but for the most part is the same day to day. Sometimes I start at six, seven in the morning, so I wake up at four to make my lunch. It takes maybe an hour to get to the field. Once you punch in you have to be working. The bosses send you to get a shovel right when you show up, or they might say, "Today we'll be pruning." Once you're done pruning, you tie up the grapes, and then comes the sprouting.

September is grape season. We take down the green grapes and the rotten grapes. We remove everything that's rotted, including the leaves that grow on the grapes. When the grapes are in clusters we separate them so that they don't get stuck together, because when the clusters are close together the grapes will rot.

How you're treated depends on who's in charge. Generally, if the boss orders you to do something and you do it fast, then it's fine. He just watches, and if he tells you to work faster, to hustle, then you have to do the work as fast as you can.

The *mayordomo* is the boss, but not the *boss* boss. He just orders people around; he doesn't help the workers. I've seen other ranches where there are thirty or forty people and the mayordomo is helping with the work. But the one at my vineyard, where there are only about eight or nine of us, he just wants us to work faster. Not one of the people who work there says anything. There's a great silence.

Once, I decided to complain to see what he would do. I asked him, "Why don't you take a row? You say 'faster,' so you take a row and we'll work better." He said he won't take a row because he's already worked too much before and now doesn't want to.

After I had a few years of experience, they'd always ask me to be the one to spray the grapes with pesticides. I'd attended training sessions and knew just how to mix up the chemicals with water, so it was my job for many years. I wore protective gear when I sprayed—I was covered head to foot.

During the summer, we're outside in the heat all day. After the grapevines are mature there are large leaves that give us a bit of shade. When it's very hot the bosses put a little canopy over by the edge of the rows, but nobody uses it, because workers can't really take breaks until the official break time at ten in the morning. Once you're working, you go until you're done. Whatever it is you're doing, you keep doing it until it's time to go home—you don't get to make your own breaks.

If it gets too hot, over one hundred degrees, then the boss comes out and tells us that we can't work anymore, so we stop working and head home. We had two days last week where we got out at one because it was too hot. But if you get in at six and get out at one, you're paid up until one. You don't get the full hours. You only get paid the hours that you can work. We lose part of the day when it's too hot. During rains, if they're strong, we also stop working. We don't get paid for that day. You stop earning. Sometimes you get seventy hours or less for two weeks: very few hours, less than full time. So even if you are making $9 or even $12 an hour, when it's the rainy season or the hot season, you earn just enough for rent.

I COULDN'T SPEAK, BUT I COULD HEAR WHAT WAS HAPPENING AROUND ME

One day in 2004, four of us were working inside of a Rivermark warehouse. We were putting the bottles of wine in boxes. We processed orders there to ship the wine to other countries. In the boxes there was cardboard where the bottle went, and we would put a piece of plastic in there to stabilize the bottles. There was someone operating a forklift. We used it to move pallets of wine.

After a couple of hours of work, I began to feel a terrible headache coming on. Someone else said, "I feel bad, I have a headache, I even feel nauseous." The others just said, "Me too, me too." It was time for break, so we took our fifteen minutes and ate tacos. I thought that it would relieve the pain but it didn't. We went back to work.

At that moment there was nobody there who was a supervisor. There was only us, the workers. We continued working and then lunchtime came at twelve. At lunch we get half an hour. We each went our own way. Some lived close by and went home. Some went inside their cars. I ate my lunch in my car. Then came the hour to head back to work. We were all working, and once again the pain came, strongly. At about fifteen or twenty minutes to two I couldn't handle the pain any longer. I began to feel faint and suddenly very dizzy. I felt as if I were falling.

Then I collapsed. I became semiconscious. A friend grabbed me, took me by the waist, and dragged me outside the warehouse.

I couldn't speak, but I could hear what was happening around me. Other winery employees were trying to talk to me but I couldn't answer. I was outside lying on the ground. Then everybody came over. I could hear them talking but I couldn't move and I couldn't speak. So the office made a call for an ambulance.

THE DOCTOR TOLD ME I HAD 45 PERCENT SATURATION OF CARBON MONOXIDE IN MY BLOOD

I remember the ambulance arriving and being inside it. The ambulance took me to the hospital in Healdsburg. I was there for one night, I think. After examining me, the doctor told me I had 45 percent saturation of carbon monoxide in my blood. My heart had stopped. I'd had a heart attack. The doctor told me that the fumes from the forklift were responsible. The forklift was damaged and giving off carbon monoxide fumes, and ventilation in the warehouse was poor. Some of my co-workers were also sent to the hospital but they were fine. That day, I was the only one who'd worked the entire time inside.

At the hospital, the doctor ran a number of tests on me and finally told me that my heart wasn't working normally anymore, that the carbon monoxide had damaged it.[15] He told me, "You need a pacemaker."

So I asked, "So this pacemaker is going to keep me alive?"

He said, "Yes. When your heart is working properly the pacemaker won't do anything, it'll just be there. When the heart isn't working properly, it's having a hard time, then that's when the pacemaker will give a jolt to the heart to revive it, so that it can function normally once more."

He explained this, and I just said, "Oh well."

Then the next day they took me to Santa Rosa Memorial Hospital. I spent about two or three days there. I was worried. Not about being deported or anything like that. At the hospital nobody ever asked me about my legal status—it never came up. But I was worried about providing for

---

[15] Acute carbon monoxide poisoning can cause cardiac arrest and lead to long-term damage to the heart and central nervous system. Brain damage, depression, and impaired motor functions may also develop in individuals who have suffered acute carbon monoxide poisoning.

my family. Rivermark never sent anybody to the hospital to speak to me. I was there by myself. Nobody from my work came. I worried about how I would pay for all this.

From the moment in which I collapsed to when I was discharged from the hospital I never spoke with a lawyer. My only worry at that time was my heart. *Will I be able to work? How will I withstand hard labor now? Will the pacemaker affect my employment?* I took two weeks of rest at home, and then I went back to work at Rivermark.

ONLY THE LAWYERS SPOKE WITH EACH OTHER

About a month or two after the accident, a few weeks after I'd returned to Rivermark, a friend told me to hire a lawyer so that maybe the company would compensate me for the damage to my heart.

So I spoke with a representative from California Rural Legal Assistance, and they provided a lawyer.[16] I never spoke with the company's lawyer or anything, not even with my boss. Only the lawyers spoke with each other.

Eventually there was a meeting between Rivermark's lawyers and mine at their office in Santa Rosa. I went to sign some papers. I went by myself, and I didn't understand English, which the lawyers spoke at the meeting. My lawyer spoke Spanish, but at that time I still didn't understand Spanish very well either. I felt very confused. I was just told to sign in certain places. I received my compensation and that was it. I said yes and signed a form. Once you've signed something then the case is closed.

I was given $33,000 in compensation money but I was told by a lot of people afterward, friends and such, that when your heart is damaged during

[16] California Rural Legal Assistance was founded in 1966 and provides free legal representation for farmworkers, immigrants, and other rural poor throughout California. For more information, visit www.crla.org.

work you are supposed to get way more—$80,000 or $100,000. But I don't know. I accepted what they gave me; I thought it was a lot at the time. My lawyer told me I'd get $33,000 and get to go back to work for the same company. He said, "You're good, healthy, and strong. You can work for the rest of your life." They told me the boss wouldn't fire me. He also told me that if I signed the settlement papers, I would have a doctor for life to check my heart for whatever problems arose.

THAT'S HOW FIELD WORK IS

Now I have a pacemaker. I keep working and it doesn't affect me. Every few months I have to go get it checked. This month, I think on the fifteenth, the doctors will examine the pacemaker. They'll see how it's doing, make sure it's working.

Some months after my accident, an inspector came to Rivermark. They put in a ventilator at the warehouse. I think the boss paid a fine of around $20,000 for not having one in the first place. So now everything is fixed up. They still use the same forklift, but it's been fixed. That's how field work is.

We don't have health insurance at work. The boss does, but we don't. If you get hurt at work, that's covered, but if you get hurt outside, at home, or walking, then you have to pay everything.[17] But there's insurance at work that covered the hospital expenses for accidents. The company's insurance also pays for my checkup, which is every three months. At first the hospital asked me to pay for the checkups, but I refused—they were asking for ten dollars for each visit. So they called the company and now the company pays for it.

---

[17] Fausto is referring to workers' compensation insurance. For more on workers' compensation insurance, see glossary, page 348.

I've had the pacemaker for many years now. It's almost time for them to have to change the battery, which is supposed to be every five or six years. The company is going to have to pay for that as well.

I do feel I was treated justly in regard to my accident. What are you going to do? I feel strong and can still work. My legal status doesn't affect my life at the moment because I have a job. As long as I have that, there's no worry. I support my family; if California or the U.S. government passes a law saying I can't work, well, what am I going to do? I'll go back to my hometown in Oaxaca. Too bad, that's life.[18]

WHERE ELSE CAN I GO?

The mayordomo doesn't order me around anymore. I've got my pacemaker, so I work at a normal pace—not too fast or anything—and I don't worry too much about the boss.

I always looked at it this way: the mayordomo has to supply drinking water, has to have a portable bathroom ready. Before, I used to help do all of that, even though it wasn't supposed to be part of my job. He used to order me around, "Do this and this. Take water over to where the people are." Before he used to send me and everybody else to do those things. This year he didn't order me to do anything. I said, "I'm not a mayordomo, and it's not my job to haul portable bathrooms or water tanks. That's for the people in charge." I met with the mayordomo's brother, who also worked at Rivermark, and complained about him. I said, "He doesn't get any of the things he's supposed to, he sends other workers. He doesn't do

[18] Fausto was recently under threat of deportation after being stopped by the police for using his cell phone while driving. After DUIs were found on his record he was sent to San Francisco for deportation. By quickly hiring a lawyer, showing proof that his daughters had been born in the United States, and providing receipts from the past ten years, Fausto was able to petition for a work permit. He is no longer in danger of deportation. He received a twenty-day jail sentence.

anything. He just shows up and earns while others do the work. I don't think it should be this way." The mayordomo doesn't order me around anymore since I talked to him and his brother.

I stopped spraying chemicals just because I didn't want to do it anymore. The backpack that you use to spray has a strap that goes right by where my pacemaker is. The mayordomo doesn't ask me to go spray; he sends two other people. Still, I make more now than I used to before the accident. I make $12 an hour, and I don't know if I could get that if I started over at another vineyard. I know some guys who work in vineyards where they pay only $7 or $8 an hour. So where else can I go? There's no choice. That's why I've stayed here.

THE EVENINGS ARE MINE

During the day I work for the boss but the evenings are mine. When I have time, I go to Frente meetings.[19] I try to help. I speak Trique on the radio, to communicate with the other workers who speak Trique. I know how to speak, but I don't know how to write it. My brother knows how to write Trique a bit. He's studied more than I have.

When you speak on the radio you're passing information on to all kinds of people. I talk about work, provide information about the chemicals used in the vineyards. For example, I'll say, "When you're spraying chemicals on the grapes, the boss has to supply you with safety equipment: a suit, gloves, and a mask. You must have the whole suit. If the liquid splashes on you, and gets on your clothes, you must take these off. You need to go home and change, put some clean clothes on. If the chemical doesn't get on you then you're safe."

---

[19] Frente ("Front") is an organization dedicated to preserving indigenous culture in Mexico and protecting the civil rights of indigenous peoples in Mexico and abroad.

I started selling Amway products because I ran into an Amway vendor at Walmart. He asked me about the products that I was buying and he started to tell me about the chemicals that they had in them. He told me about the natural products that I could be consuming and that the company would be paying me. I was invited to an Amway meeting one evening, and the guy picked me up and took me there. They explained to me how it worked. They pay you to use their products and even more if you start selling them. Things like shampoo, soap, and vitamins—whatever you use they send you a small check for 3 percent of it. Now I buy products from Amway and sell them to people in the area. It's extra work that I do for myself. I do it in the evenings for about two to three hours. I sell vitamins, weight-loss pills, and medicines for kids. I do demonstrations. The soap lasts a long time. One little box is good for thirty-two washes.

My family is getting by here, but I miss having my own land. One day I'd like to plant my own crops again. I'd like to plant some cane so that I can work like I used to. I'd like to go back with my family. Daniel and Virgilio remember living in Oaxaca. My girls have never lived there, though. If they find that they don't like it there they could come and go whenever they wanted since they have their papers. If God allows me to live longer I'll go back to Oaxaca, get some land to work, and eat better tortillas.

In October 2012, Fausto became ill after a day of work in the vineyards. After nocturnal vomiting he was taken by his son to the emergency room, where he lost consciousness. He had to be resuscitated with a defibrillator and doctors installed a new pacemaker. In 2013, he was again stricken with an irregular heartbeat; Fausto was checked at the hospital and released. He is awaiting further examinations.

NEFTALI CUELLO

AGE: *17*
OCCUPATION: *High school student, tobacco field worker*
BIRTHPLACE: *Los Angeles, California*
INTERVIEWED IN: *Pink Hill, North Carolina*

In North Carolina, when school gets out each summer, a stream of young people—nearly all Latino—head into the fields to help bring in the state's most profitable crop: tobacco. Neftali was twelve years old when she first accompanied her family into the fields. At the time, she and her older sisters wanted to help their single mother pay the household's bills. Now seventeen and a senior in high school, Neftali has spent five summers in the fields, working sixty-hour weeks and contending with extreme heat and humidity, along with nicotine and pesticide exposure.

We first meet Neftali at a gathering of young farmworkers advocating for better wages and working conditions, held in a doublewide trailer not far from her home in Pink Hill. At the gathering, Neftali speaks eloquently of the pressures that forced her parents and many of her peers to leave home and search for work in the United States, many of them uprooting themselves and their families year to year to pursue available work to avoid the attention of immigration authorities.

Over the course of several subsequent phone conversations (occasionally interrupted by the sound of roosters crowing in the background), Neftali talks about the challenges of working in tobacco, her plans for the future, and how her activism has transformed her from a shy girl into a gregarious teenager who enjoys addressing large crowds.

BACK THEN, ALL THE KIDS SLEPT TOGETHER IN ONE ROOM

People say that it's dead in Pink Hill because nothing goes on here.[1] But it's not dead—it's just peaceful. People don't really notice the beauty of nature. I live in a trailer park, and outside my house I am surrounded by fields. From the trailer park you can drive three minutes and be in the town. You know how a teenager is like, "I'm gonna go play video games or watch TV"? Well, for me it's a little bit different. I'll go and get one of my friends, a neighbor—the other trailer houses are filled with migrant farmworker families—and we'll walk around, see the birds, play with my dogs and cats. And we got a duck. It adopted itself onto our porch, so I feed it.

I was born in Los Angeles. That's where my parents met. My mom is from Cuernavaca, Mexico.[2] My dad is from the Dominican Republic. I was one when my parents separated and we moved from Los Angeles to North Carolina—it was me, my mom, and my two older sisters and brother. I don't remember anything about Los Angeles, but I want to visit.

When we first got to Pink Hill we lived right across the street from the school, but my brother and sisters would still be late. I would be

---

[1] Pink Hill is a town of about five hundred in southeast North Carolina.

[2] Cuernavaca is a city of 350,000 in the state of Morelos, about sixty miles south of Mexico City.

like, "Wake up! Wake up!"—just jumping on the couch. I wasn't even a kindergartner then. Then I started school, and my mom would walk me over. My mom had to go to work, so we'd have to get ready ourselves.

Back then, all the kids slept together in one room. It was the four of us. We'd just cuddle up together and go to sleep. We were living in a trailer with a kitchen, a very small living room, and two bedrooms. We still live there—our house is homey.

My mom would wake us up at five thirty in the morning and before she left she'd make sure we all had a shower and that our clothes were prepared and our shoes were tied. And she would always do little hairdos on us girls.

That was when she worked in pig farms. She told us why she had to stop working there. A pig was giving birth so she needed gloves, but her employers didn't provide them. She said, "No, I can't do this," and they pretty much fired her. That's when she started working in tobacco.

I THOUGHT IT WAS GONNA BE EASY-PEASY

My older brother, Henry, was the first to go into the tobacco fields. He was eleven when he went with my mom. He has pale skin, and when he got home that day he was bright red! It took maybe two days for him to get over that because he was so badly sunburned. He didn't go back to the fields after that.

Growing up, we would see our mom go to work in the tobacco fields and get home really tired. And she still had a lot of work to do around the house. When I was about ten, me and my two older sisters agreed to go talk to her, to tell her we had decided to work in the fields. At first she said, "No, you are so not working." We were like, "You know what, we're gonna go to work. We're gonna help you out." She said we were too young.

But later she let us go to work in the summers, because she couldn't take care of us all and pay the bills.[3]

I was twelve when I began working in tobacco. My sister Kimberly was thirteen or fourteen. My oldest sister, Yesenia, was fifteen. We wanted to be independent and to help Mom out. By that time she had another two kids with her boyfriend—my three-year-old brother and seven-year-old sister. My mom said that she'd rather work three jobs than see her kids working out in the fields. She told us that we broke her heart when we decided to work. We didn't exactly understand what she meant, but we understand now.

That first experience in the fields—oof! I didn't wake up that first day. My mom had to wake me up. It was five in the morning. I would guess that it was July. She said, "You only have twenty minutes to get ready." It was dark that first morning, but not a bad dark. I didn't see stars, but I could see the first little ray of sunlight.

I put on a t-shirt and shorts, 'cause it was gonna be hot. My mom said, "Go back into your room." She told me to put on some long sleeves, a sweatshirt, pants, and old shoes. "Clothes that you don't care about," she said. When I asked why, she said, "You'll see."

So my sisters and I climbed into the car and my mom drove. We were driving what we always called our little gray car. I don't know exactly what model it is because I suck at describing cars. I was sitting in the back seat. Driving to the field I was thinking, *It's gonna be really good to be outside.* Like I said, I really like nature. I was thinking, *The sun's gonna be hitting me; it's gonna be nice just to be around plants and walking.* I had always looked at tobacco plants and thought they were pretty. I was thinking, *I'm gonna see that my mom was worrying over nothing.* I thought it was gonna be easy-peasy.

---

[3] In the United States, children as young as twelve are permitted to work on large, commercial farms and children of any age can work on small-scale farms. For more on farm labor in the United States, see Appendix III, page 356.

We drove to a designated spot that my mom knew and stopped to wait for other people driving to the fields. A group of a few cars drove by and honked their horns, and we rushed to catch up to them in our car. My mom explained that if we couldn't catch up to them, we'd have to go to another contractor and try to find work.[4]

After a while, I noticed that the ride starts to get really, really bumpy. The roads that lead to tobacco fields weren't paved. They're dirt roads with huge holes, and I was being thrown around, and I'm like, *What the heck?* And then as we get out, I'm thinking, *Oh my God, the clothes I'm wearing look ridiculous. I don't even want to get out.* Me and my sisters were laughing about it. And we got out and saw dozens of people wearing most of the same things we were. Then we saw the field, just rows and rows of tobacco. And I thought, *We're not gonna get out of here. They're gonna keep us here forever.*

My mom went and talked to the contractor. There were seven or eight other people in our crew. They were all Hispanic. I've always only seen Mexicans and African Americans in the fields.[5] I was probably the youngest, though there were at least two or three other young people I recognized from my school.

If you tell the contractor you have work experience, they don't really care what your age is. They showed us how to sucker. Suckers are these little lime-green tobacco shoots growing in between the leaves. They're curvy, fuzzy, and pointy at the very beginning of the stem. They're like another branch growing, and you have to tear them off with your hands

---

[4] To ensure a steady workforce, many farmers pay a fee to labor contractors, who are responsible for recruiting and supervising crews of seasonal farmworkers. As a result, many farmworkers have little idea who owns the fields they are harvesting. For more information on labor contractors, see glossary, page 348.

[5] For more on immigration and agricultural labor in the United States, see Appendix III, page 356.

and nails.[6] But they're hard to tear off. And they can look just like a leaf. It's really hard to distinguish sometimes.

I was this short little girl. The tobacco plants were bigger than me; they were huge and would loom over you like crazy. The leaves spread out so far that you have to squeeze your way through the rows. And the suckers aren't just on the top—they're also at the very bottom of the plants. You have to go around the whole tobacco plant. How are you supposed to do that, especially when you're little?

We started at six a.m. In ten minutes I was drenched from head to toe in dew. I thought I was going fast, but I got left behind at least twice. Yesenia helped me and then my mom came over and helped me. The contractor said, "She needs to speed up." I was running—struggling with having to be the best, although I knew I never was, like at school and stuff. So I felt really bad when I heard the contractor say that.

Within two to three hours I was feeling nauseous. But I thought it was just me—that I hadn't drunk any water. It was too far back to go and get water, and I thought, *They're probably gonna yell at me if I go.* I was this really shy girl: I didn't want to get in trouble and get fired the first day.

Then I got really sluggish. I was thinking: *Okay, I need to sit down.* But I couldn't sit down, because everybody's gonna move up ahead and I'm gonna get fired, I'm gonna get everybody fired. So I kept going.

I was seeing little circles. I had to take a rest. But I saw the contractor walking by. When I got up and pretended I was working, I felt like I was going to faint. The sky started to get blurry and my head literally turned sideways. It's really hard to explain: it's like when you're trying to focus on something and just can't. My mom came over to me and said, "Sit down—I'm gonna get you some water." She went and got me some

---

[6] When "suckering," tobacco harvesters often use their hands to remove the small shoots (though machines are sometimes available for the job). The removal of these shoots forces the tobacco plant to focus its energy on producing large leaves.

water and ice; I got back to work. I still felt sluggish, and I remember that within two hours my mom actually had to sit me down again and tell me to take a break.

Kimberly was working fast. She was taking the pace that my mom was. At maybe two or three in the afternoon, I could hear somebody vomiting really loudly—it sounded like she was throwing up her lungs. I couldn't see over the tobacco plants. I was like, *What the heck?* It was Kimberly. Then she stopped and we thought she was okay. We told her to sit down, take a break, go sit in the car. But she wanted to go on, even though she kept throwing up at the same time. It was because of the nicotine.[7] The leaves would get sticky with nicotine when they were wet. Also, I think the plants had been sprayed with pesticides, like maybe a couple hours before, or the day before. You could really smell it.

At around six or seven that night they said we could go home. We were like, "Okay, yeah!" But then I thought, *Oh God, we have to walk all through the field just to get to the car*. It was muddy, and our mom told us to kick our shoes before we got in. But I couldn't do it. I was too tired. I just got in the seat and by the time we got home I was asleep. There were four of us that needed to take showers. I said, "You all just go ahead." I sat on the steps and fell asleep.

That night when I was asleep, I had strange dreams. It wasn't like I was having nightmares—it was like I was still working in tobacco. I could see myself, my hands cutting suckers, rows of tobacco. It's so dizzying, it'll literally wake you up out of nowhere. It was really hard to sleep afterwards. This happens if you work in tobacco. I couldn't go to sleep till

---

[7] Workers absorb nicotine from tobacco plants through their skin, and one in four every harvesting season suffers from acute nicotine poisoning, also known as green tobacco sickness. The symptoms of GTS can include dizziness, vomiting, headaches, abdominal pain, and fluctuations in blood pressure and heart rate. Researchers at Wake Forest University have found that, by the end of the season, "nonsmoking workers had nicotine levels equivalent to regular smokers."

three thirty in the morning. I think it has to do with the stuff that was on the leaves, the nicotine and pesticides. Eventually you just get used to it.

MY MOM TENDS TO EVERYBODY

When me and my sisters got that first paycheck, we were like, "We're gonna give it to our mom." She said, "No. Keep it for yourself. Buy whatever you need."

My mom tends to everybody. With me, I don't really like to go shopping, to buy clothes or whatever. So I followed her around whenever she went shopping. I'd look at her and if she really looked at something, like she wanted to buy it, I'd buy it for her. Like stuff for the bathroom—curtains for the tub and a hairbrush. I would stay behind and grab it and put it under the cart and pay for it myself. She was happy!

One time for Mother's Day I got her a red basket with a white bear holding a red rose, with a bag of red candies. She still has it—she loved that one. She hasn't opened it. She hung it on the wall and made sure it was very noticeable.

It was really hard for her. By the time I was twelve and started working she had six kids and she was trying to raise them all. She'd come home red from the fields and take a shower and start cooking. Then she would say, "Neftali, my feet hurt so bad. Can you please rub them for a moment so I can fall asleep?" She had issues falling asleep.

There were moments where we didn't have money, but the thing is my mom always made sure we had everything we needed. Not stuff that we wanted—wants were never really allowed. You could always think about them but never actually get them.

OUT OF NOWHERE, I'D START SINGING

By now I've worked five summers in tobacco. We're usually paid in cash. We're paid the minimum wage, $7.25 or $8.00 an hour, whatever it is at the time, but it should be more.

Every year it gets hotter. It'll get to one hundred degrees, but what people don't know is that if you're working in a field of tobacco, the leaves reflect the sun, so it's ten to fifteen degrees hotter in the fields. Unless there are trees at the very end of the field, the only shade you get is if you sit under the tobacco leaves. But there's hardly ever a moment that you can actually take a rest, because the minute you finish a row you have to go to another row. What I've noticed is that for contractors it's all about the money. You have to work as fast as possible. When she was younger, my sister Yesenia was working and all of a sudden she got really cool. She thought she was okay. But she was experiencing heat stress, where her body suddenly starts to heat up a lot inside, even if it felt to her like she was cold. It was actually a very dangerous thing.[8]

No one ever addressed any of this stuff. They didn't hand out any instructions about heat stress or nicotine poisoning. No safety lessons. We didn't always have helpful equipment like gloves or anything—we just had to make do. I remember one time I worked without gloves because my sister had our only pair. When I got done my whole arm was pure black—it was covered with tar from the plants. I went home and tried to wash it but it didn't work.

I've seen pesticides being sprayed maybe two fields over, and I've seen pesticides being sprayed in front of our house, over cotton fields. When that happened I told everybody, "Don't go outside. Make sure nothing's

---

[8] North Carolina farmworkers suffer the highest rate of heat-related fatalities in the nation.

outside that you gotta bring inside later."[9]

Every day me and my sisters try to make a happy moment, even if we're feeling really down. So I'll cut off a really big sucker when I'm working in the field and toss it at Kimberly. I'll be like, "Oh no, it was Yesenia!" Or there were days when everything was really quiet, so I'd find the weirdest, most obnoxious song and out of nowhere just start singing it. And I know that my sisters know practically every song, so they would join in and the other workers would be like, "Oh my God." They'd just start laughing.

We never find out about the cigarette companies we're working for. You try to talk to the contractor and he just says, "Get to work." This year we actually saw a farmer—the guy who actually owns the farm. He came up and he talked to my mom and then he talked to me, just to greet us. Afterwards, the contractor said we're not supposed to talk to the farmers.

I EXPECT TO SEE YOUNG PEOPLE

I expect to see young people in the fields nowadays. I saw eight- and nine-year-olds working in sweet potatoes. They were getting paid 40 cents a bucket. They had to dig around and pick the sweet potatoes up, clean 'em and put 'em in the bucket. They carried the bucket until it was full, then somebody else would carry it and throw it in the truck. That was in Greenville, South Carolina. We don't really see sweet potatoes in Pink Hill.

My friends, right after school they go to work, and they'll be talking about how they feel bad the next morning. It's actually very common

[9] A study in the *American Journal of Industrial Medicine* of 287 farmworkers—the majority of whom worked in tobacco—from forty-four different farmworker camps in eleven eastern North Carolina counties found that the workers were exposed to a large number of pesticides, and exposed to the same pesticides multiple times.

for people working in tobacco to feel sick and dizzy. It wasn't just that first day—I always got sick. One time I got sick for two days. I felt bad throughout the day in the fields. The next morning I had a huge headache and I felt like I wanted to vomit. I don't know exactly what's being sprayed, or if it was just the nicotine. It absorbs into your skin—it's just awful, the way you feel. Last year a friend of mine got green tobacco sickness. He was fourteen or fifteen. His family took him to the hospital and he was there for six days, maybe.

When I was thirteen or fourteen, I was having a bunch of problems. Teenager problems. I was really antisocial, like this emo chick. I liked to walk around outside at one o'clock in the morning, like I wasn't scared of anything, like I was practically already on my own. If somebody tried to be nice to me I would flip out. I'm telling you, I had issues. I don't exactly know what I was so angry about. I guess it was because I wasn't letting my emotions out.

In the ninth grade I had surgery on my tonsils and they gave me painkillers. Me being all depressed, I started taking a lot of them. I was gonna take a bunch at once—seven pills—and I looked at them and said, "Nope," and I closed the bottle and walked away from it.

Afterwards I started talking to my Spanish teacher. I met her in tenth grade. She's kind of like how a therapist is—you know, they don't tell anybody your secrets. I'd go see her every other day. And if I could sneak out of the cafeteria during lunch, I'd visit her in her class. They don't let us, but she always told me, "Definitely come over for lunch." I would tell her some of the stuff that was going on with me, and then I wouldn't feel like doing any of the bad stuff, like cutting classes.

SOME CHANGES ARE BEING MADE

One day when I was fourteen, my sister Yesenia told me she was having a meeting with Miss Melissa, a woman who worked as an activist for farmworkers, and asked if I wanted to go.[10] I said sure, if it'll get me out of the house! That's how I got involved in Rural Youth Power. It's a group of young people. We talk about working in the fields, the education we've received, or haven't received, and the difficulties of moving around. We've stayed in Pink Hill the whole time because my mom put her mind to it: when she wants to stay somewhere, she stays somewhere. But a lot of families never settle down because they keep moving to find work. One kid, Eddie, I think he's thirteen or fourteen, he had to move six different times. And we have so many at-risk kids. Two farmworker friends who went to school with us died last year in a shooting. They weren't in a gang but they hung around with people who were. They were supposed to graduate with us.

We don't have a lot of opportunities where we're living. I want my family to be able to start off again. Hopefully I can do something to help my mom. I don't want her to have to keep focusing on the rent and everything by herself. My hope is to get into a college this year and get started working on my major. I definitely want to work in agriculture, keep advocating. Farmworkers need better wages. We asked to take the kids out of the fields, but it's kinda hard because sometimes it's the kids who are working to help the family. And we want to reduce the spraying of pesticides.

Some changes are being made. Last year we held an event called YouthSpeak in Kinston, North Carolina. I was a panelist and I did a

---

[10] "Miss Melissa" is Melissa Bailey, a farmworker advocate in North Carolina. In 2010 she formed NC FIELD (North Carolina Focus on Increasing Leadership Education and Dignity), which provides leadership training to young farmworkers like Neftali.

spoken word; everybody liked it. You get to express yourself and how you feel. You don't have to rhyme, but I like rhyming all the time. We talked about how we wanted to see a change in the minimum wage and how we wanted to give out materials and equipment to the people working in the fields. Educate them so they know the rules—that we're supposed to get a break, for example, and that we should have better bathrooms, with soap, so we can actually clean our hands. One of the people at the YouthSpeak event was from the North Carolina Department of Labor, and he said, "All the stuff you asked for is pretty easy. I think we can actually change it. I think that's really possible." When the Department of Labor guy was speaking, we were all really hopeful. It seemed like all these little things that could make our work bearable were possible. Then a little later at the meeting, Miss Melissa gets a call, and somebody's telling her that a farmworker was behind a truck in the sweet potatoes that day and it went over him. He just got crushed and died. We got really quiet and gave a moment to him.

THEY CAN'T GET ME TO STOP TALKING

Right now school is going really well. This year I think I have all As. And I won an award—the national art and essay contest.[11] I had always been hearing about the contest, and one day I said to myself, "Okay, I'll do it."

The topic of the essay was "The Rhythm of the Harvest." I got two pages done, but it wasn't a lot. On the last day I started working on it at eleven and it was due at twelve o'clock at night. I was like, *Just think about how it is.* Out of nowhere I finished it and turned it in one minute before it was due.

[11] Officially the "Association of Farmworker Opportunity Programs' (AFOP) Migrant and Seasonal Farmworker Children Essay and Art Contest." AFOP is a non-profit that seeks to address the safety and wellbeing of farmworkers, including children.

I wrote first about how at nighttime you hear the slithers of a snake, the flaps of a bat, and in the morning you hear the frogs croaking, the crickets chirping. When you get into the fields you hear the screech of a truck stopping and, as you're working, the noise from pulling your boots out of mud. Just the different sounds that go on while you're in the field. So I turned in the essay on time and I got first place for fourteen- to eighteen-year-olds. I got to go to Boston for the award ceremony.

I like to dye my hair different colors: I've dyed it purple and two or three shades of blue. When I won the award my hair was red. One lady who was on the award staff, Norma Flores, was like, "You have to dye your hair black for the trip." I said, "Okay, I'll dye it black, but when I get back I'm dyeing it blond and pink."

There were at least two hundred people at the ceremony in Boston, and I was just freaking out. I'm supposed to go up there and I'm supposed to read my essay. I have stage fright—I've always had it. And I felt really awkward. I was thinking, *Something's gonna happen, I'm gonna embarrass myself.* But I got up there and I started reading. I was very awkward at first but then I just thought, *You know what, it's all good. I'm calm, I'm good.* I read it and at the end I got this whole standing ovation. People came up to me saying they were in tears from my story.

At Rural Youth Power, we're planning on showing kids how to speak up, to not be afraid, to speak for your rights—'cause you do have them. One of my friends was gonna get paid $6.25 an hour to work in tobacco. I was like, "Boy, you do not even need to go there." You should be getting paid the minimum wage at least. That is a right, right there. They can't just fire you.

I'm one of those people to step in. I've become less scared since I got involved. Now I can actually have a phone conversation. Before I was practically antisocial. And then I started talking, but I couldn't get serious. But now Miss Melissa says I've changed. Before it was like, "Speak up, Neftali." Now it's like they can't get me to stop talking.

RESOURCE EXTRACTION

BUYING AND SELLING THE EARTH

We can hold finished goods such as clothes and laptops in our hands, and imagine a little of the sewing or assembling that went into their manufacture. We can also imagine what our food looked like when it was still growing in the sunlight or chewing grass in the fields. But few of us have been witness to the ways oil drilling can change a landscape, or what copper ore looks like as it's ripped from the earth. At the origin of global supply chains, natural resource extraction is shrouded from consumers' view. But it accounts for as much as 20 percent of the global economy.[1]

Raw materials such as iron, copper, and aluminum are purchased by builders and manufacturers and end up becoming our cars and homes, our can openers and cell phones, not to mention the roads, buildings, and infrastructure that make modern living possible. Energy from fossil fuels such as petroleum, coal, and natural gas account for nearly 85 percent of global energy consumption. Petroleum is not just a leading source

---

[1] Statistic according to the World Trade Organization. This figure is made up largely of fossil fuels and mineral extraction (nonrenewable resources), but also includes renewable resource extraction as in the logging and fishing industries.

of energy production—it's also a major ingredient in plastics, synthetic fabrics, pesticides, medicines, and countless other consumer goods.

In short, taking resources out of the ground is where the modern global economy begins. It's no surprise, therefore, that so many of our global conflicts can be traced to a struggle for control over these very resources.

In the 1500s, fleets of European ships set off for North and South America, digging mines in what would become Mexico, Central America, Bolivia, and Brazil to inlay churches and castles of the European monarchies. Native populations in the Americas were decimated and displaced.

In the following centuries the discovery of diamonds and later oil in Africa led to infiltration by foreign powers from Tunisia to South Africa. A pattern of resource exploration and colonization played out around the globe through the Industrial Revolution of the eighteenth and nineteenth centuries and into the twentieth century, with major world wars fought over control of resource-rich lands.

Today, the struggle for resource control continues to shape global politics. As was the case when European prospectors first found gold in the New World, the discovery of rich deposits of minerals or fossil fuels has rarely been good news for the people who live above them. Economists have labeled this problem the "paradox of plenty" or the "resource curse." In many developing nations, the wealth generated by mining natural resources ends up mostly in the hands of multinational corporations that can afford pricey extraction technology, and the political elite who lease them land or are otherwise paid off. For communities living near oil wells or copper mines, social, political, environmental, and economic instability is the norm. Aside from encouraging warfare and corruption, valuable resources can distort national economies, driving up exchange rates and making it difficult for farmers, manufacturers, and other industries to compete on the global market.[2]

In the resource-rich region known as the Copperbelt of Zambia, workers scramble to take even the most harrowing jobs with mining operations. Though often rife with hazards, copper mining represents a unique opportunity to escape low-income agricultural work for Zambians such as Albert Mwanaumo. In the midst of China's enormous push for resource acquisition, Chinese corporations have established large mining operations in Zambia, negotiating deals with the Zambian government that leave local mineworkers with little legal recourse to address labor disputes. In the past five years, numerous strikes and wage protests have been met with violence. Albert was one of the workers shot when the Chinese mining company he worked for opened fire on demonstrating workers in 2006. Albert was hospitalized for his injuries, and survived with bullets still embedded in his body. Desperate as he was to make a living wage and feed his family, Albert tried to return to work for the very company that nearly killed him, only to be turned away.

The largest mining and petroleum-extraction companies in the world have operations on all seven continents, and have operating budgets larger than those of most nations. These companies are so large, so ubiquitous, sometimes we hardly notice them at all. Most readers will be familiar with the names of the world's major petroleum producers—Shell, Chevron, British Petroleum—but few of us know much about the companies that pull mineral ore from the ground.

One such company is Rio Tinto Group, a nearly 150-year-old mining conglomerate headquartered in London. Rio Tinto is a world leader in the production of aluminum, copper, diamonds, iron, and uranium, as well as a major producer of gold and coal. The company runs mining operations

---

[2] This phenomenon is known as "Dutch Disease." For more information, see glossary, page 348.

throughout North and South America, Australia, Africa, and the South Pacific. With assets of over $90 billion and active mining operations in dozens of countries, the company is a global economic powerhouse.

In Papua New Guinea, Rio Tinto has been accused of using its financial clout to devastating effect. As a teenager in the 1970s on the tiny Melanesian island of Bougainville, Clive Porabou took up arms after Rio Tinto's massive copper-mining operations threatened to make his island uninhabitable. Because the mines were such a rich source of revenue for Papua New Guinea, the government brutally suppressed local resistance to them; the conflict led to a decades-long war of independence for Bougainville.

In a small community in southern California, relatively favorable labor regulations make bargaining with Rio Tinto possible. Borax miner Terri Judd and her co-workers took on the company in a major contract dispute that led to a worker lockout in 2010. Eventually Terri and her co-workers were able to negotiate for better wages and clearer grievance procedures, though for months they risked the closure of the borax mine, their town's primary source of income.

Across the developing world, government authorities collude with extraction conglomerates to generate wealth for a few at the expense of many. In Nigeria, revenue sharing and kickbacks from Shell Oil have ensured that the Nigerian government reacts forcefully to any resistance to extraction operations. Nigeria is a top-ten oil-exporting country, generating hundreds of billions in revenues, yet poverty rates in the country have actually increased since oil extraction began fifty years ago. For Nigerians living near drilling operations such as Bere Suanu Kingston, the oil wells have disfigured the landscape, polluted the river deltas where his people have farmed and fished for centuries, and made their traditional economy untenable. Yet that same oil wealth hasn't led to basic infrastructure investments like paved roads or electrical lines for Bere's community.

The dangers to workers and communities presented by natural-resource extraction do not end once the materials are aboveground. Much of the processing of minerals and petrochemicals into raw materials for industry takes place in the poorest, least protected communities. Industrial pollution leads to increased risk of acute and chronic illnesses as well as land degraded for other uses, such as agriculture.

On the night of December 2, 1984, an explosion at a petrochemical-processing plant in Bhopal, India, caused a leakage of deadly gases leading to what is considered the worst industrial accident of the twentieth century. Sanjay Verma was an infant when his parents, some of his siblings, and more than three thousand other residents of Bhopal were killed instantly after exposure to the gas. Though Sanjay was saved by his sister, he's spent a lifetime coping with a disaster that caused physical and psychological damage still felt throughout Bhopal, even if the story is no longer in the headlines. Heavy metals such as arsenic, toxic petrochemicals, and numerous carcinogens still pollute Bhopal's groundwater decades after the initial explosion.

ALBERT MWANAUMO

AGE: *42*

OCCUPATION: *Salesman, former miner*

BIRTHPLACE: *Chiliumina, Zambia*

INTERVIEWED IN: *Chambishi, Zambia*

The Copperbelt is one of the richest deposits of copper in the world, stretching from northwest Zambia through southeast Congo. In Zambia, copper mines are a principal source of employment. Workers from all parts of the country, as well as neighboring nations, flock to the Copperbelt looking for jobs in the mines in the hope of improving their living conditions.

In 2012, Albert Mwanaumo greets us in a mellow voice and with easy laughter as he welcomes us into his house near Chambishi in the Copperbelt Province of Zambia. Chambishi, the town where Albert has lived and worked for the last fifteen years, is a special economic zone, a region exempt from taxes and tariffs. Chambishi's designation as an SEZ allows Chinese-owned mining operations to function at low cost, and in return China invests heavily in Zambian infrastructure. Though Chinese investment has brought jobs to the region, it has also led to popular resentment across Zambia.[1]

Albert lives in a modest clay home with his wife Grace on the edge of a densely packed neighborhood of improvised homes. The oldest two of their five children have moved out and started lives of their own, but Albert still struggles to support the other three. Their house has four small rooms with doorways closed off by long blue curtains. Two of the rooms are used as bedrooms, one as a kitchen, and the other as a living room. There is very little furniture in the house and the kitchen has no stove, but it does have a traditional brazier that Grace uses to prepare meals. We are invited to sit on one of their old gray sofas, covered in white and yellow blankets. Albert insists on beginning our interview with a prayer, because he believes God must always be called on when people meet. Albert then tells us of his work as a copper miner with a Chinese-owned mining operation, the dangers of the work, and the difficulty of addressing worker grievances with foreign ownership.

I WORKED ON THE FARM WITH MY PARENTS

I was born in 1972 and brought up by my parents in a small village called Chiliumina in the Lufwanyama District on the Copperbelt.[2] I have four sisters and five brothers; I am the youngest. When I was a child, my father worked at the nearby Mibenge Agriculture Training Center in Chapula as a farmer. My father was one of just a few villagers from Chiliumina hired to help cultivate the land owned by the farm—other villagers cultivated their own land. My mother helped my father there and raised me and my siblings. My parents would get a share of the produce they helped grow, and that was the principal source of our income.

---

[1] For more on the relationship between China and Zambia, see Appendix III, page 357.

[2] Lufwanyama is a district in western Zambia. It remains rural and undeveloped compared to other districts in the Zambian Copperbelt.

I went to school at the Chimoto Basic School, and I stayed there from grade one until grade six. Chimoto was a very good school at the time—it had a blackboard and chalk for the teachers to write with, and they gave us pens and books for free. But the school was not close to the village. My siblings and I had to walk about six miles each way to school.

While in grade six, around twelve or thirteen, I injured my leg. I had a wound that wouldn't heal properly, and that made it difficult for me to walk all the way to school. I would spend about three days of every week out of school, and every time I went back I was behind in classwork. So I started learning about how to become a farmer from my father, because I couldn't just stay home and do nothing. I worked on the college farm with my parents growing spinach, cabbages, onion, and tomatoes that we brought to Kalulushi to sell.[3] The college helped us bring the produce to market for free—we'd get rides with our crops in a large van.

I was out of school for the next four years because the wound on my leg wouldn't heal. I was taken to a nearby hospital to find out what was wrong with the leg, and every time I was admitted into the hospital, the wound would begin to improve. I'd feel much better, but when I went home it would get worse again. After four years, the wound healed only because I started using African herbal medicine in addition to Western medicine. After the wound healed I continued to help my family at the farm. It was too late to start school again—I was probably around seventeen by then.

Then, while I was working with my father on the college farm, I got a contract with Anglo American mining company for six months as a general worker.[4] I helped the company find copper samples while they were carrying out their exploration. They were interested in setting up

---

[3] Kalulushi is a town of about seventy-five thousand located fifty miles east of Lufwanyama.

[4] Anglo American is one of the world's largest mining companies, with origins in South African gold and diamond mining.

a mine in an area near Chapula, the little town where the agricultural college was located. It was interesting work to me. We didn't have a lot of mining activity near my village when I was growing up—I can remember some emerald mines not far away, but most of the people I grew up with worked as farmers, not miners.

During the same period I met my wife Grace through one of the old men in my village, a man who was like my grandfather. The first thing that my grandfather considered before introducing me to the girl was the behavior of her mother. Her mother was a good woman and hence the whole family was considered to be decent, especially the girls. It was assumed that she was well groomed and therefore suitable for me to marry. Besides that, I personally had background information about her because we went to the same church and we would chat when we met. We got married in 1993 in Chapula. My first child was born in 1994 and the second was born in 1996. Together we've had five children, two girls and three boys.

THEY JUST OBSERVED FROM THEIR CARS

In 1997 I decided to move to Chambishi to look for a job. I moved to Chambishi because I found life in Lufwanyama to be hard.[5] It was difficult to support my family on what I could earn near my hometown. Other than the occasional job like my work with Anglo American, there wasn't much of any way to make money. So I left my wife and kids near Chapula, in Lufwanyama, and came to Chambishi to find work. From 1997 until 1999, I did field work on other people's farms, doing things like planting peanuts or maize. That made me a little money that I could send back to

---

[5] Chambishi is a small but rapidly growing mining town sixty-five miles northeast of Lufwanyama. Chambishi is a designated special economic zone. For more information, see Appendix III, pages 357 and 363.

my wife and family, but not much. For those first few years I was living with a friend from my village who was kind enough to let me stay with him and his wife. Still, I wasn't making much of an income and couldn't even afford to take the bus back home. This was one of the hardest times in my life. I really missed my wife and kids.

Finally, in 1999, I heard from a friend of a job opening in the Chambishi mines. So I got my first job with Mining Two, a division of NFCA.[6] They hired me as a general worker—helping out the miners, moving equipment, just doing what I was asked. I remember my first day at the mines—I was so excited, and scared as well since they had warned us to watch for falling rock when we were down under the ground. I didn't know what to expect. The mines were like a city underground. There were even rail tracks to move workers around with rows of electric lamps lighting the way. One of the first things I noticed was how hot it was down there. My clothes were soaking with sweat after just a couple minutes of working.

I didn't have any special skills at the time, so my wages weren't that high. I was paid 150,000 kwacha a week, enough to afford to move out of my friend's house and rent a room of my own in a small house.[7] I could also afford to have my family visit me sometimes. The room was so small I couldn't even fit a bed or mattress in the space, only a reed mat and blankets where I slept. Then I had a little space left to put my pots and pans. When my wife would come to visit me, both of us could barely fit in the room together.

The work was difficult. The company provided transport to pick us up at six in the morning and bring us back at eight at night. I worked

---

[6] Nonferrous Corporation Africa (NFCA) is a division of China Nonferrous Metal Mining Co. Ltd., a mining company operated by the Chinese government with extensive operations in Zambia.

[7] 150,000 kwacha = approximately US$28.

for twelve hours a day, five days a week. And after two weeks we would change shifts. If you worked in the morning, then you would begin work in the evening. The night shift started at eight at night and ended at six the following morning. For meals, I was given two buns without sugar or tea or anything.

The ventilation was very bad down in the mines—there was a lot of smoke, there were no outlet pipes to bring in fresh air, and it was so hot. Every six months the company would give us new work equipment like boots, a hard hat, and a jumpsuit. But sometimes the gear wouldn't last the full six months. I would sometimes find myself in a situation where my working shoes were worn out, and my working suit was tattered, and I had to wait for months before I got new attire. This was very dangerous because there were loose electrical cables, and with torn boots it was easy to get electrocuted and get injured moving around equipment.

The mine also did not have a proper drainage system. So that posed a great risk. The water that seeped into the mines was sometimes above knee level and contained all of the chemicals from the explosives used to open up the mine walls. Once, the water penetrated my boots and I got some kind of fungal infection. After that, I got an infection like that almost every three months. I eventually decided to apply grease on my feet so that the water would slide off my feet and reduce the risk of getting infections.

I was worried about my safety, so I joined a mine worker union we had. I paid a little out of my check every month, and we could try to address safety worries through our union reps. I also complained about the ventilation and the problem with damaged clothes and boots to our shift boss, who took the matter to the mine captain, who later went to the supervisor. But with the Chinese management, nothing ever happened no matter how hard you complained. When you told them what the problem was, nothing ever got fixed. The Chinese management did visit the mines in person, but they always visited the site in their cars—they just observed from their cars.

I worked with Mining Two from 1999 to 2002, when my last contract expired. The company allowed me to sign a contract only on a year-by-year basis, so every year I had to sign a new contract with the company. When the contract was over in 2002, I didn't have work for six months, and later I decided to start looking for another job. I found one off-loading copper concentrate from trucks. At that job I was paid a weekly wage of 80,000 kwacha,[8] and the money was never enough. I had to find other means to make money to send back to my family, so I did things like sell eggs after work. Then after three months at the off-loading job, I was let go.

After that I was out of regular work until 2004, when my friends came to my house telling me that Mining Two wanted jackhammer operators. Each jackhammer operator had to have a blasting license. It was a legal requirement for some of the work. So Mining Two trained me to be a jackhammer operator at a school they had set up in the plant. The training was done underground. It took about eight months to learn to be a jackhammer operator, and then in 2005, I did some on-the-job training and obtained my blasting license.

I HEARD A GUNSHOT

By the end of 2005, I had my license and had been transferred from Mining Two to Mining One, this time at better pay as a jackhammer operator. I was leading a team of three workers, still for twelve hours a day under the ground. By the time I was with Mining One my basic wages were 520,000 kwacha a week, with medical, education, and

[8] 80,000 kwacha = US$14.50.

transportation benefits that added up to almost another 300,000 kwacha.[9] My wife and two kids moved in with me here in Chambishi, and I could better afford an education for my children, so they were going to a school called Twateka Basic School in Chingola.[10] My wife and I were also expecting our third child. With the money I was making as a jackhammer operator, I started a little bar in 2005. I sold a beer called Chibuku, which is made from maize. So I could finally afford to take care of my family, but by the middle of 2006, workers at the mines started to talk about striking.

The main reason for the strike was that the company began deducting money from our promised wages without telling us first or explaining why they were doing it. They were charging us a fee without any justification, so we were being paid less than promised, and some workers associated with the union began demanding back pay for the wages that had been deducted without notice.

We were promised that back pay would be delivered to us on July 24, 2006, but when the day came, nobody received the money. The company representatives gave an excuse that the manager who was in charge of issuing payments was in Lusaka.[11] We thought to ourselves that he was around and was just avoiding coming into the plant.

So some of the workers, those involved with the union, they began to call for a strike. I didn't want to get too involved. To me, the point of having a union was that our representatives would work things out with management. That's why I paid union dues. So I decided that instead of striking or joining a demonstration at the mine, I'd go to work as normal.

The morning of July 26, I left for work as usual. Every morning before

---

[9] Total wage and benefits of 820,000 kwacha = approximately US$150.

[10] Chingola is a city of about 150,000 a few miles from Chambishi.

[11] Lusaka is the capital of Zambia.

work I would board a bus outside China House, which was the compound of barracks where Chinese employees of the company lived. We were all anxious to hear what would happen with our promised back pay, and that morning there were about sixty workers near the gate of China House, where the company had posted a memo. When I arrived a friend told me that the memo stated that the company did not have the money they had promised to pay us, and that in fact the issue was that we had been overpaid earlier. We were all upset and confused.

I had actually been outside the China House only for a minute or two when I heard a gunshot. I looked toward the gate of the compound where the sound came from, and I saw my friend Ellias Siame on the ground. He'd been shot. I ran over to him to try to help. But as I hurried toward him, I heard another gunshot go off. After that, I don't remember anything but waking up at the Chambishi clinic.

I HAD TWO BULLETS IN MY BODY

When I woke up, the first thing I noticed was that the clinic was full of journalists from places like Radio Chengelo,[12] Zambia National Broadcasting Corporation, and others who had come to find out what had happened. I actually learned some of the details of the incident from reporters who had come to interview me about it. They said that there were five workers who'd been shot outside China House. Two bullets were shot at me, the rest at other miners: two at Moses Makayi, two at John Chisenga, and one at my friend Ellias. Another colleague was only grazed. One more miner named Edward Katongo had been shot at the mine itself. While I was learning what happened to me and the others, I still couldn't remember being shot. I didn't know whether I'd lost blood, because I'd

[12] Radio Chengelo is a Catholic-run local radio station.

been knocked unconscious immediately.

Then I was transferred to the Wusakile Hospital. They wanted to send me to Sinozam Hospital, which was Chinese run, but there was some concern that protesters who were upset about the shootings were planning on marching on Sinozam and vandalizing it. But later that afternoon, at around four p.m., I was moved to Sinozam after tensions were lower.

I later discovered what led to the shooting at the China House. There had been wage protests at the mine for a couple of days before the 26th, and on the morning of the 26th real violence errupted at the mine. A man named Nelson Jilowa, who was the head of the police force in charge of mine security at that time, had shot Edward Katongo during the worker demonstration. Jilowa had just fired into the crowd as they were listening to a union representative speak. Afterward, Jilowa issued instructions that if there were workers at China House waiting for pickup, they should be held off because of the ongoing protests at the mine. So worry over additional protesters is what led to the shooting at China House by an NFCA employee, a man who was identified in the papers as Mr. Que.

Between the mine and China House, six of us were shot and taken to Chambishi Clinic, and we were later picked up by the NFCA bus to be taken to Sinozam Hospital. I had two bullets in my body: one near the heart in the chest and the other in the shoulder. So the union asked Dr. Lee, the head of the hospital, what was going to be done for me, and he said nothing could be done because the bullets were lodged in critical parts of my body.

I stayed in Sinozam for two months. After that, I was discharged with bullets still in my body, but the doctors told me that the bullets could stay in my body up to twenty-five years without giving me any problems. I didn't trust the doctors at Sinozam, given they were working closely with the mines. They did things like purposely hide my X-rays and downplay the extent of my injuries, because they were helping to keep my injuries out of the media during a tense time for the mining company. Eventually I asked for a transfer to Ndola Central Hospital.[13]

One of my older brothers came to get me from Sinozam when I was discharged. My wife was home with the kids, and it was impossible for her to come and retrieve me. We had a newborn child. When I left Sinozam, it was a struggle for me to walk, because I was feeling very weak.

I went to Ndola Central Hospital, and the surgeon, Dr. Kachenko, said they could remove the bullet that was in my shoulder but not the one near my heart, because they didn't have the equipment to perform such a procedure. But then they decided it was too dangerous to remove either bullet. I did not feel very good about this because I was in pain and hoped that I could have at least one bullet taken out of my body. The bullets made my breathing a bit difficult, and I've always been nervous about them causing more damage.

THE MOMENT I WAS SHOT, MY CONTRACT WAS TERMINATED

I spent two months at Sinozam and more than a week at Ndola Central Hospital. During my time in the hospitals, the mine did nothing to help. They did not send anyone to visit any of us who had been shot. I had to use my own money to pay for the hospital bills. This money came from the small bar that I was running before I got shot.

Because of being in the hospital for a long time, I could no longer maintain my bar and I had to shut it down. So in September, just a little while after I'd left the hospital, I decided to try to go back to work at the mine. I even got a sick note from the hospital—the procedure was that you

[13] Ndola Central Hospital is in Ndola, a city of 450,000 that functions as the commercial center of the Copperbelt region. Ndola is about sixty miles southeast of Chambishi.

needed a doctor's note to excuse any time that you were away from work. When I arrived at the gate to the mine, the mine police there stopped me and told me that the moment I was shot, my contract was terminated. Someone from the company had given the guards the message that I was not welcome back. So at that point I began to look for a lawyer who could act on my case.

I found a lawyer and began the procedure to sue the company. Starting in October 2006, I spent five years going back and forth to the Kitwe High Court. I had to spend 250,000 kwacha for every appointment with the lawyer, and every time he came to court I was required to give him 250,000 kwacha for gas.[14] Sometimes it was hard to find that money for the lawyer, so he would waive fees for me. Even when I had to file the case, the lawyer would pay for me using his money and he told me he would get his money back after I won the case. I did not know how much I would have to pay the lawyer or what percentage he would get out of my settlement.

Finally, in 2011, Nonferrous Corporation Africa was found liable for damages during the shooting. The high court decided that all the workers who had been fired on should be compensated, and each employee should be paid according to the degree of his wounds. It was also decided that I was to be taken to a hospital that would carry out the surgery to remove the bullets.

When the judgment was made, the company representative was not present because they knew they would lose. They were later informed by the court. Nothing has ever happened to Nelson Jilowa or the man who shot me. As for the man who shot me, I do not know whether he is still in the country or not. But I do know that Jilowa was promoted to the post of mine manager.

---

[14] 250,000 kwacha = approximately US$48.

My immediate settlement was 70 million kwacha, though much of that ended up going to my lawyer.[15] The company still hasn't responded to my lawyer's requests to send me to South Africa for treatment. It's also frustrating that the cost of the trip is not part of the settlement—only the operation. If we can finally get them to pay for the operation, I'll have to cover travel costs myself.

It is very hard for me to find a means of survival because I cannot do too much hard work. I always depend on God for survival. You know, since 2006, I have not been able to eat certain rough or hard foods. Every time I eat anything too difficult to digest I experience abnormal stomach pain, and I become incapacitated. I have to eat soft, easy-to-digest foods like potatoes and rice, but they are expensive. The doctor also advised that I take tea with fresh milk or drink fresh milk every two hours but those things are expensive as well.

In the recent past I have been managing to survive by selling charcoal, and sometimes I am asked to build small houses, usually one-room houses for my friends, but it's hard because I am in pain and I cannot work at a fast pace. I can build even bigger houses, but unless I'm helped by someone, I can't make much progress because I don't have the strength or energy to work very long. But I have to force myself because there is nothing much else I can really do to survive. I have five kids at the moment, and I need to find ways to send them to school. I cannot lie; I am not finding enough ways to take care of my children.

For me, to go back to work even after the operation might not be easy, because it might take years for me to fully recover. Or so I've been told. Despite this, when the bullets are successfully removed, by God's

---

[15] 70 million kwacha = approximately US$13,000.

grace, I will for sure venture into running my own business. With some of the compensation money, I was able to send my wife to tailoring school, and she now runs a store in Chambishi where she mends and resells used clothes. I've also built some extra rooms behind the house, which I intend to rent out, and I'm raising a few pigs with the help of my sons. I hope one day to make raising pigs into a bigger business. And about my children, I want to send them to a private school because I think they will be better educated there. It's very important for them to get an education so they can be independent, happy people later in life.

The Bible tells us that you should forgive seventy times seven, and as long as you are a believer no sinner is unforgivable. I do not hold anything against the people who shot me, despite what they think of me. Despite going through all this suffering and pain I still have forgiven the person who shot me because this is what the Bible says and I am a believer. If I had to meet with the person who shot me I would sit him down and talk to him because I believe in forgiveness.

CLIVE PORABOU

AGE: *45*
OCCUPATION: *Musician, filmmaker*
BIRTHPLACE: *Mamung, Bougainville*
INTERVIEWED IN: *Australia and the Solomon Islands*

Clive Porabou was born in 1969 on the Pacific island of Bougainville, just as transnational mining conglomerate Rio Tinto was beginning to dig the world's largest open-pit copper mine on the island. He came of age in the years when Bougainvilleans without special education or skills were excluded from mine work. Instead, Rio Tinto brought in workers from Papua New Guinea (PNG) who set up sprawling worker camps, displacing native residents. Australia had granted Papua New Guinea administrative control of Bougainville in the 1970s, even though the islands are hundreds of miles apart and culturally distinct. Armed conflict over the mine's presence started even before excavation began, though major conflict did not break out until the late eighties, when a small Bougainvillean military force attacked the mine's power supply and shut down mine operations.[1]

From 1989 to 1993, Clive fought with the Bougainville Revolutionary

---

[1] For a full history of Bougainville and its independence movement, see page 358.

Army against the PNG defense force. After getting shot in the arm in 1993, he sought medical treatment in the Solomon Islands, as many injured Bougainvilleans did after PNG imposed a total blockade of the island. In the Solomons, he fell in love with Rachel Caleb, a secretary at the Seventh-day Adventist hospital where he was treated, and they married in 1996. He also began to write and record music about the conflict. Clive soon returned to the front with a video camera to document the struggle—and with cassettes of Blood Generation, *the album he had recorded in the Solomons. After the war ended in 1997, Clive returned to live with Rachel in the Solomons, and they had two children, Rosalie Matari, and Clive Tangaona. He has continued to film, record, and blog about the independence movement of his home island.*

We interview Clive three times via Skype in 2011, twice when he is in Australia and once when he is in the village in the Solomons where he now lives with his family. More than anything, Clive wants word of Bougainville's struggle to circulate around the world.

THEY DIDN'T WORRY MUCH ABOUT MONEY

Mekamui is the traditional name for my island, but the island is also called Bougainville. *Meka* means "sacred" and *mui* means "island." So it's a sacred or holy island. Everything's always green on Mekamui.[2] Before the mining company came, people were living in peace and harmony. Most of our parents, and our grandparents, they just lived on subsistence farming, making food from the garden, growing coconut and cocoa and other food crops they could sell at the market, and earning a little extra through

[2] Mekamui, or Bougainville, is an island of over 3,500 square miles with a population of nearly two hundred thousand. It's located at the northern end of the Solomon Island chain but is still administered by Papua New Guinea, an island nation four hundred miles to the west. For more on Bougainville, see Appendix III, page 358.

whatever jobs they could find. They didn't worry much about money. They just lived on the land and everything the land provided—like food, housing materials, whatever.

Before the mine, the people lived by a barter system. For instance, people who lived along the coast went fishing, and when they caught fish, they exchanged them with the people from inland for taro or yams or other crops. Or the people down along the beach would boil seawater for salt and exchange it for food from inlanders who maintained gardens.

Bougainvilleans stayed in extended families. The older families—aunties, cousins, and whatnot, they stuck together. Families would cultivate big gardens together, working to clear brush and plant food crops. We'd grow yams, potatoes, taro, cassava, bananas, and greens too. One crop we grew was *aibika*, which in English is called "slippery cabbage," because it gets a bit slippery when you boil it.

Where I grew up was about an hour and fifteen minute walk up into the hills from Arawa.[3] Our village, Mamung, had about two hundred people and all the houses were laid out in a long row in the hillside. Aside from my parents, I lived with three brothers and two sisters. I was the youngest. My brothers and I, we used to climb breadfruit trees, and we also went fishing in the river with many other kids from the village, and we went to school near the village. My brothers all liked to strum on the guitar and sing, and they taught me how to play when I was young. Music was in my blood. When I was a child, the village was safe.

---

[3] Arawa is the capital of Bougainville and was the administrative center of the copper mining operation. Before Rio Tinto developed the area as an administrative headquarters, it was a cocoa and coconut plantation.

"WHAT CAN WE DO?"

In early 1969, Australia granted land—owned by Bougainvillean villagers near the town of Rorovana—to Rio Tinto to build a shipping port. The land grant led to protests that included removing surveyor markers. The protest was quashed by over seventy police brought in from Papua New Guinea, which had some administrative control over the island of Bougainville granted by Australia.

Bougainville Copper actually came in just a few years before I was born in 1969.[4] The first thing they did was survey the land for the Panguna mine. Women on Bougainville, Mekamui, are the landowners, and they pass the land down to their daughters—land ownership is a very important tradition. The Australian government was set to hand over a parcel of land along the shore to Bougainville Copper, and there was resistance immediately. The story I've heard is that when the women protested, the police and the company's security forces kicked the women and dragged them along the beach.[5] The way we see it, the company came into Bougainville by force.

For most of us Bougainvilleans, we grew up with the idea of becoming an independent island nation. It's been passed down for generations.[6] And that's why in 1975 Bougainvilleans held a protest demonstration in Arawa. They stormed the White House, threw rocks through the windows.[7] I was just a kid at the time, but my brothers joined in. They threw stones through the White House windows and camped nearby for a few days. The prime minister of Papua New Guinea came to the island in

---

[4] Bougainville Copper Ltd. is an Australian-owned subsidiary of the British/Australian mining conglomerate Rio Tinto.

[5] For more on the history of Bougainville, see Appendix III, page 358.

[6] Since the nineteenth century, control of Bougainville has passed between Britain, Germany, Australia, Japan (during World War II), and independent Papua New Guinea.

[7] The White House was the headquarters of the prewar Bougainville provincial government.

early September 1975 and negotiated a provincial government structure for Bougainville. Then, on September 16, Australia granted independence to Papua New Guinea. All these changes happened at the same time. But independence from Australia didn't solve our problems. We were now a part of Papua New Guinea and were still not free on our own land.

Most of our problems seemed to come from the development of the mining operations. People from the Papua New Guinea mainland came looking for jobs, they built squatter settlements, and it got worse for those of us who were born in Mekamui.

I grew up seeing our mothers and sisters raped by the squatters. Old people getting kicked or punched. When I was a child of ten or twelve, I was walking with a cousin on a section of road down by the river where the squatters had their houses, and we witnessed a group of squatters, guys in their twenties, assault one of our female relatives. Three of them pushed her down, took off her clothes, her bra. She was screaming. We were just kids. We couldn't do anything, but she was a big strong woman, so she put up a good fight with them. Luckily, two or three other guys came and chased off the attackers. When it happened, you know, we had pain in our hearts and in our minds. Me and the cousin, we said, "What can we do?" We decided that one day we must try to do something.

But soon after the incident I left the island for a few years. My siblings and I went to primary school right next to our village, and I was there through the sixth grade, but for high school, I went to Papua New Guinea. I grew up in the religion called Seventh-day Adventist, or SDA, so we had to go to the SDA school. At the time there was not any Seventh-day-run high school around Bougainville, so we went to Papua New Guinea. I was about fifteen when I left. I stayed in PNG for four years. I came back in late 1987, and in '89 when I was home for a couple of years, the uprising started.

WE STARTED FIGHTING WITH BOWS AND ARROWS

Francis Ona was a landowner up near the Panguna mine, the major mine operated by Bougainville Copper at the time. He also worked for the company as a surveyor—he was one of the few Bougainvilleans who found work with Rio Tinto. Through his work, he realized there were seven other deposits on the island that would be mined after Panguna, and that the damage done to the land would destroy the island.[8] The rivers were already poisoned by waste from the mine—fish had disappeared, animals were disappearing, and the company was already tearing up tens of thousands of acres for the mine that used to be hunting and gardening grounds. Ona understood his people would have no future if things continued as planned. Ona called for a review of the mine, a review of the agreement between the PNG government, the mining company, and the landowners who received royalties from the company for use of the land. He just peacefully called for a review. And the Panguna Landowners Association, the mine owners, and the PNG government, they didn't listen to him.

After protesting for years, in 1988, Ona just took off. He and some associates took up arms and formed the Bougainville Revolutionary Army, the BRA. Over the next year, they started blowing up the pylons that carried electricity from the coast to the mine, and in May of 1989, the Panguna mine came to a standstill.[9] Mining activity stopped completely, but the mine owners were not about to give up. It was the beginning of

---

[8] At its height of operation, the Panguna mine was the world's largest open-pit copper mine, measuring more than four miles across and nearly a third of a mile deep. It produced more than one billion tons of waste, including heavy metal trailings that clogged the island's fresh water streams and rivers.

[9] For a clear timeline of the independence movement, see Appendix III, page 358.

a civil war. When the mine closed down, the Papua New Guinea government sent in the police, the riot squad, the security forces, the defense forces. The company ordered PNG security forces to use every possible means to reopen the mine.

At the start of the uprising, I was just a couple of years back from high school, about nineteen, and I had a job at the Palm Store, one of three department stores in Arawa at the time.

I can't remember the actual date I joined the BRA, but it was at the time the Papua New Guinean laborers in one of the cocoa or coconut plantations around Arawa killed a woman from the island. Some of the woman's relatives were with the BRA in Ona's camp, and those relatives came down to the PNG work camps and killed some men as payback.

PNG security responded by setting up roadblocks and stopping all Bougainvilleans from heading home to their villages. When all this was happening, I just left the shop and put the money in the safe at the Palm Store and left Arawa. And I rang the boss to tell him that the money was there. I realized that the area was not safe, and that anything could happen. Everyone fleeing the PNG crackdown drove up near our village, and put their trucks and cars and buses near there, and walked the bush track through the jungle up the mountain and back to their villages.

Me and one of my cousins, we decided to go into the bush to join the fighters. We said, "We'll join the uprising, the boys, for what we believe, and for what we want the island to be." It was very exciting during that time. I was in my late teens, with energy and all that. Most young guys, they loved it. When you shoot at an enemy, you're going to feel proud. You killed someone who tried to come kill you, to steal your things.

We used to have only five or ten boys in each fighting unit on the BRA side, each led by a unit commander who was usually a little older. At first, we started fighting with bows and arrows or whatever stones and sticks we could find. We used what we call the *foca* in our language, which is a sort of slingshot. Soon we had a few homemade rifles. Then some of the boys captured enemy weapons. All the best weapons we had, we took from the PNG security forces.

Most of the time we would attack by setting up an ambush. We'd spy on PNG camps from the bush. The island itself is mountainous, and we took advantage of terrain that we knew well. We could see the enemy camps from the mountains and plan out our strikes. Our land really helped us.

In those times we had little sleep. We took turns: some would watch, others would sleep. Early in the morning, some of us would go down to check if any enemy soldiers had come in the night. In the day we would patrol the area to see if it was clear or not. During this time, the villagers in the highlands moved higher up in the mountains, to set up bush camps. Villagers would go down to the old village to get things they needed and then return to the safety of the hidden bush camps. We would patrol the villages before the villagers came down. We gave them certain designated days to come down, like Monday and Thursday, and we would go down with them to make sure they were safe.

That was most of the routine, unless boys from other areas asked for help. That's when platoon commanders would select someone with a high-power gun and ask us to go help. The messages got around very fast. The boys ran from one place to another. At first there was no radio, but later on we got a few high-frequency radios.

That's what we signed on for—rain, cold, whatever. We would tell people who wanted to join, "You may sleep in cold or rain at night, and you have to accept that. Sometimes when we have ongoing military operations, we will have no shelter. If you can't do that, there are other ways you can help—communications or whatever." But once the war started, it was impossible not to be involved in some way.

WE SURVIVED ON WHAT WE COULD GROW

From 1989 to '97 we had a total blockade of our island imposed by Papua New Guinea. There weren't any resources coming in. Rio Tinto and Papua New Guinea, they were saying, "We will make the Bougainvilleans suffer and make them come down from the mountains and say, 'Oh, we don't want to fight now. We surrender,'" so that they could reopen the mine.[10]

During that time in the mountains, we survived on what we could grow in our gardens. We didn't have much protein, and little salt, because before we used to gather salt and trade for fish from the people down at the beach and sea, along the coast. PNG forces controlled the coasts, and it was risky for those of us in the mountains to travel down around the shore.

We didn't have medicine at the time, or new clothes, and in the bush high in the mountains it could get a bit cold. Many people died from this blockade because we had no medicine or doctors to treat them. Sometimes we could travel to the Solomons for medical assistance.[11] But it was very dangerous, because of PNG boats and helicopters used to patrol the water. So if it was between life and death, you traveled across. If you had a way, you found someone who was going across to the Solomons, and you had to take a chance. On the side of the border on the Solomon Islands, the Red Cross and some other humanitarian groups, they used to help us.

---

[10] The Red Cross estimates that the blockade killed two thousand children within the first two years.

[11] Geographically, Bougainville is the northernmost of the Solomon Islands, an archipelago off the east coast of Papua New Guinea. Bougainville ended up as part of PNG due to complex land swaps during the European colonial era. The closest islands in the independent Solomon chain are just a couple of miles off the southern coast of Bougainville.

"THIS IS THE GUY THAT NEARLY GOT US KILLED WHEN WE LISTENED TO HIS MUSIC"

In 1993, I was shot through my right arm in an ambush. Another Bougainvillean, he betrayed us. He told the PNG soldiers that my unit was going to be in a certain location, so the soldiers set up an ambush. After I was shot, I had to wait in some bush camps with relatives until it was safe to cross. Once in the Solomons, I was treated at a Seventh-day Adventist hospital where they successfully removed the bullet from my arm.

I stayed in the Solomons after my injury, and I began to focus on music. I recorded an album, which I called *Blood Generation*. It came out in '95, during the time when the war was bitter on the ground. PNG tried every means to end the resistance and reopen the mine, with all these operations that they gave names like "High-Speed I" and "High-Speed II." They'd send waves of helicopters and armored trucks into the bush to drive out the BRA. We put *Blood Generation* out, and the first copies went all over Bougainville. Many Bougainvilleans played it, and if the PNG security forces heard you playing it, they would smash your tape; they might kill you. I once met another Bougainvillean at the airport, and he said, "This is the guy that nearly got us killed when we listened to his music during the height of the war."

Aside from pursuing music while recovering in the Solomons, I also met a Solomon Islander, the woman who would become my wife. Rachel was a secretary at one of the Seventh-day Adventist hospitals in the outer provinces of Solomon Islands—that's where most of us from Bougainville went. I met her while I was recuperating, and we were married in 1996.

After my album made its way to Mekamui, I thought about other ways I could make a difference with the independence movement. I contacted some supporters in Australia and I sent *Blood Generation* around there too, because on the ground, most of the media that was coming out, it was crap. It was pro-government—journalists or TV crews who had been going out with the Papua New Guinea defense forces. They'd been telling one side of the story only.

Then some journalists went to the Solomon Islands through the blockade, across the border, like Dom Rotheroe did to make *The Coconut Revolution*.[12] They went across and they stayed with the people out in the jungle, out in the bushes. And they brought out the stories of what was really happening to the people of Mekamui. So people in Papua New Guinea, in Australia, they learned what bullshit was coming out from the pro-government media.

But I saw that Rotheroe's TV crew made it in, and I thought, *Why can't we Bougainvilleans do the film shooting ourselves?* So I borrowed a camera from one of the supporters on the Solomon Islands, went back to Bougainville, and we started shooting some film. I filmed the boys in action, fighting PNG defense forces. So it was dangerous. You had to look in two directions at once—one eye looked through the viewfinder, one eye looked out for bullets flying by. Trying to capture good, steady footage while bullets were flying was like a suicide mission.

IT'S A MIRACLE WHAT HAPPENED TO US

Unable to defeat the Bougainville Revolutionary Army, the PNG government made a secretive and controversial decision to hire mercenaries from the British firm Sandline International in 1997. The governments of Australia and New Zealand, as well as PNG defense force commander Jerry Singirok, opposed the move

---

[12] The 2001 documentary *The Coconut Revolution* spotlighted the Bougainvilleans' resistance to Rio Tinto and the PNG forces, and the ingenious ways they used their natural resources to survive during the blockade—running trucks on coconut oil, for example.

when it became known. The government of then–Prime Minister Julius Chan went forward anyway. As soon as the forty-four mercenaries landed on Bougainville, Singirok had them arrested. Chan fired Singirok, but soldiers at the central barracks rebelled, students at the University of Papua New Guinea in the capital Port Moresby boycotted classes, and mass protests filled the streets. Chan remained intransigent. The government of Australia then threatened to withdraw financial aid, and that proved the decisive factor. All the mercenaries were withdrawn five days after the protests began.

In '97, when the situation on Bougainville was getting hard, the government of Papua New Guinea brought in mercenaries—they spent a lot of money hiring them. The mercenaries came from as far as Port Moresby,[13] but the Papua New Guinea defense force commander, Jerry Singirok, he opposed the use of mercenaries. He had the mercenaries arrested as soon as they showed up.

Then Jerry Singirok went on air to one of the local radio stations, and he explained everything. And the people of Papua New Guinea were listening. And that's why students and other PNG citizens walked with the soldiers along the road and protested. Many people were calling, "Don't kill our brothers in Bougainville, don't do that."

We say it's a miracle what happened to us. They killed twenty thousand–plus Bougainvilleans while trying to reopen that mine, and it took a PNG general to end it.[14]

---

[13] Port Moresby is the capital of Papua New Guinea.

[14] A court case brought against Rio Tinto in the United States, *Sarei v. Rio Tinto*, put this figure at fifteen thousand. Bougainville had a total population of about 154,000 in 1990, so this represented about 10 percent of the island's residents. For more on *Sarei v. Rio Tinto* and the Alien Tort Statute under which it was filed, see Appendix III, page 362.

WE WANT INDEPENDENCE, SO LET'S GO NEGOTIATE FOR INDEPENDENCE

When the war ended in 1997, the BRA and other revolutionary forces signed a peace agreement with PNG, and negotiations began to grant the island more autonomy.[15] In 2005, they granted a limited autonomous government to Bougainville.

I haven't been involved in any real way myself with the negotiations, but I still do my part letting the world know about our struggle through my website, www.mekamui.org. And I work with a number of groups within Bougainville to try to make sure they never reopen the mine. And to push for full independence from PNG. I just got a text from the boys on the ground, they texted me this morning. They held a meeting yesterday and they said, "We don't want to be controlled by directives from Port Moresby." So, to be independent, it is like we will become separate. Not controlled by Papua New Guinea, or under Papua New Guinea.

The referendum on independence is scheduled for 2015, but it's conditional. Roads and hospitals, all these must be built before the referendum is sealed. There's not anything on the ground yet, so that's why maybe the referendum will be later. Still, many of us are saying: Why bother with a referendum when we've lost twenty thousand fighting to close the mine and get full independence? Our sacrifice shows that we want independence, so let's go negotiate for independence right away.

---

[15] Though the 1997 mercenary debacle made clear that the Bougainville uprising would not be quelled by force, the peace agreement was not signed until August 30, 2001. Deep divisions wracked Bougainvillean society as the conflict wore on, and the peace process needed to address these as well as the war with Papua New Guinea. The core provisions of the peace treaty included a higher level of autonomy for Bougainville, a deferred referendum on independence, and demilitarization. For more information, see Appendix III, page 358.

I'm very happy that now on the ground the people are free, girls can walk anytime in the day. Arawa is very safe now. Everywhere you go it's only Bougainvilleans.

We have more autonomy, but even in the last couple of days there's been a lot of talk again around the island on the mine issue in the Bougainville Autonomous Government. Our president in Bougainville, John Momis, he went to Moresby and talked with the prime minister and the Panguna Landowners Association, the landowners' chairmen. They want to review the agreement because the actual landowners of the mine are still divided on the issue of independence and whether to reopen mining activities.

THE TREES HAVE STARTED BEARING FRUITS AGAIN

After the mine opened, life on the island seemed to stall. Now, everything has just started again. Fruit trees—they've started bearing fruits again. During the time of mining operations, fruit trees weren't bearing any fruit. Like the breadfruit we used to eat when I was a small boy. It stopped when the mine was in operation, and now it has started bearing fruit again, so we think it was the chemicals or whatever poison they used in the mine that sickened the breadfruit trees.

Before the mining, the small streams from the highlands were free to flow down to the main Jaba River without anything blocking them. All the waste from the mine, the rocks and sediment, it spread out over the river and its tributaries, blocking the smaller streams so it causes big landslides. When it rains for a few days, there's flooding and it causes a lot of damage to the soil and land.[16] The river starts from the mine, and

[16] According to the Bougainvilleans' lawsuit against Rio Tinto, the mine's waste and runoff contaminated an area of nearly ten thousand acres of farms and gardens. Coastal lands near the Jaba river were turned toxic from heavy metal runoff.

there's nothing living around it for about fifty, sixty kilometers. Not any living thing. But it's slowly getting better, life is coming back.

Our group that followed the lead of Francis Ona, we don't want the mine reopened.[17] Other residents of the island, they want to reopen the mine and just want to renegotiate with the mining company. We are saying, "Why do you want the mine reopened? What are you gonna get from it? What are you gonna do? Where are your children going to live, and what will they think of you when they know you destroyed all this land?"

But the residents in favor of reopening the mine are saying that we are going to become economically independent, that more money will come directly to Bougainville instead of PNG. In the past, about 19 percent of the profits from the mine went to Papua New Guinea. Only a little amount of money, the peanuts that landowners got, came to Bougainville. So we've been saying that when we are independent, all of that money, 90 or 50 or whatever percent that the government of the day can agree on, will come to Bougainville and not be shared with the government of Papua New Guinea, which was the previous arrangement.

My group has been saying, how come very tiny Pacific island countries that don't have any valuable resources like copper or gold manage independence? Like the Solomon Islands, Nauru, and Cook Islands and all these other little island nations—they are independent, even though they don't have valuable resources. We can make cocoa or coconut plantations—we could do that instead of mining and destroying the land. We could plant food. We saw that mining will destroy our land, so we've been piping up to keep our land as it is: green, always green. We want the island to be green, so our future generations can live peacefully, live happily with things from the ground.

---

[17] The group Clive works with is the Mekamui Hardliners.

Before, when the mine was in operation, people were busy, you know, busy, busy. They nearly forgot their relatives, their neighbors. Because they were always struggling to make money, money, money. They seemed to forget our culture and our traditional ways, and now, people are learning that again. We need to hold on to our identity. That's what the war and the closing down of the mine brought to us. It brought us back together.

TERRI JUDD

AGE: *44*
OCCUPATION: *Borax miner*
BIRTHPLACE: *Heidelberg, Germany*
INTERVIEWED IN: *Boron, California*

Born to a military family, Terri Judd lived on five different bases before she turned ten and her family moved back to the small town of Boron, California, where her father had grown up. A single mom and Desert Storm veteran, Terri followed her father and grandfather's footsteps when she went to work at the borax mine that gave the town its name, a mine owned by international conglomerate Rio Tinto since 1970. Borax is a natural compound of sodium and the element boron, and it is an ingredient in a wide range of industrial and commercial products, from cosmetics to pesticides. The mine near Boron is the largest borax mine in the world.

When we first talk to Terri, she beams as she describes her work operating enormous quarry vehicles. "It's something not a lot of people get to do," she tells us. "It's almost like I'm a little kid. I get big dump trucks and I get to go play in the dirt." Then, after Rio Tinto locked the workers out in early 2010 during a contract dispute, Judd became one of the workers' most visible spokespeople—though she never imagined she'd be standing up and talking in front of hundreds of people. "That's not something I wanted to do," she says. Asked why she did, she replies, "Because the union asked me to. They came out and said, 'We need somebody to do this,' and I had to step up to the plate. We're fighting for our rights and need people to go out there, so I figured, why not?"

We first meet Terri Judd after the world premiere of the documentary Locked Out 2010, *held at Boron High School on October 30, 2010.*[1] *Cheerful conversation and the smell of popcorn from an old-fashioned machine float through the huge multipurpose room as workers and their families gather their things to leave, buoyed by seeing their story on the big screen.*

MOVING TO BORON WAS A LITTLE BIT OF A CULTURE SHOCK

For the first ten years of my life, my father was in the U.S. Army, so my family traveled quite a bit. We lived on military bases in Pirmasens and Heidelberg in Germany; in Fort Bragg, North Carolina; Fort Carson, Colorado; and Fort Polk, Louisiana. I think I'd actually been to four different schools by the fifth grade. You learn to make friends fast—there's no such thing as being really shy.

In 1980, my father retired after twenty-six years in the army, and he, my mother, my sister, and I came back to Boron, California.[2] He pretty much had a job waiting with U.S. Borax.[3]

Moving to Boron was a little bit of a culture shock. A lot of military

---

[1] *Locked Out 2010* follows the contract dispute between Borax workers and Rio Tinto.

[2] Boron is a town of just over two thousand residents. It's located about 120 miles northeast of Los Angeles and west of the Mojave Desert.

[3] The multinational mining conglomerate Rio Tinto bought U.S. Borax in 1968. The subsidiary is now called Rio Tinto Boron, though employees sometimes still refer to their employer as U.S. Borax.

bases are the size of a small city, and the majority of them are sitting next to a large city. Then we came to Boron, where we have between two and three thousand people, at the most, and you gotta drive fifty miles just to go to the movies. And Boron is very tight-knit. The first question you're asked here is, "Who are your parents?"

I was lucky enough that I had grandparents who had lived here. My father had grown up in this area, and my mother had spent time here after she married my dad. So actually, we were known to the community. We weren't coming in as strangers.

You got people here who are friends who go back. They're friends because their parents and their grandparents were friends. Then we got families that are mortal enemies. Sometimes it can get pretty ridiculous. I know of two individuals, and I won't name names, but these women have probably not spoken in forty years. Nobody really knows what happened. But these two, they just don't speak, they don't even look at each other.

And we know who's alone. We know who has family that comes and checks on them. If people live by themselves, don't have many visitors, neighbors make a point of keeping an eye out for 'em.

In Boron I had cousins who lived three houses down from me. We weren't indoors a lot. We would ride dirt bikes, three-wheels, ATVs. We had an entire desert to explore. If we weren't in school, if it was summertime, we were outside playing, chasing jackrabbits, little bitty lizards—the big ones tend to hide from you very well. And then of course you have horny toads out there—they got horns growing out of their little heads.

I will say, I was the tomboy. And I was daddy's little girl. I loved following my father around. He had this firm belief that if you're going to drive a car, you should know how it operates. When I was a teenager he used to love dragging me out of bed Saturday mornings, saying, "Come out here, I want to show you this one thing on the car." I remember looking at an engine one morning, being half asleep, and saying, "What are you doing to me, Dad?" If he had a project he wanted to do, he'd always come and say, "Come and help me." If the washing machine broke down, Dad would want to take it apart and see if he could fix it, and I remember being the one to hold the flashlight and hand him the tools.

I graduated from high school in 1988, and I worked as a security guard out at Borax for most of two years. Then I left that job and spent four years in the military. You could pretty much say I followed in my father's footsteps.

I had just turned twenty years old when I was sent to Iraq. I had been in the United States Army for only four months. I'd enlisted in April 1990 and I'd just completed my basic and my advanced individual training. My specialty was going to be the OH-58 Delta helicopter; I was going to be a crew chief on that.

I went to my new post at Fort Stewart, in Georgia, on September 1, 1990, which I believe was around Labor Day. And only three days later, I got stuck on a plane and sent to catch the rest of my unit, who had already been deployed over in Saudi Arabia for the start of Operation Desert Shield. I ended up joining them in the desert, because I hadn't graduated from my training till August 17 or 18, and Saddam Hussein had already invaded Kuwait on August 2.

It was a waiting game, the first eight months we were over there. We stayed in Saudi Arabia during that time. It wasn't until the ground war started that we jumped positions to Iraq.

We advanced straight up to a section of the Euphrates River and set up camp literally out in the middle of nowhere. I thought Boron was the middle of nowhere, but I discovered that nope, there's someplace even worse. By the time we showed up, the war was over and peace had been declared. So we saw the Iraqi soldiers, but most of them had pretty much given up, and the U.S. was like, "We can't take any more prisoners," so they were just sending them home. So it was the opportunity to, quote, "be in a war" without ever firing a shot. Which I'm actually pretty happy about.

I was over there in Iraq for just about nine months, and then I went back to my regular duty station. I got out towards the end of 1993, beginning of '94.

I was supposed to be in for six years, but I stayed in for only four. I took an early out because when I got orders to deploy to Korea, I was already pregnant with my daughter Ashley. My orders were put on hold when Ashley was born in June '93, but when my daughter turned six months old I would've had to go to Korea for one year and leave her with my parents. There was no way I was going to leave my six-month-old and be gone for a year. You miss all that important stuff. Her dad was in the military too, but by the time she was born it was a disaster of a relationship.

I ended up getting hired back on with the guard service out there at Borax, and I worked for them while I put in applications—applications to work at the mine, applications with the California Highway Patrol—if they took an application, I put in for it. Finally in July 1997 I got hired on with Borax as a mineworker.

I GET TO GO PLAY IN THE DIRT

I went in as a laborer and spent about three weeks in the labor pool. It was a requirement. When you got hired in, you went into the labor pool, and that's where you learned the different parts of the plant. From there, you put in bids to go to certain departments. I knew exactly where I wanted to go.

As soon as they put up the bid for the mine department, I put my name in on it. Same as my father, same as my grandfather. I wanted to go play with the big trucks.

I love my job. It's something not a lot of people get to do. It's almost like I'm a little kid. I get big dump trucks and I get to go play in the dirt. It's like overgrown Tonka toys. I've run haul trucks, water trucks, dozers, shovels, and front-end loaders. A front-end loader is a big bucket that sits on four wheels.

My job is to load the ore into the haul trucks and send it up to the crusher, after they strip off the waste material, drill, and blast the ore. I scoop it up into the bucket, go up to the side of the truck, dump it into the dump truck, and that's all I do all day long: load them dump trucks. And then they haul it from the bottom of the open pit up to the crusher.

Surrounding the open pit we have what we call our waste dumps, where we stockpile the dirt. Eventually, once we're done mining in that area, all that dirt's gonna come back into that hole. Unless of course Los Angeles gets hold of it and turns it into a giant landfill. It ends up being a big, big hole. From the top going down I want to say it's over a thousand feet.

My crew runs probably about forty people. We normally have at least one front-end loader operating, and one shovel, and then we have dozers that are working the dumps, we have a crusher crew working, water trucks, haul trucks, and graders.

It's one of those jobs that you're either gonna love or hate. You have to be of a certain mindset, because it can become very repetitious. Some days it feels like you're doing the same thing just over and over and over. And some get very bored with it very fast.

EVERY DAY WE WORK, SAFETY IS BROUGHT UP

The equipment and the environment that we work in, it's very unforgiving. We have more fatalities in the mining industry here in the United States than your firefighters and your police departments put together. In the U.S., both metal and nonmetal, open-pit mining and underground mining, including sandpits and gravel mines, in the past years, we average about five deaths a month.[4]

You always see on TV the underground miners who get trapped. But you don't hear about the truck that rolled off the top of a dump at the sand and gravel mine and killed a driver. At a sand and gravel mine around Houston, Texas, they had an individual who had twenty-three years of experience working at a mine. And he got run over with a front-end loader that he was trying to fix, because the brakes weren't set. But when you got tires that are twelve feet tall, you know, if it starts to roll forward and it catches you, it's gonna kill you.

Every day we work, safety is brought up out there. We discuss it among ourselves. Case in point, we just had an incident not too long ago where one of the big haul trucks ran over a small pickup, completely crushing it. Thankfully no one was in the pickup. But we're still talking about it. What if someone had been in the pickup? What would I have done differently? What could the driver have done differently? Basically we pick it to death to find out the why, the how, and most importantly what we can do so it doesn't happen again.

Besides the human error factor in a lot of fatalities and injuries out there, you have the mechanical. Sometimes machines just break down, there's no good reason. You know that a piece of equipment's not always going to work right, no matter what you do. If it goes out of control, you're just stuck along for the ride.

You got environmental factors too. We work twenty-four seven, day and night. When that sun goes down, that mine becomes a whole 'nother place of operations. Where you used to be able to see different things

[4] According to the U.S. Department of Labor, the average yearly number of miner deaths in the U.S. from 2006 through 2010 was thirty-five. During the seventies and eighties, one hundred to two hundred and fifty miners were killed in the U.S. each year.

during the daylight, you can no longer can see 'em, and you're doing the same job, backing up to a dump edge where you got a drop-off behind that dump, say two hundred, three hundred feet. It's a little harder to see where that edge is, if the edge is cracking, things like that.

Normally, there's about a six-foot berm that sits on the dump edge.[5] And the haul truck drivers will back their trucks up, touch their rear tires against that berm, then stop and lift the bed of the truck, so all of the waste material goes over that berm and down the side of that dump.

They have to line both sets of tires up. And one of the big things to remember is that a full truck has around 256 tons of dirt. That's not including the weight of the actual truck. And you go up to these edges, and you're lifting that bed in the air, and dumping this material over. Depending on the material that you're working in, we have what's referred to as sloughing, where the edges of these dumps literally break off and fall down. There's so many different factors that you have to be aware of out there. It can actually get pretty intimidating.

A lot of times, even if you know there's a safety issue, a lot of that still comes down to that human error factor. Just bad judgment calls on the part of the employee.

And the company pushes production. A lot of your supervisors out there, they get bonuses based on their performance and their performance is judged on their production, so if it wasn't for the union they would be pushing production a lot harder, which in turn means skipping safety procedures.[6]

---

[5] A berm is a wall of dirt piled at the edge of the pit to keep dump trucks from backing up too far.

[6] The workers at U.S. Borax voted in 1964 to join the International Longshore and Warehouse Union, and became ILWU Local 30. Their contract covered everyone who worked in the mine, the processing plant, and the maintenance department, as well as some of the office staff.

THAT COULD'VE KILLED ME

When the wall fell on me, I should not have been digging in that area. Yes, I should have stopped digging, but I had reported the situation to my supervisor, and they still continued to have me dig in that area.

I was digging kernite, one of the ores that we mine at U.S. Borax. It has the consistency of dirt with big boulders in it. It gets processed into boric acid, which you find in the majority of your bug killers.

The accident happened one day in March 2005, around eleven thirty or noon. I wasn't actually in the bottom; I was in what we refer to as extension 33Z. We call that kind of area where we're digging into a "bench." We build a dig face in front of us with the front-end loader. The dig face should be no higher than about thirty feet. Thirty-five would be pushing it. And I was working a dig face that was topping forty-five feet. It was too big of a wall for me to be actually working.

I had just come back from taking my lunch. And I think I loaded one or two more trucks, and then the others took off for lunch. I went to clean up my work area where I had some spillage, and I moved my loader in towards the wall. And before I could put it into reverse and back up, the whole dig face just started breaking off and collapsing down on top of me.

It had cracked farther back where I couldn't see it, and then I just happened to look up and see this wall of dirt falling at me.

My first reaction was literally, *Oh shit.* I had the skiff into reverse and I was trying to back up, thinking, *I can get backed up before it hits me.* But that didn't quite work. The dirt hit me, it broke the windshield of the loader, and the whole time I'm looking at all this dirt that had completely buried the front of my loader. The only thing I could think of was, *Well, the engine's still running, I can back up*. What I didn't know was my back tires were about eight feet off the ground.

When that dirt came down—we're talking probably at least a hundred tons flying down—when it hit the front end of the loader, it caused the rear end of it to jump up into the air, so I was actually kind of sitting with my front end buried and my rear end sticking up in the air.

The dust settled and I knew I couldn't back the skiff up. I had a windshield that was lying on me. I couldn't get out of my seat because it had me pinned down in there. I was thinking, *Okay, now I gotta call somebody. They're going to have to come help me; they're gonna have to move this dirt so I can lift this off my legs so I can get out.*

So I finally had to call for help. A water truck driver, Richard Harvell, had heard me call and he told me later that he knew something was wrong because I guess my voice had pitched up really high. He and Mike Green, one of our roving mechanics who happened to be in the area, both showed up at the same time to give me a hand. They told me later when they first pulled up, they were amazed I wasn't dead, because that's how bad it looked. All they could see was the fallen wall covering the front of the cab. Richard was actually more freaked out than I was. He didn't know what kind of injuries I might've had.

He and Mike called to me and told me they were there, and he climbed off his water truck and climbed up the dirt to get access to my loader and got all the way up to the cab. He helped move the dirt off the windshield so I could lift it up, so I could get out the cab door. And then he helped me over the side and we both got down to the ground safely.

I was standing down there on the ground and I got adrenaline going like crazy. I didn't realize till I got down off the equipment and turned around and looked back, I thought, *Oh my God, that could've killed me.* A lot of people thought that, too. Their first question was, "How bad was the operator injured?"

I had a little red mark on my forehead from bumping it on the windshield. That was the extent of my injuries, which to this day I am very thankful for. It was a lot of luck, and wearing a seat belt. The accident gave me quite a reality check, it drove home just exactly how dangerous the job is.

I wasn't written up, I was not disciplined in any way, shape, or form, until three months later they put me right back in the same area, almost the same exact situation. And I started feeling uncomfortable in the area because the wall was getting up there in height. I called my supervisor and told him, "This is the same situation happening again." He came out and looked it over, said, "You know what? You're right." He pulled me out of the area, sent me to another area to dig. And we just left that area.

Three weeks later, the mine superintendent and the general mine manager were driving around the mine, just looking at different areas. They saw where I had left the digging and claimed that I had left a dangerous situation, that I had left an unstable wall, even though I had called my supervisor and he pulled me out of the area.

There was no damage, there was no injury, there was no incident, but they used that situation to disqualify me as a front-end loader operator. I think it was because the company was fined when that wall fell on me and they were found to be more at fault. I believe my whole disqualification was in retaliation for that. So they demoted me down to being a miner, so I was driving the smaller haul trucks.

I spent two years fighting to get my seniority and qualification back, and going through the grievance process is what really drove me to get involved with the union. My shop steward at the time, Vince Avitto, was really there for me.[7] He was always encouraging me. He always kept me informed of what was going on, and he inspired me. We would be talking

---

[7] In nonunion workplaces, the employer can hire, punish, fire, and set pay and rules without input from workers. A union contract, negotiated between employees and their employer, gives workers a say in their pay and conditions, and a grievance procedure to protect them against arbitrary or undeserved discipline or firing and other breaches of the contract. Shop stewards act as advocates during the grievance process and help ensure the contract is respected. For more on shop stewards, see glossary, page 348.

about my case and he would bring up other issues going on in the plant, and he would make this comment, "We could always use more stewards." I said to myself, *You know what? I can sit here and say, "He did a good job," and go on my merry way or—I can step up. He helped me and I want to help other people.*

The wall fell on me in 2005, they disqualified me a few weeks later, and I got my qualification to drive the front-end loader back in 2007. Starting in 2007, I became a steward. Most of what I worked on was real basic, everyday stuff. They paid a guy wrong—he took sick leave, they charged him for vacation, and so I would have to talk to his supervisor to get his pay straightened out. We would have individuals being called in, being disciplined over absenteeism, and I had to make sure all of that lined up with our contract and was fair. Just everyday stuff.

EVERY CONTRACT HAS BEEN A LITTLE MORE OF A FIGHT

Every contract that we've had going back to before I hired on, back into the early nineties, has seemingly been a little harder, a little more of a fight. Rio Tinto has made it pretty obvious over the years that they want the union out of here. From what I understand, one of the higher-up management people has literally said, "We want to get rid of the union." Some of the individuals that the company has brought in to work here at Rio Tinto Boron, you can trace back their work history, and every place that they've worked, they've gone in and have worked at destroying the unions. We had a new guy around 2007 who had taken over our human resources, Kim Moulton, who came from Kennecott Copper in Utah,[8] and Chris Robison who was CEO of Rio Tinto Minerals came down from Denver.

---

[8] Kennecott Copper is a subsidiary of Rio Tinto.

Around September 2009, we started into new contract negotiations with Rio Tinto.[9] Pretty much right at the beginning, our worst fears were confirmed—that the company was out not just to break the union, but to destroy it by undoing almost everything we'd negotiated for decades.

They had pretty much taken our old contract, the one that we had been working under, and gotten rid of 90 percent of it. And they came in and they dropped this new contract on the table and said, "This is what we want." In the new contract, they took away job security, they took away seniority, they were wanting to take away your right to a forty-hour workweek, and they wanted to take away the union shop.

Right now, we're what's considered a closed shop or "union shop." To work as hourly out there now you have to be in the union; you automatically pay union dues. The company wanted to make it so that paying union dues could be voluntary, that if you didn't want to be a union member, you didn't have to be.[10]

My union dues are about $43 out of each paycheck. And some people say, "Well, yes, it should be my choice to pay that." What they need to understand is that $43 goes to secure that I'm going to have forty hours a week where I get to come into work, that the company can't say, "Hey Terri, we don't need you today, so you gotta go home and you're not going to get paid."

Our union is out there to make sure that we have jobs to go to every day. And that we have safe jobs to go to every day. And that you don't have to worry about, *Well, this supervisor doesn't like me*. If it wasn't for my union, some guy could fire me just 'cause he didn't like the color of my hair.

The way our original contract read, there was a clause that said if Rio

---

[9] A process known as collective bargaining. For more information, see glossary, page 348.

[10] Employers often push for a contract clause that makes union membership optional, which makes the workplace an "open shop." Unions bargain for the "closed shop" Terri refers to, in which everyone who is covered by the contract must be a union member.

Tinto has employees who can do the job, we've got to do the job. They can't bring in contractors from the outside and have them do our jobs. And one of the things that they wanted to do with this new contract is they wanted to eliminate that clause. They wanted to bring in whoever they wanted, and they wanted to be able to contract our jobs out. Instead of paying the employees their regular wage for what they're doing, they would literally go out and find somebody who could do it cheaper. They're a subcontractor, and so technically they don't have to pay medical or dental. And liability-wise, it's cheaper on them. Because if a contractor gets hurt, it's almost one of those, "Oh well, we don't have to worry about getting sued because they're a contractor. They'll go after their headquarters, not after us."

On November 4, 2009, our old contract expired, and the company tried to extend it for another 120 days. The union wasn't willing to do that. We wanted to keep working, and we wanted to keep negotiating. Between September and November, the company really was dragging its feet on any negotiations. The different department heads from the mine would come in, they would sit down at the table with the union, they would be in there for like thirty-five minutes, then they'd get up and walk out. And then they wouldn't come back to the table for the rest of the day.

I heard a lot about the negotiations from the Contract Action Team,[11] and I attended negotiations myself sometimes. Every union member was encouraged to be there, because our negotiations were open. We couldn't talk during the sessions—we had a negotiating team that spoke for the union body—but we could sit and hear what was going on.

---

[11] ILWU Local 30 formed the Contract Action Team to distribute information and coordinate actions as needed during the negotiations. The union members on the team passed out flyers and newsletters and talked with co-workers to be sure everyone stayed informed on the progress of the talks and to minimize the rumors that inevitably arise during negotiations.

On our negotiating team, besides our union president, our vice president, and our lawyer, we had an individual to represent each department: the truck shop, the mine department, instrumentation and electricians, the boric acid plant, processing plants one through four, the shipping department, the labs, and the pilot plant.[12] That way each section had someone at the table who knew the department's needs.

Just like we had a representative from each department, on the management side you had whoever was in charge of the department. For the mine department, for example, we had Mike Wickersham, the general mine manager. Most of them were pretty well known to us.

They were being directed by Rio Tinto headquarters. We could tell Kim Moulton and Chris Robison were running it. They were the only ones to speak, but sometimes we would hear comments from our managers and supervisors. They would say, "I don't have a say-so in any of this, it's their show." Our managers were pretty disgruntled.

The company and the union continued meeting, with the exception of the break over Christmas and New Year's. They were still meeting pretty much two, three times a week until January 28. I was actually at the negotiation that day. They met at ten o'clock in the morning.

We went into the room, and our negotiating team was there. Then the company management's negotiating team walked in. They sat down. The way they would always start these negotiations, everybody introduced who they were and where they were from. Right off the bat when they started to open up the negotiations, the company's head representatives, just in a heartbeat, said, "Nope, we're not doing this." They dropped their original contract back on the table, the same one they'd put out in September, and they said, "You have until January 31 at 7:00 a.m. If this contract is not signed, we're gonna lock you out." And then they got up

[12] The pilot plant tests new equipment.

and they walked out of the room.

It was very quiet. Our lawyer Danny Bush and our negotiating team, we were just sitting in there, like, "Oh my God, did that just happen?"

THEY WERE READY TO STAND UP. THEY WERE READY TO FIGHT.

We had to call an emergency union meeting to vote on whether or not we were going to accept that contract. We had the meeting Saturday, because Sunday was Rio Tinto's deadline. You know, I've attended a few union meetings over the years, but I've never seen that many union people come together that fast. The place was packed. We had a good 350 to 400 union members there. There were people who couldn't be there because they were working, but I think the majority of union members drove from wherever they had to drive. A lot of people drove an hour one way just to come to that meeting.

I would say 99 percent of the people who showed up at that meeting that Saturday had already made up their minds. By that time the workers were just so fed up with the company—with the arrogance, with the attitude. The way they were wanting to treat us as disposable. The employees themselves had just gotten sick and tired of it. And they were ready to stand up. They were ready to fight.

Boron's a scrappy little town. We got about 150 to 200 of the workforce out there who live in Boron today. At least another 150 to 200 had some way or another grown up around Boron or have relatives in Boron. And if one thing can be said about the people of Boron, it is that they're fighters.

The Boron High School football team, the Bobcats, right there is a perfect example. You're talking about a high school with probably less than 250 kids in it. Yet they're a championship team. Every year. And it's that attitude. And it's that drive and that heart. It not only affects that football team, and that school, but the town.

And it overflows into a lot of the workers who live in Boron or who grew up in Boron. We bring that same attitude to work with us every day. And I think that attitude is why we were able to stand up to 'em.

The vote was pretty unanimous. Nobody was taking that contract. And I think that really surprised the company because I think their game tactic was, the country was already in an economic downturn, jobs were disappearing, unemployment was going up. People were afraid; 401(k)s, savings plans, and all that took major hits. And I think the company seriously thought, "Hey, we can scare them into a contract."

I think it shocked them when we turned around and said, "No. Lock us out." Which, of course, they did.

January 31 was my first day to go back to work. I had been at negotiations when they told us to either accept the contract or get locked out. I was at the union meeting when we voted down that contract. But me and a lot of my co-workers went to work expecting to actually work. We were expecting to call their bluff.

I drove all the way into the parking lot where I would normally park my car, got out of my car, and walked up to the gate for the mine department. There were seven or eight of us walking up to the gate at that time. General mine manager Mike Wickersham was actually standing there at that gate telling us, "No, you can't come in." He told us we could go pick up our checks later that day at the pizza parlor in town.

It was like getting punched in the stomach. My first thought was, *Oh my God.* I was in shock. I could not believe they had actually locked us out.

Just off the company property there's an asphalted area, a truck turnout, and that's where we went. Some went down to the union hall but the rest of us were out on the pavement, just outside the company property. There was a lot of anger. Some workers felt betrayed. I felt more betrayed than angry that the company would actually treat us that way. All kinds of things ran through my head: *How long is this going to last? Am I going to be able to get unemployment? What am I going to do for money?* I was worried about my daughter Ashley, about my mother, about losing my house, everything.[13]

But during the lockout we never got discouraged. We knew that plant, we knew how things operated, what it took to get product out. Even though the company was putting out media reports saying, "We're running at 100 percent," a lot of us could just stand at the gate and look towards the plant and say, "They're not even running that plant." We had guys who could tell you exactly what plants were running, when they were running, and how much they were producing just by the steam and smoke coming out. We would have truck drivers who would go in to pick up orders and turn around twelve hours later and come out and say, "I spent all day in there and they still haven't got my order ready." A lot of that kept us encouraged.

For those three and a half months I was running my butt off. Between me and my mother, we had the food bank committee. At least one day a week we'd show up to make packages of the food to be taken to union families who were in need.[14] I was on the communications committee and

---

[13] During a lockout, work is shut down on the initiative of the business in a labor dispute rather than the workers. When workers initiate a shutdown, it's called a strike. In many states in the U.S. (including California) workers who are locked out during a labor dispute are eligible for unemployment insurance, though striking workers are often not eligible for unemployment. For more on lockouts, strikes, and unemployment insurance, see glossary, page 348.

[14] Union members all over the United States contributed money to purchase food for the locked-out families, working through the local and national American Federation of Labor and Congress of Industrial Organizations (AFL-CIO) networks and other labor organizations such as the Service Employees International Union and the International Brotherhood of Teamsters.

I had at least two gate duties.[15] Wednesdays from six p.m. to ten p.m. and Saturday from two p.m. to six p.m. And I was speaking with reporters, doing interviews, going to other local events. Time just flew.

My mother was with me 100 percent all the way. I tried to keep my daughter out of a lot of the activity and stress of the lockout. She would go to some of the rallies with us, but I didn't try to force her to be too involved. But one time towards the beginning of the lockout, she said to me, "That's okay, Mom, I have plenty of clothes, I have plenty of everything. You just do what you need to do."

When we went into this lockout we knew what we didn't want to do. We knew we didn't want to get violent, we didn't want to be portrayed that way. The 1974 strike out here was a short strike, I think it only lasted something like four and a half months, but during that time period, it was very volatile.[16] There was a lot of violence, and it ripped people apart. You had brother who wouldn't speak to brother, fathers and sons who wouldn't talk.

During that strike, some union members crossed that picket line. People were throwing rocks at cars, and the guard shack, I think it was the guard shack, or purchasing, got firebombed. The memory of that 1974 strike was one of the biggest things in our minds.

We weren't going to let the company push us or instigate us into doing something that would make us look bad and harm our cause. They tried constantly. The guards that they had, the security team, Gettier, if you go check their website these guys advertise themselves as strike

---

[15] The workers maintained picket lines at the two plant gates at all times throughout the lockout. They scheduled four-hour shifts with five to nine people at each gate on each shift.

[16] In 1974, the company proposed a contract that cut sick leave, pensions, and holidays, eliminated safety rules, and allowed the company free rein to contract out work. The workers struck for four and a half months. Though they ultimately had to give in to most of the demands, they were able to regain lost ground in the years that followed.

busters. They guarantee that they will get injunctions against picket lines and stuff like this because what they do, they constantly videotape, and what they're looking for is somebody breaking the law. Then they go to the local court and get an injunction to where you can't have a picket line or you can't be standing in front of their property. That's what they tried to do. Thankfully, every single person that we had out there conducted themselves in a very good manner, and they were never able to do that with us. Everybody kind of watched everybody else's back.

One of the best things that came out of that lockout was the union members really got the chance to talk with one another. When we're out there working, we kind of get locked into our own little sections. Like with me, I'm out in that open-pit mine. I don't really get that big of an opportunity to talk with the guys who work in the shipping department, or talk with people who work at the boric acid plant, or who work in the primary process. You don't get a lot of interaction time with these individuals while on the job. And that lockout brought people from all different parts of that plant together, got them talking with each other, and, more importantly, got them supporting each other.

Support came in a lot of different forms, from families sharing recipes on how to make food stretch, to where to go for the best food prices, to even, if somebody had something a little extra, giving it to the next person. From Boron to go to the bigger grocery stores you're looking at anywhere from a thirty- to a fifty-mile one-way trip, so instead of just one family getting in the car and going, maybe three or four wives would get together and they'd carpool over. There was a lot of carpooling going on.

I'm not going to sit here and say that the lockout didn't affect people because, financially and emotionally, it affected a lot of people. We had quite a few people who could not survive on unemployment. We had individuals who were working and tried to find other work, but they still faced bankruptcy. They still faced foreclosures.

I was lucky enough that I had my mother who lived with me, and with her Social Security and what she draws from the Veterans Administration from my father, she was able to help me out.[17] I made enough on unemployment that I was able to cover my house payment and my utility bills. But if it hadn't been for my mother, it would have gotten real tight about putting food on the table, about having gas for the cars.

Because of my daughter, I qualified for state Medi-Cal.[18] Continuing on my health insurance plan, just for myself and my daughter, would have cost over $450 a month. I couldn't afford that. There were a lot of people out there who couldn't afford that.

Most people, if they had kids, they qualified for Medi-Cal. But we had a lot of older employees whose kids were grown. They didn't qualify for it. And they were the ones with the bigger health issues, who had medications that they were required to take. And they couldn't afford to pay for health insurance. So the ILWU had set up a relief fund, and they utilized a lot of that money for people to keep their medical insurance during that time we were locked out.

We reached out for support and a lot of people responded. It wasn't just our local community. We got support from people all over the world, people sending contributions or speaking out for us. We had unions down in Los Angeles, the AFL-CIO, the teamster unions, the ILWU—our Local 20 down in Wilmington, Local 13 down in San Pedro, our international contacts. A number of unions sent contributions or organized protests. We had the Maritime Union of Australia. We had representatives from

---

[17] The United States Department of Veterans Affairs, formerly called the Veterans Administration, manages pensions and other compensation for U.S. military veterans and their families.

[18] Medi-Cal (the California Medical Assistance Program) is the state's public health insurance program for low-income families, seniors, people with disabilities, pregnant women, children in foster care, and some low-income adults.

Turkey, from South Africa, from New Zealand, from the Netherlands, from England.

Just the show of support from people was amazing. And knowing you had those people backing you up, that you had somebody, they might not be right there but they were supporting you, encouraging you; it gave us the strength to stay out there and fight. If it hadn't been for them, the company probably would've destroyed our union.

The lockout woke local people up to just how fragile the economy is. The majority of people who live in Boron earn their paychecks right out at that mine, so when that mine goes, that town goes. That became very clear, especially to the business owners. They did what they could to help out and try to support their businesses—things like helping provide food and drinks to the people working gate duty. One of the restaurants, the Twenty Mule Café, gave a 20 percent discount to union members and their families. It was little things like that that helped.

During the strike, the ILWU set up an emergency fund that gathered contributions from union locals and individuals, to be distributed to union families in need. The international conference of mining and maritime unions met in Palmdale, California, on February 16 and 17, 2010, and traveled to Boron for a rally. Allies in the International Transport Workers' Federation and the International Dockworkers Council organized protests at the Rio Tinto shareholders' meetings in London and Melbourne in April 2010. Closer to home, the California School Employees Association led a march through Boron for "Good Jobs and Good Schools" on March 6, 2010, that brought out hundreds of workers and their families.

More than two months after initiating the lock out, Rio Tinto came back to the bargaining table in April 2010. After another month of negotiations, Rio Tinto and Borax workers agreed to a new labor contract on May 15, 2010.

WE WON THE BATTLE

We had even more people for the ratification than for the meeting where we voted down the contract. People had a lot of questions. They wanted to know, "Is this good for us or will it hurt us?" It was not the most perfect contract, but we weren't losing our benefits or jobs. We weren't forced to pay for medical care or take a pay cut. My big concerns were taking away our Veterans Day holiday and taking away jobs to give to contractors, and we were able to avoid all that.[19]

It was a ballot vote, and we had to wait for the count. It was nerve-wracking. I went to work and stood at the gate. The very first day they locked us out, I was on that gate, and the day we voted and counted the ballots, I was doing my gate duty too. About four or five in the evening on May 15, someone came down and said, "Take down the picket line, the contract is in."

When we all came back to work, everybody was happy to be doing the job that we wanted to do, earning that paycheck, being able to support our families. All the locked-out union people who wanted to come back got their jobs back. But every one of us knew, we understood, and we still believe today—we won the battle, but the war still rages on.

They are just constantly trying to undermine the union.

We have a contract and you can actually sit there and read a contract. It's written in black and white. And then you have the company who comes along and says, "Oh, well, that's open to interpretation." And it becomes a constant fight over wording. For example, overtime. It's supposed to be scheduled first with the person with the lowest extra hours and then you

---

[19] The contract ratified by ILWU Local 30 members on May 15, 2010, did include a couple of take-backs. All newly hired workers now get 401(k) plans instead of the more secure defined benefit pensions, and workers are no longer able to sue over violations of wage and hour law. All wage and hour disputes have to be arbitrated.

work your way up to the person who already has put in the highest hours so everyone gets an equal chance to earn the overtime. And the company will actually come in and say, "Well, no, it doesn't read that way." And we're like, "Yes, it does."

The way our contract reads, you should be trained according to seniority. Highest senior person will get offered the training first, and then it goes right down the line. What we find is if one of the people who gets hired is a supervisor's son, management seems to be saying, "You know, Joe Smith, the supervisor over in this department, that's his son. We're going to train him first. We're going to get him up to the higher rate of pay first."

I think the lockout did a lot of good in making people aware that, hey, you do need to stand up, hey, you do need to speak out, you can't let the company blatantly violate rules, whether it's our contract or government or environmental rules. We can't just let them do what they want, and I think finally people are coming to that understanding.

Here we were, six hundred employees standing up against a multibillion-dollar corporation. All the lawyer talk and everything else put aside, it was the people coming together, and joining together, and supporting one another, and helping one another. That's what really won this fight for us.

I'm proud of the fight we put up, but it's hard to say what's in our future. Optimistically, you're looking at the life expectancy of that mine to be only about another thirty years. Once they've mined everything they can mine out of it, there's a big question as to what happens next for our town, and nobody seems to have that answer. Workers my age, we're just hoping there's going to be a mine to retire from. The younger ones coming up behind me, they're going to have to set their minds to the fact that there isn't going to be a mine that will employ them until they retire.

My daughter Ashley, she took some time off after high school to help me take care of my mom, who was diagnosed with breast cancer in 2011. Now Ashley's looking for employment, looking to take some online classes. She's hoping to go into some form of graphic design. I hope she learned from the lockout that in this day and age, you need an education to get the good jobs—and if you see wrong, you need to stand up and speak out. One person can make a change.

BERE SUANU KINGSTON

AGE: *48*

OCCUPATION: *Salesman, nurse*

BIRTHPLACE: *Ka Bangha, Ogoniland, Nigeria*

INTERVIEWED IN: *Oakland, California*

Bere Suanu Kingston invites us to his house in Oakland, California, on a cold and cloudy summer day. Bere's daughter, a tall, quietly self-possessed teenager, greets us. She calls for Bere and he soon emerges from the long hallway. He leads us through the dark corridors of his multistory home, giving us a tour and, in the process, introducing us to his two sisters who live with him, one of whom has a new baby in her arms. He leads us down to the basement level and into his son's room where, he says, we will not be disturbed during the interview.

We speak about his childhood in Ogoniland, a region of about one thousand square kilometers in the Niger River Delta in the southeast of Nigeria, where the Ogoni people have lived for the past five thousand years. Shell and Chevron and other oil companies have been extracting oil in Ogoniland since the 1950s, establishing large, modern plants among rural villages with neither electricity nor running water.

At one point, Bere turns off his phone as he begins to describe his involvement with the Ogoni resistance movement and Ogoni demands for a small share of oil revenues. He shifts his position as we speak, often kneeling on the floor with his hands folded in prayer over his son's tiger-print bedspread. Because of his political activism, Bere was arrested and tortured and narrowly escaped execution by the Nigerian military. As he recounts his experience, his voice falls to a whisper.

OGONI IS ONE TRIBE BUT IT IS MADE UP OF DIFFERENT AREAS AND DIFFERENT GROUPS

I was born April 22, 1966, in Ka Bangha, a village in Ogoniland by the Niger River in Nigeria. Ogoni is a flat land. Some people live in the mountains, some people live in the swamp, some people near the ocean, but we Ogoni are in the flat land: we don't have hills, mountains, or even rocks. And we don't have the sea. But there are many rivers going through Ogoniland, so it's almost as if we were by the sea.[1]

Ogoni is one tribe but it is made up of different areas and different groups. There's almost a million of us now. We have a similar language but we speak different dialects. What brings us together is a similar ancestry: we come from the same people. Ogoniland is peaceful. We plant cassava, yam, coco, plantain. There are palm trees, too. We use red palms for oil and big white palms to make palm wine.

The village where I'm from—Ka Bangha—is big. It is almost a city. When I left in 1996, we had about two thousand people in the village. Now we have around five thousand people.

In Ka Bangha, when I was a child, we had a green apple tree in the town square. The tree was for everyone. After school, we would hang out

[1] The land inhabited by the Ogoni is a four-hundred-square-mile area in the Niger River Delta, just north of the Gulf of Guinea. The Ogoni speak a handful of different languages but share cultural practices related to farming and fishing around the Niger River.

by the tree, and when an apple fell we would race to it. Whoever could grab the fallen apple could keep it. Now sometimes we stole apples from the tree, but we'd be whipped if caught by the grownups, because you weren't supposed to pick the apples straight from the tree. The apples were for everyone in the village. If children picked as many apples as they wanted, there'd soon be none left. The same tree is still there in the town square today. Generation to generation, it's stayed there.

So we would go to the apple tree and wait for an apple to fall, or go to the school grounds to play soccer, and this is how we kept busy. In our village we had sand floors in the schools. We sat on the ground—there were no chairs or desks.

My dad was a teacher who became a headmaster, and from headmaster, he became a supervisor. My mother was also a teacher. My father had five wives and twenty-three children. My mom had seven kids, and she would prepare meals for the seven of us. In the morning, we ate *foofoo*.[2] We'd have foofoo with soup made with vegetables like okra. Sometimes we'd also cook rice or beans, and we had a lot of fish because we were close to the river.

My mom would often cook for more than just us seven kids, because she entertained a lot of people. The house was always open. I see over here in the U.S., people don't always ask, "Do you want a drink?" when you come to their house. But in my culture, when you go to somebody's house, the first thing is that they offer you a cup of water, they offer you food, because it's like welcoming you.

Shell Oil actually started drilling in Ogoniland a few years before I was born, but I remember seeing them moving into Ka Bangha. Surveyors and heavy equipment would come in, and we'd hear the sounds, loud machine noises. First one truck, then many. When I was a child there was not too much awareness of what the oil companies were doing. When

---

[2] *Foofoo* is a dish made from boiled, pounded yams or cassava.

people first heard that Shell was coming to our land, we just expected to meet some white people. We thought of them as interesting visitors. "Oh, Shell is coming here today! They are coming to see our land!" We were so excited.[3] Then after they started drilling, we'd see light from the gas flares at night, and at first we were excited about that as well: "Look there is light, there is light!"[4]

When I was growing up, we would go to the river to swim and fish and bathe and play. We also drank from the river—we didn't have a tap. And it wasn't really safe. Because anything that flows from the rainy season goes into the water. Dead things end up in the river, as well as the runoff from clothes washing and bathing. And even when I was young, we were already seeing oil runoff in the river. The river was oily and black. And we had no idea what to do when we saw the water was polluted with oil. When my grandmother and my mom saw the water, they just said, "What is this?" To drink, we'd just push aside the oil on the surface and then scoop up the water. Fish were dying, though when I was younger we didn't connect that with the oil. We didn't know that pollution was killing our fish, killing the trees, contaminating our water, making us sick. Some people even intentionally drank the crude oil, because they said it would help their immune systems, clean out some bacteria and some stuff like that. I remember once when an oil pipe broke and oil spilled out all over the land, some people took some home to try out as cooking oil.

So Shell was all around us, building new roads and bringing in big machines to drill, but our villages remained the same: no plumbing, no electricity, no hospitals, no jobs. At the same time, the land and water we

---

[3] For more on the history of Shell Oil and Nigeria, see Appendix III, page 360.

[4] In the oil-rich Niger River Delta, natural gas deposits next to crude oil deposits are often burned off as the oil is extracted, resulting in enormous fireballs called gas flares, some of which can be seen from space. Burning natural gas to access crude oil is a practice that generates nearly four hundred million tons of carbon dioxide a year.

needed to support ourselves were becoming toxic. The problem was, in Nigeria, we were a minority. The government didn't care about how we survived. They didn't care about our rivers, about how we grew our food. The government cared about oil, they didn't care about us.

IT WAS AT UNIVERSITY THAT I LEARNED THE TRUTH ABOUT SHELL

When I was about nine years old, my family moved from Ka Bangha to Bori, the capital of the Ogoni region.[5] We stayed in the city, and when I started my secondary school at age ten, I would go to a nearby village called Lumene. There were no buses to Lumene. I had to walk five to ten miles to get to school. At 4:00 or 5:00 a.m. I'd wake up when it was still dark and I'd start to walk. The land was a mixture of clay and sand, and in the summer, when it was hot, it hurt my feet to walk, even with sandals or shoes. When it was rainy season it was even more difficult. I had to hold a giant cocoyam leaf over my head to keep from getting wet. And I had to squeeze water out of my shoes when I arrived.

Since it was such a long walk, my family decided I should move to Lumene. So I lived with a group of students. Five of us children lived in one room together. There I learned to cook for myself, fetch water from the river, clear the bush around the compound, do my homework. Being on your own teaches you how to deal with these things in life.

So I went to school in Lumene, and then after graduating I stayed for a while in my home village, Ka Bangha. I came back and sold things—rice and beans, spices, clothes, paper, whatever I could find. I would go to different villages and buy at the big markets, and then take big loads on top of my bicycle.

---

[5] Bori is a town of about twelve thousand people.

Then I came back to Bori for my bachelor's degree in business administration. It was around 1987, and I was twenty-one. That was the same year my first son was born. My son's mother and I didn't stay together, but he's been part of my life since.

It was at university that I learned the truth about Shell Oil. I can remember the exact moment I became fully aware of what the government of Nigeria was allowing Shell to do on our land. It was 1990, and I was twenty-four. I had already heard a little about the oil companies in Ogoniland on the news. But that year, Ken Saro-Wiwa spoke to us about it openly.[6] He came to address the whole Ogoni people—there were two thousand of us in the crowd—in Bori, on the campus of a grammar school. The crowd was gathered in the school's play yard, its soccer field, and everyone was on their feet.

We have six separate groups among the Ogoni people, and Ken Saro-Wiwa addressed all of us together. He told us that for almost fifty years Shell Oil had been taking this oil from our land without paying revenue. He said, "Now we want to let the government know that there is a lot of pollution in our homeland, that they are destroying our land, our fish, and our waters. We need the government and the oil companies to help our people build hospitals, colleges, and roads, to provide clean water, and to pay revenue for what they are taking from us." Afterward, we danced in the field like it was a festival. And then he told us to go home and get prepared.

That's when I got involved. I started talking to people at the college in Bori I was attending. Then I started going to villages and rural areas. I

---

[6] Ken Saro-Wiwa was an author and activist from Ogoniland who achieved national renown as a businessman and television producer before turning his attention fully to the environmental and humanitarian crisis unfolding in the Niger River Delta. For more information, see Appendix III, page 360.

became a spokesman because I'm good at speaking in public. I don't get shy or scared. I would go village to village and visit schools to teach the students about the problems that oil companies were bringing to our land. I let other Ogoni students know what I'd heard from Ken Saro-Wiwa.

It was hard work. Ken started going from place to place, giving talks, and people like me would help carry the news to all the people of Ogoniland. People wouldn't always believe and embrace the truth in one day, after one speech. People didn't see a reason to stand up to their own government. To convince some people it takes a long time, and a lot of voices. People listened to me, though, because they knew what I was saying was from the heart.

WE WERE DYING SO THAT OTHERS COULD PROFIT

In 1990, the Ogoni people presented a bill of rights to the federal government that had been written by Saro-Wiwa and other leaders of the Ogoni. The bill of rights was essentially a list of demands.[7] First, we demanded more autonomy over our own political affairs in Ogoniland, because the Nigerian government had failed the Ogoni people. We wanted control over how our land was used, how our water was used—everything. The second demand was to use some of the oil revenue from our land to build roads, plumbing lines, electric lines, hospitals, schools—all the necessary amenities to help the people live healthy lives. Third, we wanted adequate and direct representation of Ogoni people at the national level. The fourth demand was the official recognition of Ogoni languages. The fifth demand was the full recognition of our distinct culture. The sixth right was the

---

[7] Here, Bere reads from the handwritten notes he has prepared for the interview.

right of religious freedom. Maybe 90 percent of us are Christian. But the Muslim majority in the country want to, you know, dominate every area.[8] We were saying, "Don't force me to be a Christian. Don't force me to be a Muslim or a Buddhist." And the seventh right: the right to protect the environment in Ogoniland—for all creatures—from further degradation.

What the Ogoni people were demanding was to have a stronger voice in how our land was used, who profited from it, and to have our people recognized as having a right to exist, to not be squeezed out. Because in my village we were dying of cancer, of other illnesses, because of the pollution. We didn't have anyone who was older than eighty years. And even young people of twenty, twenty-eight were dying from asthma, cancer, different things. We were dying so that others could profit.

Our first major action was to present our bill of rights to the Nigerian government, but that didn't lead to any changes. The government ignored us. Later that year, the bill of rights was amended to formally announce MOSOP, the organized Ogoni movement started by Saro-Wiwa.[9] The Ogoni people decided we needed to remain active and organized to stand against Shell and other oil companies as well as the Nigerian government, which was not on our side. There was violence early on, and Saro-Wiwa was arrested and released often after the formation of MOSOP.

By December of 1992 MOSOP was making demands directly to the oil companies. We demanded that they halt all operations until our bill of rights was addressed by the Nigerian government. Then on January 4, 1993, we had the first-ever Ogoni day, a huge, peaceful protest of over

---

[8] Nigeria is approximately 50 percent Muslim (concentrated in the north), 40 percent Christian (concentrated in the south), and approximately 10 percent localized, traditional religions.

[9] MOSOP is the Movement for the Survival of the Ogoni People. The organization, founded by Ken Saro-Wiwa, is dedicated to nonviolent protest against oil extraction from Ogoni lands without adequate compensation or political representation.

three hundred thousand Ogoni. It was in Bori, the capital of Ogoniland, and all the people from friendly villages came to town, and we made a sort of declaration of independence. Different tribes came and brought with them their different cultures, different clothes, games, dances. We were singing, chanting the Ogoni language, Ogoni music, Ogoni songs. The Ogoni people appealed to the international community to let the world know what the government of Nigeria was doing to us. The point we were making that day was, *We are Nigerian. We need development. We need education. We need the government to recognize that we are part of Nigeria. If they take something from us, we need something in return. We need to stop the violence. We need recognition.* That was our message to Shell and the government of Nigeria.[10]

In April or May of 1993 the government and Shell wanted to lay a pipeline from Ogoniland to the northern part of Nigeria. The pipeline was cutting right through Ogoni farmlands. So, on April 30 of that year, many Ogoni gathered for a peaceful demonstration to demand that the pipeline be stopped.[11] The surveyors for the American company that was going to lay the pipe came, and they also came with soldiers: the Nigerian military. And the Nigerian military opened fire. Ten people were hurt.

And I remember seeing a man killed at a protest a few days later near a town called Nonwa. Those of us who were there, we stood and said, "No." A leader of our group said, "We came over here to tell you, you guys cannot come over and take this oil until the government has solved our differences and responded to the things we demand."

There was a person who was peacefully standing up on the pipeline,

---

[10] In response to the gathering in January of 1993, the Nigerian government banned public assembly in the region and Shell temporarily withdrew its employees from the area. For more information, see Appendix III, page 360.

[11] On April 30, 1993, ten thousand Ogoni gathered to demonstrate against the pipeline being installed that would carry oil from the region to the sea.

and the soldiers, the military that were there, they shot him.[12] I remember seeing him get hit, and every one of us who were protesting went running for the bushes to escape.

THEY WOULD MAKE US DO ALL SORTS OF THINGS TO HUMILIATE US

Between 1993 and 1994 there were many protests on Ogoniland. Shell halted some if its oil production in response, but for the Ogoni people, things just got worse. There was a lot of violence from the Nigerian government; many people were getting arrested.

Then, on May 21, 1994, an incident occurred where four Ogoni chiefs were found murdered. The Nigerian government immediately blamed the murders on MOSOP and Saro-Wiwa, even though the chiefs were closely allied with him. The next day, May 22, a security task force was sent into Ogoniland to arrest everyone associated with MOSOP, claiming that they were searching for the killers.

I was arrested in Bori on the twenty-second of May, along with many others. Close to midnight they sent some troops with guns, and they knocked on each person's house and surrounded the house. If you tried to escape, they shot you. I later heard they shot six people that day, and they arrested Ken Saro-Wiwa and other leaders of MOSOP and charged them with the murders of the Ogoni chiefs.

In my case, they knocked at midnight. I was sleeping, and I woke up and heard people shouting, "Run! Run! Run! Escape! Escape! Escape now!" But before I could get up and dress myself, they had surrounded my house. I was arrested and thrown into a truck with other Ogoni.

All of us who had been arrested were taken in a big truck to the camp.

---

[12] The man killed during the protest in Nonwa was named Agabarator Out.

We were thrown together in a large crowd, almost two hundred people in a hole in the ground, sort of a well, with a locked grate on top. We only had room to lie down on the floor; we didn't have space to move. To visit the bathroom, we had to be taken out of the hole in chains.

Then early in the morning, they would take us out. They made us start jumping. Hopping like frogs. They would make us do all sorts of things to humiliate us. They might make you hop for half a mile down the road while holding your ears. Or they might say, "Everybody crawl on the ground." And you'd have to crawl back and forth on the road until they allowed you to stop.

And they would beat us. They'd whip us with a baseball bat or metal cane. Some people died. You know what they did to me? They drove a nail into my anus. I still have the scar on my anus. They did all this to make us confess our political activities. You confess, and then they make you promise that you will not join MOSOP again.

After two months my family and some local chiefs were able to bail me out. I was still a student, and the head of my department and my instructor, they came to get me. And when I was released, I joined MOSOP again.

Things did not get better for us in Ogoniland. In the fall of 1995, Ken Saro-Wiwa and eight other leaders of the Ogoni people were sentenced to death. They were killed in November of that year. And the Nigerian government continued to crack down on the Ogoni.

The second time I was arrested, the military caught me on the way to school. They took me to a second camp in a military truck. On that truck, they were beating me with their guns and boots, smashing my head, hitting me with a baseball bat. A lot of people were beating me at once. I was thinking, *Either you die or you survive. The only thing is just to pray to God. Your only solution is just for God to help you.* When you're in the truck, you pray, you have to pray.

Then when we were in the camp, they tortured me to make me promise that I would not join MOSOP again. They said they would cut off my legs and my hands. They had a knife, they had a gun, they had the tools to do anything they wanted to a human being.

But I escaped from the camp. One of the soldiers escorted me to the bathroom and said, "I want you to escape, because they want to kill you." He unlocked the chains. I said to the soldier, "Thank you." And then I ran.

WE LIVED IN A TENT FOR TWO YEARS

After my escape, I stayed in the bush for a couple of months with other people who were running from the military. In the bush we survived off oranges and other things we could forage. Eventually someone passing through our group mentioned that many Ogoni were fleeing to Benin Republic and seeking asylum there.[13] It takes two days to get from Ogoniland to Benin by car, so there was no real way to do it on foot. So I snuck back home to get a little money for the journey, and there I met up with my sister Blessing, who wanted to make the trip with me. We traveled any way we could—by bus, hitching rides—to Lagos, and then from Lagos to Benin Republic. That's how I ended up in a refugee camp.

It was early 1996 when I made it to Benin. I told the authorities there that I'd been arrested for political activity in Nigeria. And they took me and my sister to a refugee camp. Other Ogoni people were there, as well as some refugees from Togo, Congo, and other neighboring countries. There were maybe eight hundred or more of us. We lived there in a tent for two years. Each month they would give us ten cups of rice and ten cups of beans, as well as two fish, four small cans of tomatoes, and one little

---

[13] The Republic of Benin is a country of nearly ten million that borders Nigeria to the west. Benin's southeastern border is about an hour west of Nigeria's most populous city, Lagos.

bottle of peanut oil. We thought, *God, the kind of food they give to us we can finish in one week—one day.* We were always hungry. We would go into the bush and look for any food we could find. Then in 1998, the United Nations opened another camp and built houses. So we moved into a house and stayed for three years. We were in the refugee camp for five years all together. Then the International Rescue Committee managed to place us in the United States.[14]

YOU SHOULD SHOW THAT YOU ARE HUMAN

When my sister and I left Benin, we came to Oakland. In Jesus's name, Father we thank you. In Jesus's name, amen. I was traveling with my sister Blessing, no one else. I didn't know anybody in California. Nobody.[15]

When I met the people from the International Rescue Committee, they took me to a hotel by Lake Merritt where I spent my first night in America.[16] The first thing I did when I woke up the next morning was pray a ton to thank God for making me succeed and be in America. We spent two days at the hotel before they found us a place by the lake on Ninth Avenue. I stayed there for, I think, a year. At first I was working with my sister in Park Plaza, cleaning hotel rooms and doing other jobs.

---

[14] The International Rescue Committee was founded in 1933 in order to assist refugees escaping humanitarian crises to relocate in stable countries and begin rebuilding their lives.

[15] Around one hundred Ogoni refugee families are living in the U.S. Many were placed in Chicago by the IRC, and Bere's may have been one of the first of numerous families placed in Oakland. In 2002, a group of Ogoni refugees living in the U.S. filed a lawsuit against Royal Dutch Petroleum for complicity in human rights abuses. Even though Shell is not an American corporation, the Ogoni refugees were able to bring suit under the Alien Tort Statute. For more information, see Appendix III, page 360.

[16] Lake Merritt is a tidal lagoon near downtown Oakland.

It was too much for me, the work was so hard.

But if you want something, you have to be disciplined. You pay a price for what you want. I have disciplined myself now for five years. Right now I now have no woman, no girlfriend. I don't smoke. I don't drink. After working as a hotel housekeeper, I went to work in the Oak Tree, a restaurant, as a waiter. I worked so hard. I wanted to achieve more. So I went to nursing school and became a nurse. I also bought the house I live in, in 2009, and I've bought one other here in Oakland. I've been able to bring some of my other family over as well, and now there are seven of us here from my family.

I believe life is full of obstacles. I intend to step forward every day. That is what I hope for myself.

What I hope for the Ogoni people is to have a dialogue for whoever is in power. If I could talk directly with Shell Oil and the Nigerian government, I would say, "Look, I know you are going to drill the oil. But you should have sympathy for the Ogoni people; you should show that you are human. I know, everybody needs money. We are all Nigerian. Ogoniland, it's beautiful. Let's share it as equals."

The Ogoni people have been through a lot of things. It's frightening to think what the Nigerian government wants to happen to the Ogoni, but we endure. In 1994 there were five hundred thousand people living in Ogoniland. Now there's a million. But, you know, I keep telling people here, I am blessed. We are blessed. In Ogoniland, we have the resources so that everyone should have healthy food and water, money from our oil reserves, and peace with our government.

SANJAY VERMA

AGE: *30*
OCCUPATION: *Tutor, community advocate*
BIRTHPLACE: *Bhopal, India*
INTERVIEWED IN: *Berkeley, California*

In December 1984, a pesticide plant in Bhopal, India, operated by the American company Union Carbide, began leaking the toxic gas methyl isocyanate, a chemical used in pesticides. The leak killed over two thousand Bhopal residents on first exposure. In the days and months afterward, thousands more perished from acute damage to their pulmonary and nervous systems. In all, nearly six hundred thousand were affected by the leak, with many developing lifelong chronic health problems. The Bhopal leak rivals the Chernobyl meltdown as the worst industrial accident in history.[1]

Sanjay Verma was just an infant when the gas leak occurred, but the accident has shaped nearly every aspect of his life since. His parents and five of his seven siblings were killed that night. He grew up in an orphanage and then with his two remaining siblings, and he was inspired from an early age by his older brother

[1] For more on Bhopal and the Union Carbide disaster, see Appendix III, page 361.

Sunil's activism related to the health and economic consequences of the gas leak. Not only have thousands of survivors suffered long term health consequences such as vision and respiratory problems, the groundwater in Bhopal has been found to contain other contaminants from the factory such as arsenic, mercury, organochlorides, and numerous other chemicals produced in the factory.

Sanjay, who still lives in Bhopal, agrees to our initial interview while visiting the United States in 2011. He's come to testify as an expert witness at a West Virginia hearing about the safety of a Bayer CropScience chemical plant that produces methyl isocyanate. When the hearing concludes, Sanjay flies to the West Coast to help promote a new documentary on the disaster in Bhopal. We speak over the phone, and in a canorous voice, he talks about the family he's lost to the disaster, his path to activism, and the ways the disaster continues to be felt in Bhopal.

"SANJAY, THERE WAS A TRAGEDY"

I grew up in an orphanage in Bhopal.[2]

The orphanage was part of a chain of orphanages around the world called SOS Children's Villages.[3] I was there with my sister Mamta, who is about nine years older than me, for around ten years. The one we were in had twelve big houses that looked like cottages. Every house had a "foster mother" and ten or eleven orphaned children. And every cottage had around four bedrooms and one living room. One was the baby bedroom, one was the foster mother's bedroom, one was the boys' room, and then one was the girls' room. I was in the boys' room with three other boys. My sister was always in the same house with me, but she was in the girls' room.

---

[2] Bhopal is a city of over three million and the capital of the state of Madhya Pradesh in central India.

[3] SOS Children's Villages is an NGO headquartered in Austria that provides family services, including orphan care, in over 130 countries.

We lived in the orphanage and went to primary school nearby. One day when I was about five years old, we had a parents' meeting at school, and many of my classmates came in with their parents. But I didn't have anyone there that night. So then I realized, *I don't have parents with me.* I thought, *I should ask my sister about this.* I knew that she was my biological sister and my foster mother was the person who took care of me, but I didn't understand how things came to be the way they were. So, I said to my sister, "My classmates came with their parents to the meeting, but there was no one with me. Our foster mother—she's my mother, right? So who is my father? And how come they didn't go with me?"

And so my sister told me about what had happened. She said, "Sanjay, there was a tragedy, a disaster, in 1984. We were four brothers and four sisters and two parents. But both our parents, three sisters, and two brothers died that same night." And that's all she said. When she told me that, to be honest, I don't even remember how I felt. I knew that she had answered some pretty big questions, but I still had many more.

But living in the orphanage was pretty fun. I liked the competition with the other children my age. You are studying in the same school and you get higher marks than them and it's a good feeling. The orphanage used to send children who were doing well to other orphanages for a vacation; it was a way to encourage you to study more. Once I got really high marks and they sent me to an orphanage in the old country in Varanasi.[4] I was there for a few days and then I came back to Bhopal. I was so happy.

At this time, our surviving older brother Sunil was still living by himself in the old house where we had lived before the disaster. He was just a young teenager when the disaster occurred, about thirteen, but he was allowed to live by himself rather than come to the orphanage, because

---

[4] Varanasi, a city of about 1.5 million people on the banks of the Ganges River in the state of Uttar Pradesh, is the holiest of cities in Hinduism, as well as one of the oldest continuously inhabited cities in the world.

he could take care of himself. I think the government was paying him and other victims living on their own about 200 rupees a month at the time.[5] My sister and I weren't awarded any compensation other than money paid to SOS Children's Villages for our support.

Sunil came to see us once a year during a festival we have in India called Raksha Bandhan.[6] And then when I was ten, we moved out from the orphanage and back into the house with Sunil. Soon after that, in the mid-nineties, we were given a new apartment by the government. Over 2,500 new homes were constructed by the Indian government for families who had lost loved ones who had supported them. The houses were built all in one big neighborhood that people called the Gas Widows Colony.[7]

When we started living with our brother I began finding out more about the tragedy. We found pictures of my other siblings who had died that night, and then once in a while my brother would talk a bit about it. He would say, "One day, we were four brothers and four sisters," and he would list their names. And then he would tell us about who our siblings had married or were going to marry, what sort of work they were going to do, everything about their lives that he could remember. He told us that our father was a carpenter in Bhopal and our mother was a simple Indian lady; she was a housewife. He wanted us to feel like we knew something about the family we'd lost.

---

[5] 200 rupees = approximately US$3.

[6] Raksha Bandhan is a festival that celebrates the relationship between brothers and sisters.

[7] Around 2,500 housing units for widows and other survivors of the Bhopal disaster were built on the northern end of Bhopal from 1989 to 1994.

NOT ENOUGH SPACE IN THE CEMETERIES

I came to find out more about the night of the accident as well. It was my sister who took me when I was a baby and ran with me when gas started to fill the air. My brother and sister said the gas made it hard to breathe and burned people's skin. Everyone was running. My brother Sunil had started to run, too, but he had to go pee, so he stopped in the street on the way. There were so many people running in the streets, and he got separated from us. Then, later, he fainted.

The next day when people started collecting bodies, they found my brother, and he was still unconscious. They thought he was dead. Because there was not enough firewood to cremate the bodies and not enough space in the cemeteries, they were dumping the bodies into the rivers. So they put him in the back of a truck and they were going to throw him in the river. All of a sudden my brother woke up, right before they were about to throw him in. That he woke up at that very moment was the reason that he survived—otherwise he'd have been thrown in the river and drowned.

My sister and I managed to stay together in the days after the tragedy. We were taken to one hospital and my brother was in a different hospital. After his stay in the hospital he came back to our family's house out by the factory. And right then some of our relatives from Lucknow had arrived in Bhopal to help search for our other family members.[8]

Sunil found out about what happened to our family from those relatives who came to search for us. One of my sisters who we lost had been married to a cop in Lucknow in March 1984, but she had come home to visit just before the disaster occurred. After the accident, her new husband

---

[8] Lucknow, the capital of the state of Uttar Pradesh, is a city of nearly 2.2 million located four hundred miles northeast of Bhopal.

came with my uncle who also lived in Lucknow to Bhopal when they heard about the disaster on the radio. They started looking for us at the family house, and they quickly learned that so many members of the family had died. And then when Sunil came home from the hospital, they had to break the news to him. They all set out to find me and my sister, since we were still unaccounted for. And after they found us at the hospital, they decided to take us back to Lucknow. They took all of us survivors—me, my brother Sunil, and my sister Mamta—to their home.

After a few months of living with our relatives, we moved back to our old house in Bhopal. My brother realized that we were kind of a burden on my uncle's family. After we lived by ourselves for a short time, government workers found us and sent me and Mamta to an orphanage.

I hadn't known much about the tragedy or my family before leaving the orphanage, so living with my brother again really opened my eyes. My brother was very active in fighting for victims' rights, so I began learning more and more, not just about what happened that night but also the struggle to bring the town back afterward.

A HOUSE OF GHOSTS

My brother was active in the movement to get justice for the victims of the Bhopal disaster. Even at just thirteen, he had become involved in activism immediately after we returned to Bhopal and my sister and I were settled in the orphanage. He started an organization called Children against Carbide and protested with other young survivors of the disaster. He never went back to school—he dedicated his time to fighting for victim compensation.

After I moved in with him, I learned that in 1989, there was a settlement between the Indian government and Union Carbide for 470 million U.S. dollars. As part of the settlement, Union Carbide was to provide money to build a hospital for the Bhopal gas victims, and the government would provide the land. The hospital is still there. It's the biggest hospital in Bhopal.[9]

The government also distributed some of the $470 million settlement directly to victims of the disaster.[10] Survivors were given $500 each for long-term injuries and about $2,000 for each family member who had died. Me, my brother, my sister, and the husband of my sister who died that night, we all received compensation money for our lost family members.

My brother kept my part in the bank. We were getting interest from the bank every month, and he was paying my school fees from the interest. I started studying in an English school, and in India English schools are quite a bit more expensive than Hindi schools. We could use only the interest from my share of the compensation money for my education, because the law stated that the principal could not be accessed since I was a minor. The interest money helped, but it wasn't enough to fully cover fees.

A couple of organizations came forward and started helping us. One of those organizations was AID India.[11] There was a retired state government official named Harsh Mander who found out about my brother and my family, and he started donating money for my studies. He would give a certain amount of money for my studies once every three months. He was

---

[9] Sanjay is referring to the Bhopal Memorial Hospital and Research Center. For more information on the Indian government's settlement with Union Carbide, as well as on the history of legal action against the company and against Dow Chemical (which bought Union Carbide in 2001), see Appendix III, page 361.

[10] The Union Carbide settlement under the Indian Supreme Court in 1989 for $470 million was distributed among five hundred thousand claimants affected by the disaster. As a condition of the settlement, Union Carbide executives were immunized from further criminal and civil action. For more information on the Union Carbide disaster and legal aftermath, see Appendix III, page 361.

[11] Association for India's Development (AID India) is a U.S.-based NGO that promotes various social justice and human rights causes in India.

very interested in keeping the story of the Bhopal disaster alive. He went on to write for newspapers, and he even wrote a book about the Bhopal disaster called *Unheard Voices*—the very first story in the book is about my brother and my family.

My brother and I were very close. Our sister Mamta got married in 1997, a few years after we all moved in together, so after that it was just my brother and I living together. We were very close, but things could be difficult sometimes. Every time my brother talked about our family, he would get depressed, and you could see the depression in him for days. Sometimes he tried to hurt himself. Once, he tried to set himself on fire. I was not in Bhopal when he did it. I was visiting my sister in Lucknow, where she had moved after her marriage. One of my neighbors came to the door of our house just in time to save my brother. We found out my brother was suffering from paranoid schizophrenia. Later, he tried to kill himself with rat poison, too, but he survived. All this started around 1997, when I was thirteen. From that point on my brother and I were sort of taking care of each other.

Around 2001, when I was sixteen and he was around thirty, I asked Sunil to buy me a motorbike. I kept asking him, and finally he bought me one, but he said, "I'm not going to give you extra money or cash, you know, after the motorbike. So make sure you don't ask me for money for gasoline."

I said, "Don't worry, I'll start working."

So, I started tutoring. I did that for a few years to help provide an income, and then I also started working for some media people doing stories on Bhopal. It was 2004, I think, when I first did work for a journalist. He was a photojournalist from Italy and I was doing translations for him. He liked to tell stories through his pictures. And he was doing a piece on the disaster—on almost everything about Bhopal, really. He was the one who first took me to the ruins of the Union Carbide factory.

I wanted to see all of it. I always wanted to see how the factory had run. So I walked around with the Italian photojournalist and I saw different rooms and spaces, the old signs hanging on the walls. There used to be many separate buildings and structures on the factory grounds. Throughout the years many fell down, but the two main structures are still there. From the outside, though, it looked like they might fall down at any minute. And, well, I was kind of shocked because I hadn't seen big abandoned plants like that one, and it was kind of scary. Like a house of ghosts.

And it smelled so bad. The factory smelled of many different things, but mostly it smelled like DDT,[12] a harsh chemical smell. I had to put a handkerchief over my face as I toured the buildings. But it was also so green inside. There were trees and flowers inside the factory; things had started growing there again.

But you know another thing that was scary? The safety gloves and helmets of the former employees. In 2004 there were so many gloves still lying around on the floor of the factory. And I thought, *These were the hands of people who died. These are the hands of the workers who were the first to die.*

PEOPLE WERE GETTING SICK

In the 2000s, many of the people I met in Bhopal had health problems, especially the people who were in their thirties and forties and fifties. Most of them were suffering from breathlessness, and they got tired after walking for even five minutes. Before the disaster most of the people

---

[12] India is the world's only country still manufacturing dichlorodiphenyltrichloroethane (DDT), and is the world's largest consumer of it. Popular as a insecticide in the mid-twentieth century, DDT was banned in most of the world after it was found to cause numerous human health problems, including cancer, birth defects, and the disruption of endocrine systems.

in town worked as laborers. They would carry wheat, or they would sell vegetables on a handcart in the streets, or they would work as masons. They lost their working ability because they inhaled poisonous gases the night of the gas leak, and many are still easily fatigued and so cannot do hard work.

I didn't have any effects from the disaster until 2005. That year, when I was twenty years old, I had a stroke. Half my body was paralyzed for about twenty minutes, and I was in an intensive care unit in the hospital for about three days. Then I had to go through some tests in a bigger hospital, and the doctors found out that my carotid artery had narrowed, and that's what caused the stroke. I'm not sure why it happened, whether the stroke was because of the disaster or not, but there were a lot of hard-to-explain illnesses in town.

Not only were people still sick, they were still getting sick from drinking water that was contaminated from the disaster. Those of us who were active in the movement for victims' rights worked hard to fix the problem.

I visited Delhi in March 2006 as part of a victims' rights campaign organized by the International Campaign for Justice in Bhopal.[13] Our city was still contaminated twenty years after the disaster, our drinking water was unsafe, and nobody had ever really been held accountable for the accident. We wanted to make Dow liable for contamination cleanup, since they had bought out Union Carbide in 2001. We thought they should compensate all the people who had drunk contaminated water for twenty years and also help clean up the site. We also wanted Warren Anderson

[13] The International Campaign for Justice in Bhopal (ICJB) is an international coalition of non-profits and Bhopal survivor groups, including Children against Dow-Carbide, which Sanjay's brother Sunil helped to form. For more on the ICJB, visit bhopal.net.

to face trial.[14]

Around seventy people from Bhopal went to Delhi to rally and demand to see the prime minister—we walked, even though it was over five hundred miles. It took us thirty-six days. The prime minister wasn't willing to meet us, so a few of us went on a hunger strike. I was one of the fasters, along with seven or eight others. I fasted for six days. The prime minister didn't come, but he called us, and then three or four of our representatives went to meet him to list our demands: to set up a commission to monitor and treat the long-term health effects of contaminated air and water from the disaster; to force Dow Chemical, which had bought Union Carbide, to dismantle and clean up the old factory site; and to ensure a supply of clean drinking water to affected communities. The prime minister listened to our demands, but we didn't get anything out of the meeting except for vague promises.

While I was in Delhi, I got a call from an activist from Bhopal who worked with my brother. She told me that Sunil had tried to kill himself again, that he had eaten rat poison and was in the hospital. I thought, *He'll be fine.* I thought this because the first time he'd eaten rat poison he'd survived. Still, I took the first train home from Delhi, and my sister and her family were also on their way from Lucknow.

I arrived in Bhopal first, and it was only then that I found out my brother was dead. He hadn't eaten poison; he'd hanged himself in our apartment. I went to see his body during the post mortem. I was so shocked. I couldn't stop crying. And then, after a while, I was not even crying. I was just looking at him, in disbelief that I wouldn't see him alive again.

---

[14] Warren Anderson was the CEO of Union Carbide at the time of the Bhopal disaster. He was charged with manslaughter by an Indian court in 1991, but the U.S. government has never agreed to extradition. For more information on the Bhopal disaster, see Appendix III, page 361.

When my sister and her family arrived, my sister actually kind of fainted. And then she was crying terribly. Then her children—she had a son and a daughter by then—when they saw her, even they started crying.

After my brother died it was quite hard for me to live by myself in the apartment we'd shared, so in 2007 I decided to move to Delhi. I thought I would go study there, and I enrolled in a crash course in business management.

In the meantime I decided to rent out our apartment. So a family moved into my home for the year and a half I was in Delhi. And then when I was ready to move back to Bhopal, I told the family in my apartment, "Either you can share the space with me, or you will have to vacate because I need a place to stay." They agreed and were happy to live with me. I still live with them—they are really nice people.

I'm damn sure that my brother's depression was because of the tragedy and the gas that he inhaled that night. He used to say things like, "Someday soon I'll be dead." And, "Sanjay, move to Lucknow so that you can live. Our sister, she will look after you. Or better, you should move to a big city like Delhi or Mumbai because I don't think Bhopal is a safe place to live." He used to talk like that. Perhaps he did not want me to live around the tragedy. Maybe he knew that his life was ruined because of the past, and that the tragedy was something he could never escape.

I didn't want to abandon Bhopal. I moved home and dedicated my time to the campaign for victims' rights. I wanted to be as strong as my brother had been.

I WOULD DREAM ABOUT FOOD WHEN I SLEPT

We decided to build off our 2006 campaign in Delhi and rallied again the next year, and again in 2008. In 2008 we walked again from Bhopal to

Delhi and went for an indefinite hunger strike there. I again fasted, this time for weeks. Fasting was hard because I would dream about food when I slept. There were so many dishes that I used to eat every night when I was sleeping. All these dishes like spicy chickpeas and stuffed tomatoes. I missed soup the most. Tomato soup. I even missed fried rice. So every morning I woke up, I would say to my co-fasters, the people who were fasting with me, "Oh, I ate this and this and this."

And they would kind of go, "What? We're on fast, why did you eat?"

"No, it was in my dream!" I'd tell them. And every night before I went to bed I would say to them, "Okay, so this is what I'm going to eat tonight in my dream." Pretty soon nobody wanted to hear about it from me anymore! Then, twenty-one days into the fast, the government finally agreed to meet with us about our demands and asked us to call off the hunger strike.

After the hunger strike the prime minister of India called for clean water to be piped in to areas that had been served by contaminated water sources. We'd finally have clean water, which was one of our central demands. He also suggested a thirty-year plan for the cleanup, rehabilitation, and decontamination of the Union Carbide site and the surrounding land.

Still, we have all been affected by the disaster and continue to be affected. If we don't pressure the government, we will be forgotten. We're making progress, though. In June 2010, eight former senior employees of Union Carbide India were finally convicted. They were sentenced to two years in jail and a fine of $2,000. They got bailed out the next day and now have an appeal in higher courts. But because of this lenient verdict there was a big media outrage. The prime minister felt pressure, and ultimately we received more compensation money for the people who had lost their family members and a commitment to clean up the Union Carbide site. Still, not much has actually improved since then—though people in areas with contaminated water have clean water pumped in now, it's available only for a short time every day, or every other day. Much more still needs to be done.

I HOPE THAT PEOPLE WILL FIND OUT MORE ABOUT BHOPAL

For the last few years, I've been heavily involved with a documentary about the situation in Bhopal called *Bhopali*, directed by an American named Max Carlson.[15] At first I worked as a translator for him as he interviewed victims of the disaster, but in time I became a subject of the film. Right now I've come to the U.S. to educate others about the Bhopal disaster. I'm helping to promote the documentary, and I've testified in court on behalf of plaintiffs in a case against a chemical manufacturer.

I arrived in the States on March 13, 2011. My first engagement was in Charleston, West Virginia. I was called to testify as an expert witness on the long-term effects of methyl isocyanate—MIC—in a case that was filed against Bayer CropScience—it's a German company that has a plant in West Virginia. There was a risk of MIC leakage following an explosion in 2008. So a group of sixteen or seventeen area residents filed a case against Bayer, since a leakage of MIC could have resulted in another Bhopal. I was called in to testify about the devastation I'd seen in my hometown. The day I was in court, Bayer agreed they would no longer be producing MIC at the factory. So they backed down. It was actually a big victory for all of us fighting against the manufacture of MIC.

Here in California, we've had four screenings of *Bhopali*. The screening that we had in Los Angeles and last night in Berkeley were well attended,

---

[15] *Bhopali* is a 2011 documentary by Van Maximilian Carlson that covers the Bhopal disaster and the efforts of survivors to bring Union Carbide officials to justice. More information is available at www.bhopalithemovie.com.

and people had lots of questions.

I hope that people will find out more about Bhopal. There are still many people who just do not know about the accident, so this documentary is important because it's not just about what happened that night; it's also about what is happening in Bhopal now. We need to keep telling our story. It is not just history. We are still here, and we still need help.

Today, cleanup is yet to be done, the factory still stands abandoned. What I hope for Bhopal is justice—clean and abundant water, adequate health care, land free of contamination, adequate compensation for all victims, and I want Dow, who bought Union Carbide, to take responsibility and pay for the cleanup. The people of Bhopal have fought for almost twenty-nine years, and I strongly believe that we'll get justice one day even if we have to fight for another twenty-nine years.

ELECTRONICS

NOVEL TECHNOLOGIES, FAMILIAR PROBLEMS

Americans spend over $125 billion on consumer electronics every year, more than the entire gross domestic product of some populous countries such as Bangladesh. Electronics, ranging from the latest kitchen gadgets to innovative smartphones, seem to change Western consumption habits year to year more than any other consumer products. And in the past decade, no segment of the electronics industry has transformed global life more than digital communications. Nine out of ten American adults own a cell phone. It is difficult to imagine the modern workplace functioning without the use of the Internet and its conduits. Nearly one in five people across the globe purchased a new mobile phone sometime in 2012, and nearly 2.5 billion individuals, more than a third of the world's population, make use of the Internet.

Whereas the agriculture and garment industries have developed for millennia, the electronics industry is less than a century old—though early computing technology was based on innovations in textile manufacturing, such as punch card machines. It's tempting to imagine that this fledgling industry might have skipped over some of the worst labor abuses associated with older industrial sectors, but electronics workers have been subject to child labor abuses, low wages, dangerous working conditions, and environmental degradation from the dawn of the digital age.

Transistor radios—perhaps the first mobile communications devices that linked individuals through electricity and airwaves—were engineered in the United States after World War II. When William Shockley opened his laboratory in Mountain View, California, in the mid 1950s and stopped using germanium semiconductors in favor of silicon ones, he introduced a new age in electronics. The personal computer and other personal electronic devices were on the horizon.

Enthusiasm for semiconductor manufacturing in the newly dubbed Silicon Valley and elsewhere in the United States, high in the 1970s, turned tepid in the eighties and nineties. Reports surfaced of contaminated drinking water around manufacturing plants. PCBs and trichloroethylene, among other chemicals used in the manufacture of computer chips, were identified as possible carcinogens.[1] Rare birth defects and cancer clusters emerged among factory workers and their families near electronic manufacturing sites in California, Minnesota, and New York. Today, Silicon Valley hosts some of the highest concentrations of Superfund sites in the country, including the grounds of nearly twenty former computer chip manufacturing plants.[2]

Facing health claims from U.S. workers and residents, many tech companies shifted their manufacturing operations to other continents. In Taiwan in the seventies and eighties, manufacturers developed an original

---

[1] PCBs (polychlorinated biphenyls), used as coolants in electric systems, were banned in the United States in 1979 because of their possible toxic effects. Trichloroethylene is an industrial solvent that the U.S. Environmental Protection Agency has identified as a carcinogen.

[2] A Superfund site is land contaminated by toxic waste and earmarked by the U.S. Environmental Protection Agency for cleanup. For more information, see glossary, page 348.

model for mass-producing silicon chips and other electronics components. Perhaps the best known of these companies is Foxconn, an electronics manufacturer that established or contracted local agents to set up mega factories (industrial sites with tens of thousands or even hundreds of thousands of workers) that could produce high-volume, low-cost electronics components for multiple brands and retailers overseas.

Foxconn's largest factory presence is in Shenzhen, China, a city located in the Pearl River Delta bordering Hong Kong. In 1979, Shenzhen became one of the world's first special economic zones, a designation that exempts manufacturers from local and national taxes, regulations, and labor laws.[3] Today, Foxconn manufactures around 40 percent of the world's consumer electronics and employs over 1.2 million workers in China alone, along with countless others in India, Brazil, and Mexico, with many factories located in special economic zones that shield the company from labor regulations and allow for the lowest possible production costs.

For Foxconn clients such as Apple, Dell, Hewlett-Packard, and Walmart, the advantage of manufacturing abroad is clear. In October 2012, Apple announced that net profits for the previous three months were $8.2 billion, making it the third-highest profit-netting company in the world. Microsoft, Walmart, General Electric, and Intel were close behind, all with annual net profits of over $12 billion.

For individuals working in electronics manufacturing, the benefits are less clear. Though the lure of greater economic opportunity brings millions from rural areas to new urban manufacturing powerhouses in China and other developing nations, workers often encounter unexpected hazards.

At Foxconn, abusive labor practices have been met with vocal and sometimes violent protests from employees. Twice in 2012, pay disputes,

---

[3] For more on special economic zones, see Appendix III, page 363.

use of forced student labor, and dissatisfaction with employer relations sparked protests by Foxconn workers. It was not the first time Foxconn had come under scrutiny for its labor practices. Six years earlier, Foxconn had been criticized for violating Chinese law on maximum work hours, and, in 2010, the electronics giant was the subject of international media attention when more than a dozen workers took their own lives by jumping out of Foxconn dormitory windows on two campuses in Shenzhen.

Groups such as Students and Scholars against Corporate Misbehaviour (SACOM) and China Labour Bulletin have been monitoring labor conditions in China since 2005 and 1994, respectively. Through their discussions with workers in some of China's biggest exporting industries, they have uncovered the use of forced student labor, unpaid and illegal overtime, chronic injuries from lack of protection from gases used in electronics, and life-threatening equipment in the manufacture of home appliances.

Li Wen,[4] a young worker who had come to Shenzhen seeking employment as a teenager, suffered a greusome hand injury in a factory subcontracting to Walmart in 2009. His hand had to be amputated, and though Li was granted some compensation from both the factory and the Chinese government, the award was inadequate and he's been left with few long term employment opportunities.

One young Foxconn employee, Sung Huang,[5] has fared better than Li Wen, but his experience is representative of that of many young workers lured from the country to do factory work in Shenzhen. Sung grew up in the town of Jiangzhi, historically one of China's foremost porcelain producers, but the promise of better wages drew him five hundred miles south to Shenzhen and other industrial centers in the region. Though jobs are readily available, most are temporary. Sung hops from job to job in

---

[4] Name changed to protect the narrator.

[5] Name changed to protect the narrator.

towns hundreds of miles apart, staying in temporary housing and unable to establish stable living conditions.

The hazards faced by young electronics workers are not unique to China or other developing nations. In South Korea—often called "The Republic of Samsung" because of that company's near-total economic and political influence over the government—workers in semiconductor plants have begun to fall sick. Dr. Jeong-ok Kong, a medical researcher working with Supporters for the Health and Rights of People in the Semiconductor Industry (SHARPS), has discovered that over the last five years, more than eighty cases of rare blood and brain cancers have been documented among workers from two Samsung semiconductor facilities near Seoul. Most of those workers who have died so far have been in their twenties and thirties. In trying to get more information from Samsung about working conditions and worker medical records—which Samsung obtains from medical examinations of all its workers—SHARPS has been repeatedly turned away. Samsung has refused to release the health records, even to the workers requesting them for themselves. In this atmosphere of secrecy and indifference, individuals such as Hye-kyeong Han—a former Samsung semiconductor worker now battling brain cancer—remain struggling for recourse for their work-related illnesses, even as those illnesses continue to erode their health.

LI WEN

AGE: *26*

OCCUPATION: *Former factory worker*

BIRTHPLACE: *Shaoyang, Hunan Province, China*

INTERVIEWED IN: *Zhuhai, China*

We come into contact with Li in early 2012 through an organization called Students and Scholars against Corporate Misbehaviour (SACOM), an NGO based in Hong Kong. Debby Chan, who works for SACOM, agrees to travel with us to Zhuhai to meet Li Wen, who lost a hand while cutting machine parts at an electronics and household goods manufacturer.

We take an hour-long ferry ride from Hong Kong to Zhuhai.[1] *After we dock, Debby reaches Li by cell phone. He's running a little late, so we decide to eat at a small place inside the ferry terminal. It is during this meal that Debby tells us about a previous trip she took to this very location to meet with factory workers as*

---

[1] Zhuhai is a coastal city of over 1.5 million located in Guangdong Province on the Pearl River Delta near Hong Kong. Zhuhai was one of the first special economic zones in China, along with neighboring Shenzhen. For more on special economic zones, see Appendix III, page 363.

part of the work she does with SACOM. She says she began to suspect that two men were following her, so she took a long and winding route through the terminal, and the two men were behind her everywhere she went. She says she doesn't know who they were. "Maybe from the government. Maybe the company."

Eventually, Li arrives with two friends who have also lost hands in factory accidents. Li strikes us immediately as a warm, friendly person. He's about five foot four, with longish black hair that sweeps to one side. He wears a t-shirt and long orange shorts, and he keeps one forearm tucked into his shorts pocket at all times. As we walk to find a private place to conduct the interview, we notice a black sedan drive past us and park at the curb, then drive and park again after we walk by. We ask Debby if we're being followed and if we should be worried. "Definitely," she says. "But they're not going to attack us or anything. They just want to know who we are." Eventually we find a nearly empty restaurant with a private room.

Li is eager to tell his story. We talk for close to three hours, Debby working hard to translate between us. The following narrative comes almost entirely from that one conversation. Names and details have been changed to protect the identity of the narrator and his friends.

ONLY THE ELDERLY REMAIN IN MY HOMETOWN

My hometown is in Longhui County, in Shaoyang Prefecture of Hunan Province.[2] I grew up in a house that was built in the 1960s or seventies. It's really old. There are many old houses in my village, and the living conditions are really poor. Many houses don't have electricity, and in my home we don't have any electrical appliances—no fan, television, or refrigerator. There's not even much furniture, just a couple of beds. And for

---

[2] Hunan is a large province in south-central China with a population of over sixty-five million. The region's economy is still primarily agricultural, and the largest city is the provincial capital, Changsha, with over two million residents.

heat, we burn firewood and sometimes coal.

I'm the only child in my family, and I'm short, because when I was young I didn't get enough nutrition. My parents are very old. My father is sixty-two years old now, and my mother is fifty-nine. They both worked in coal mining when they were young, so now they're not in good health. Their bodies are weak. Sometimes they work as temporary laborers in the local community, doing things like cutting trees or demolishing old houses or construction work on new houses. But that work is really unsteady. The jobs might last only three to five days. But like many of the villagers, they farm for much of the year. Most people grow rice or peanuts. The farm we have is allocated to us by the state, and the rice we grow is mainly for feeding the pigs and other livestock, and for feeding ourselves. My family grows all the rice we eat, and most of the vegetables. Sometimes, if there are vendors selling meat, then we'll buy some.

In my neighborhood there are about one hundred residents, but in the whole village, I don't know exactly, maybe one thousand. The neighborhoods are near each other, so I can walk to the others. It's convenient. Only a few people own cars, and they use them for business, things like transporting coal into the villages. Still, there's not much work to do near my hometown other than farm. Many young people go out to look for jobs, so mostly only the elderly remain in the village.

When I was sixteen years old, I went to Longhui Vocational School. I studied electrical appliances, but other majors included computers, fashion design, arts, molding, and mechanics. My grades were good, but because I'm poor I didn't have the opportunity to go on to university. In fact, I am really lucky that I could go to vocational school because of the poor economic situation in my home. I thought I might only be able to finish junior high, because when I was in grade nine, my father had a problem with his eye, and then a problem with his stomach at the same time. So much money went for his treatment that the only way I was able to go to the vocational high school was because of subsidies from the school and because my family sold our cow. We got 800 yuan for the cow, and my father borrowed 600 from his friend in the same village.[3] And my father's eye was treated successfully, so he was able to return to work. Otherwise, I would not have been able to go to school.

In my first month of vocational school I also borrowed money from my friends in order to survive. The school fees were around 1,400 to 1,500 yuan for one semester, and the cost of living was around 100 yuan per month.[4]

The first two years of school I was in the top three in my class. But in the third year I didn't concentrate as much on studying. I just wanted to graduate and go look for jobs. It was my dream that after five years working outside the village I would have enough money to return home and renovate my family's house with bricks and cement.

IN SHENZHEN, EVERYTHING WAS NEW AND EXCITING

In my final year at vocational school, I was already hoping I could leave my hometown to work in the city. I graduated in June 2007. I was nineteen years old.

At that time my school organized a training for migrant workers, which I attended. The training covered only the basics of electronics, which I'd already learned in school. But only the students who enrolled in the training would be recommended by the school for a factory job.

---

[3] 600 yuan = US$90. 800 yuan = US$120. (All conversions in this narrative represent the approximate average dollar value of the yuan from roughly 2005–2010.)

[4] 1,500 yuan= US$220. 100 yuan = US$15.

After that, in August, I left home for Shenzhen[5] with around ten other students from the same province as me. The journey by bus and train took around seventeen hours and cost me 140 yuan, a little less than half of what my family had given me before I left.[6] It was the last time I asked for money from my family. I had never been outside my hometown before, and I knew nothing about what Shenzhen would be like. But I was curious to see a new place, and I had big aspirations.

In Shenzhen, everything was new and exciting. It was the first time I'd seen so many high rise buildings, the first time I'd seen neon lights, the first time I'd seen so many cars on the road. I had never even been in an elevator before. Shenzhen felt like a great city to be in, and my hometown now seemed like such a tiny place.

I became friends with the people I'd traveled to Shenzhen with, and then we met even more new friends in Shenzhen who were really nice. They took us along to try many things in the city, including the food there. I was pretty excited about all of it.

I got my first job at an electronics factory there because my vocational school had a student placement arrangement with the factory. The factory compound was made up of about seven buildings, and there were probably two thousand people working there. All my other friends went to work on the production line, but I was the only one of us assigned to quality control. I don't know why I got that position, but I guess the management believed I could handle it.

Those of us in quality control had to inspect printed circuit boards for

---

[5] Shenzhen is the capital of Guangdong Province, and one of China's leading manufacturing cities. It has a working population of over ten million, but as many as six million residents are migrant workers who live in dormitories during the week and are based permanently elsewhere in China. Shenzhen was one of the first special economic zones—free-trade regions exempt from national and local tax and many regulations and labor laws. For more on special economic zones, see Appendix III, page 363.

[6] 140 yuan = US$20.

computers. We used a magnifying glass to examine the boards for defects. But the management believed that the female workers were more careful about this, so usually they did this part, and I usually handled the circuit boards that were sent back. Most of the employees in quality control are female workers. Another guy and I were the only males.

I worked very hard while I was there, and I had a lot of fun. When I had free time, I would play basketball or badminton. I went hiking or running. I was optimistic about my future then.

After I'd been working there for several months, in November 2007, my face swelled up. I still don't know what caused it, if it was an infection or a tumor or what. I went right away to a doctor at the largest hospital in Shenzhen, and the medical opinion was that I should have surgery immediately. But I didn't have any family in Shenzhen who could take care of me while I recovered, so I took leave from the factory and went back to my hometown to have the surgery there to have the swelling relieved.

The job at the electronics factory was my first job and I didn't know much about labor law then. When I left to have the surgery, I did not receive any salary while I wasn't working. On my wage stub from that time it actually stated that I owed the factory a few yuan.

I WANTED TO LEARN SOME NEW SKILLS

I stayed in my hometown until after the Lunar New Year,[7] and then I returned to work at that factory in Shenzhen and stayed there for four or five more months. I worked really hard at that time because I wanted to learn some new skills from the factory and then look for a better job with

---

[7] The New Year festival in China is based on the lunar calendar and usually falls in late January or sometime in February according to the Gregorian calendar. The festival is a major public holiday in China, and most businesses and schools close for three days. In 2008 the Lunar New Year fell on February 7, ushering in the Year of the Rat.

a better career path.

I left that job around July 2008 and looked for another job. It took me around three weeks, and then I was hired at the Lenovo factory to work on the production line. Our department was responsible for assembling the LCD monitors, fixing different components.

At that time the basic wage was slightly over 900 yuan per month. But the overtime premium was calculated in accordance with law, which meant that on weekdays the overtime payment was 1.5 times the hourly wage, and then on weekends the hourly wage was doubled. In the low season I could earn 1,300 to 1,400 yuan per month. But in the peak season my wages were 1,800 to 1,900 yuan. In terms of wages, it was a good factory. A lot of factories pay only around 1,500 yuan to the workers, so the treatment at Lenovo was good.[8]

I was hired there as a temporary worker. Usually the factory would convert temporary workers to regular workers after three months, but because of the financial crisis, this didn't happen. At the end of the year, the factory laid off all the temporary workers.

IN ZHUHAI, THERE ARE MANY TREES, AND THERE IS THE OCEAN

I wanted to go back to my hometown to celebrate the Lunar New Year in 2009, but my cousins who worked at a factory in Zhongshan, a few hours by bus from Shenzhen, asked me to come celebrate the holiday with them, which I did.

I had a friend working at a factory here in Zhuhai, which is south of Zhongshan, about two hours by bus, and he suggested that I apply for a

---

[8] 900 yuan = US$135. 1,400 yuan = US$210. 1,900 yuan = US$285. 1,500 yuan = US$225.

job here. Because he already worked there and gave me a recommendation, it meant I'd be able to go to work right after the Lunar New Year ended. So I ended up in Zhuhai. At the factory in Zhuhai I produced parts for rice cookers, and I fixed screws in the lids of the rice cookers.

Like Shenzhen, Zhuhai is very different from my hometown. It's much more prosperous, like Shenzhen, and there are lots of places to hang out for fun, like playing basketball or using the Internet. But there are also many trees, and there is the ocean. The scenery is beautiful.

When I'm at home with my family, I usually have two meals a day, at eight in the morning and then around three in the afternoon. If I'm really hungry then I might have an additional meal in the evening. The main thing I eat at home is rice. But when I was in Zhuhai, I would usually have three or sometimes four meals a day, because of the work cycle of the factory. I worked hard and had to eat more, but my diet was more varied as well.

I stayed in Zhuhai for only three months because the wages were too low. I could make only around 1,300 to 1,400 yuan per month.[9] So I left in April of that year, 2009. I went back to Shenzhen to look for work, but because of the financial crisis I couldn't find a job. Then, around that time, my cousin Li Fang, my uncle's daughter, called to tell me my father was suffering from a very bad stomach ulcer. So in May, I returned home.

When I got there, I accompanied my father to visit the doctor. The treatment lasted for ten days and was successful, so he didn't need surgery. I wasn't worried about not having a job during that time. I believed there were plenty of opportunities that would be available. And sure enough, in June, just a couple of weeks after my father's treatment, a friend called

---

[9] 1,300 to 1,400 yuan = approximately US$200.

me about a job at the Elec-Tech factory in Zhuhai.[10] He was working in the quality-assessment department, and he told me that his department was recruiting new employees. I left my hometown again.

I WORKED ELEVEN HOURS A DAY, SIX DAYS A WEEK

I applied to Elec-Tech for a job as a quality-assessment officer. In the final stage of the interview process, there were only two interviewees, me and a female worker who had worked previously at Elec-Tech for a number of years. Ultimately, she got the job. So I just applied to work as an ordinary worker in the same factory, and I was hired. My salary was around 1,500 yuan a month.[11]

I lived in the dormitory at Elec-Tech. The room had five bunk beds, and it had a bathroom where we could take a shower. It also had two fans. But we had to buy the pillows and beddings ourselves.

In the dormitory, roommates were usually from the same department, and if we were off work at the same time, we would mostly chat with each other or play cards. Sometimes I would have a day off and my roommates would still have to work, but for the public holidays, like the national days, then usually all of us would have the day off. When I was off work I liked to play chess or just hang out in the city. I also went to the seashore, which was really nice. I had never seen the sea before moving to Zhuhai. The ocean is so wide and big, and when I looked out at it, it was just like the sea and sky merged with each other.

I was assigned to the molding department. There were thirty to forty

---

[10] Elec-Tech is a Hong-Kong–based company that manufactures components for a wide range of products, including home appliances and wind turbines.

[11] 1,500 yuan = US$225.

people working in my section, but there were other sections in the factory doing the same work. I would get up at six in the morning and go to work around seven. And when I finished work it was around eight in the evening. I worked eleven hours a day—which doesn't include the meal breaks—usually six days a week. But if the department was really busy, I worked seven days.

Usually it's one or two people operating a machine. And each machine makes different things. I worked on different products. I produced parts for kitchen equipment, for example, but sometimes I had no idea, because we produced just that one component on the line and then the other workers would assemble the components.

Usually the material was steel, and after I put the material in the machine, I would step on a pedal, and the upper part of the machine would press down to stamp the metal to shape the component we were making at the time.

Sometimes the sheet metal was really big, and then we needed two workers to put the metal into the machine. And when we were working with the bigger-sized metal, usually there wasn't a pedal, but two big buttons. You had to use both hands for the buttons, which was safer, because if both your hands were on the buttons, they couldn't get trapped in the machine when it clamped down. I'd heard stories about injuries at the factory. For example, I heard about one worker who lost three fingers and another who lost part of his middle finger. But I didn't give it much thought at the time. Only later did I become aware that injuries are really common in that department.

It was very hot on the shop floor, and very noisy, but we were given earplugs. The sounds came from the molding machines, when the machines pressed down to make shapes out of the metal sheets, the metals clashing with each other. But if we had to talk to our co-workers we could still hear them. All the machines were very close to each other, just a fifty-centimeter gap between them.

When I finished shaping the products, I would pile them up next to me, and then other workers would come by and collect those pieces. I had to stand while operating the machines, and at the end of the day I would be really tired, and my hands and legs would be sore.

WHEN THE MACHINE CAME DOWN ON MY HAND, I SCREAMED OUT

In July, a month after I'd gone to work at the Elec-Tech factory, I started working on the night shift.

July 10, 2009 was the day everything changed. I'd started work at eight p.m. At eleven p.m., I had a meal break for thirty minutes, and then I went back to work. The machine I was working on, the pressing machine, was three to four meters tall, and the color was almost white, with rust seeping through the paint. You might not know by looking at it that it was really old, but I remember it was made in the seventies or eighties. The date was printed on the machine.

The material I was working with was small pieces of metal, and I was operating the machine with a pedal. I would step on the pedal, and the machine would press down. I was doing this for a long time, working very fast. I was tired at the time. It was around one a.m. that I noticed there was a small scrap of metal inside the machine that I needed to remove, because if I didn't, the next piece of metal I put in would have some defect in it. I reached my left hand in to grab the metal scrap.

I don't really know how it happened. When the machine came down on my hand I screamed out. It was really painful, and there was a lot of blood. I can't remember what I was thinking at the time. I just screamed and clenched my teeth.

I COULD HEAR THE SOUND OF THE SAW CUTTING MY BONE

I was brought to the entrance of the factory. I don't remember who brought me there. My mind had almost gone blank, and I just wanted to get to the hospital as soon as possible. I had to wait for twenty minutes until a minibus arrived to pick me up. And then it took another hour to reach the hospital.

After the examination at the hospital, the doctor said I needed surgery. I couldn't think clearly, but I was asked to sign something. I realized that it was really severe only after the surgery was done.

The doctor numbed my arm, but I was conscious the entire time. All I could think was that I hoped the surgery would be over as soon as possible. I could not see what was happening because there was a cloth covering my eyes, but I could hear the sound of the saw cutting my bone, and even though they numbed my arm, I could still feel the pain. It was the most painful experience of my life.

I stayed in the hospital for sixteen days after they amputated my hand. That whole time I was very depressed. I didn't call my family. I didn't call anyone. I didn't want to upset them. While I was in the hospital, I met a lot of people who had suffered work injuries like me. Most of them said the same thing, that they weren't going to tell their families until after they'd been treated.

After sixteen days I was discharged. Later, people asked me why I was sent out so soon, but at the time, I didn't think to ask why. I felt completely helpless. I didn't know what to do or what to demand.

IN THE EYES OF MY PARENTS, THERE WAS SADNESS

I went on medical leave and started receiving medical leave payments of 1,380 yuan each month from the company.[12] I put all my time into trying to deal with my injury. On August 10, 2009, I went for an examination to determine my work capacity now that I had lost my hand. It had been a month since the accident, and it was around this time that I decided to tell my family what had happened.

I called my cousin, my uncle's daughter, and told her first, because I was worried about my parents, how they would take the news. My parents are old. My cousin is the one who told my parents what happened to me.

In September, I went to be fitted for an artificial hand at a company that makes prostheses. But the one they gave me was very uncomfortable. It was not as good as I'd imagined. It was clumsy and too big for me. I don't use it.

On December 2, I was certified as having a grade-five injury. This was really detrimental, because a grade five meant I could not receive the full workers' compensation for my accident.[13] Grade ten is the lowest you can receive. It means you get the lowest amount of compensation. And grade one is the highest. I don't know what the amounts are for each grade, but I think that because of my injury, I should have been given at least a grade four, since I couldn't do the same work I'd be trained to do anymore.

On December 14, a lawyer came to handle my case. My uncle had arranged this. The lawyer told me I could get 23,760 yuan from social security as compensation for my accident.[14] And then the next day the lawyer

---

[12] 1,380 yuan = approximately US$210.

[13] For more on workers' compensation, see glossary, page 348.

[14] 23,760 yuan = approximately US$3,550.

negotiated with one of the managers from the company, someone who takes care of industrial injuries. My lawyer asked that I get another examination, because the grade-five certification was too low, but the manager from the company said the law did not require them to offer another examination. In the end, the company said they were willing to offer me a settlement of 90,921 yuan, in addition to the 23,760 from social security.[15]

The company gave me two options. One was to go back to work at the factory. In this case, I would have been allowed to take only a portion of the compensation. I don't know what the company would have had me doing at the factory, and I didn't ask, because there was no way I was going back there. The second option was to officially resign from the company and accept the full compensation they were offering, which wasn't enough.

I didn't know what to do. I wanted to think about things. A week after the lawyer told me my options, I went back home. This was the first time my parents had seen me since my hand was amputated. When I saw them, I just cried out, "Father and Mother!" I couldn't say anything else.

Their hair had turned grayer since I'd last seen them. And the way they looked at me now was different. In the eyes of my parents, when they looked at me, there was sadness.

"WE DID EVERYTHING IN ACCORDANCE WITH THE LAW"

I stayed there for the Lunar New Year at the beginning of 2010. I took leave from the factory and rested in my hometown. It was peaceful, but I was also confused about what my future might hold. My cousin helped

---

[15] 90,921 yuan = approximately US$13,640. According to Chinese worker compensation law, Li's grade-five disability entitled him to sixteen times his monthly salary as a disability grant and a medical reimbursement grant of sixty times his monthly salary.

me find another lawyer who was willing to offer legal assistance. The lawyer we found was helpful. When he contacted me I was touched by his sincerity.

I didn't ask much advice from my parents, because they're not well educated and don't know much. They just wanted me to get as much compensation as possible.

On April 22, I left my hometown again to return to Zhuhai, where I stayed with a friend. I negotiated with one of the managers from the company several times, but his attitude remained the same: "We did everything in accordance with the law."

So on May 18, 2010, I officially resigned from the company. That was the only way I could get the compensation of 90,921 yuan from them. But I still thought the compensation was too low, so after my resignation I decided to bring a lawsuit against the company.

I filed a complaint in court in June, and the case was first heard by the court on the July 29. I lost that lawsuit because I had already been paid settlement money.[16]

Many people have asked me how much money I received, and, when I tell them, they ask me why I accepted it. Unfortunately, according to the legal standards, it was the only money I could get.

Eventually, after a series of injuries, Walmart conducted several audits at the factory. But Elec-Tech used a lot of deception tactics. I've talked to people who have been injured but still work in the factory. These are people whose injuries aren't as serious as mine, people who have lost maybe one finger or a few fingers. They tell me that during the audits, Elec-Tech would put the injured people on leave, so they weren't in the factory when the Walmart people were there. I don't know if they were

---

[16] Although workers in China have the right to sue employers for workplace accidents apart from worker compensation payments, few such lawsuits have ever been filed after compensation has been paid. Li's case was quickly dismissed.

paid while they were off work.[17]

I also know two other guys who lost a hand at the same factory. When I last talked to them by phone I found out that they had both accepted compensation for their injuries. But now they've gone back to their hometowns, and I haven't talked to them.

THERE ARE LOTS OF INCONVENIENCES IN MY LIFE

My family had planned to rebuild our house in Shaoyang in March 2010, because at that time our relatives planned to rebuild theirs, and our houses are connected to each other. But it took a long time, because we had to sort out the money. During the renovation of the house we lived with one of my uncles. But the construction is done now, and my family has moved back into the house. In August 2010, I moved back to my hometown to live with my parents, though I still come to Zhuhai often.

Still, there are lots of inconveniences in my life. For example, when I was working on the house, when I had to carry the bricks, I could carry only two bricks with one hand. There were builders, but we were helping the builders, and we had to prepare the materials for rebuilding the house. My father bought the cement mix and mixed it with water to prepare the cement. And then I had to carry the cement to the builders. But living with one hand, so many things are difficult, and there are things I just cannot do.

After my accident and after I returned home, some journalists showed up to interview me. One was from the *Wall Street Journal*. Another was from Beijing, the *Global Times*, and another was from some journal on

---

[17] According to SACOM, around sixty accidents took place at the Zhuhai Elec-Tech factory between July 2009 and June 2010, with many resulting in the loss of hands or fingers. Machines such as the one that mangled Li's hand were replaced in 2010.

work-related injuries. They asked me questions about how I was injured and where I'd been working.

And even someone from the government came to talk with me, but I don't remember much of what he asked. In the end, I was disappointed with the government. They didn't care about what had happened to me. They were hoping I wouldn't make trouble or draw more public attention. I think the government could help me in several ways, like helping me find a job or start a business. But the government doesn't care about poor families like us.

Still, after the journalists showed up, the company agreed to pay me an additional 130,000 yuan, as long as I agreed not to talk to any more journalists about my injury.[18] I accepted the money, so now I have to be careful when talking about my story.

So now I've received all the compensation, a total of about 240,000 yuan.[19] I am grateful for the assistance, although I think it's still not enough. For example, in rebuilding my home, I've already spent 130,000 yuan, so there is not much money left.

There is a policy that the government will provide subsidies to impoverished families for renovating their houses. But last year I was not in my hometown, and when I returned and went to the civil affairs office for a consultation, the officer there told me the resources were limited. He said there was enough for only one or two families in a village to receive the subsidy. But no one had applied for it, so the officer said that in order to keep the money from going to waste, the government had allocated the subsidy to the village secretary, which is something like the mayor of the village. He got to keep the money himself.

---

[18] 130,000 yuan = approximately US$19,500.

[19] 240,000 yuan = approximately US$36,000.

I'D LIKE TO GET MARRIED, BUT THAT MIGHT BE DIFFICULT

To this day I feel frustrated and helpless. The place where my hand was amputated continues to ache. It's very painful. Even now I still feel pain, and the problem cannot be resolved. I don't have any medication. Even when I visited the doctor, he said it was normal to have pain and did not give me any medication. I've gone to the hospital several times, but they're always telling me there is no problem. And sometimes I feel my hand there, and it feels cold. Sometimes it really hurts, and sometimes it's just numb.

I imagine my future will be difficult. I've spent a lot of my time on the house, but now that we've finished with the renovation, I really need to sort out my future plans.

I'm worried about my parents. I worry about their health because of their age. I feel I have a responsibility to take care of them. When I was able to work in the factories, that was the major source of our income. But my father will still go out to find temporary work when he can. Although most of the young people have left my hometown, I still have my cousin, who has a newborn baby.

My hometown is surrounded by mountains, but this year, hopefully, the main county road will connect to our town, so it will be much easier for us to go out to other towns. I expect that after the new road connects here, there will be a public bus that will come to our hometown.

I'm thinking about starting my own business, but I don't know what kind of business I would do. I don't feel very confident, and I don't have any experience. I don't have a clear plan about how I should work it out, and now I have only about 100,000 yuan left from the settlement.[20]

---

[20] 100,000 yuan = approximately US$15,000.

I'm worried about having enough capital, because in my hometown, if I have to rent a place to start my business, the rent is about 50,000 to 60,000 yuan per year.[21] Right now I come to Zhuhai often to meet with other workers who have been in factory accidents, and to share my story so that others understand what's going on in China, including other young Chinese workers like me who may not understand the dangers of their work.

My relatives feel pity for me, because they think the compensation I got wasn't reasonable. They think I was too young to have handled the negotiations. I have to come up with a plan of some kind. I also hope to have my own family. I'd like to get married, but that might be difficult. I'd like to find a nice girl, but she'll need to accept my disability.

[21] 50,000 to 60,000 yuan = approximately US$7,500 to $9,000.

SUNG HUANG

AGE: *25*

OCCUPATION: *Factory worker*

BIRTHPLACE: *Jingdezhen, Jiangxi Province, China*

INTERVIEWED IN: *Shenzhen, China*

As with Li Wen, we meet Sung Huang through SACOM in 2011, this time on a trip to Shenzhen from Hong Kong. At a restaurant in Shenzhen's Longhua District, we sit with Sung and two of his friends (also in their early twenties) as they slouch in their chairs, smoke cigarettes, and inventory the long list of moves from city to city each has made in search of stable work.

Sung and his friends have stories similar to those of many young Chinese workers we meet: he grew up in the countryside with his grandparents while his parents worked in a major manufacturing center hundreds of miles away. With little opportunity for work in rural China, Sung made the trip to join his parents in the town of Hangzhou, one of China's designated special economic zones free from import and export taxes and many of China's national labor regulations. Life for rural Chinese in urban manufacturing zones can be transient at best. National residency laws designed to limit urban sprawl make settling down in cities like

Hangzhou virtually impossible for migrant workers. Many live in company-sponsored dormitories during the week and travel hundreds of miles to their home villages on the weekends. The stress of this sort of instability on young families can be enormous. Sung found he couldn't get along with parents who had been absent for much of his childhood, and he ran away at sixteen and began supporting himself.

Names have been changed to protect the identity of the narrator.

I HAVE MANY SPIRITS

I have a lot of stories to tell, because I have many spirits. I have a lot of job experience, and I've tried a few occupations.

I was brought up in Jiangxi Province by my grandparents. Jingdezhen, Jiangxi, not too far from where I grew up, is world famous for its porcelain, especially porcelain dishes.[1] But my village is very common, and my family lived a common agricultural life. At home it was me, my younger sisters, and my grandparents. We didn't see my parents very often, since they worked factory jobs hundreds of miles away.

I went to junior high, but I didn't make it past the third year there. I wasn't very obedient, and I decided I couldn't learn much from the school. At that time, my parents were working in Hangzhou, and when I quit school I went to Hangzhou to stay with them.[2] But I got into some arguments with my parents, and we didn't have a very good relationship. So I ran away from my parents' home, all alone and with only 100 yuan.[3]

---

[1] Jiangxi is a large province in Southeast China with forty-five million inhabitants. A mountainous and forested region, Jiangxi has an agricultural economy but is also known as the leading porcelain-producing province in China.

[2] Hangzhou is a major Chinese city with approximately twenty million residents in the metropolitan area. It lies along the Yangtze River Delta in Zhejiang Province, and is around three hundred miles east of Jiangxi.

[3] 100 yuan = US$15.

I found a job for myself in Hangzhou, and then after a month had passed, I got in touch with my family to let them know I was okay.

My first job was in security. This was in 2005, when I was sixteen. But I used the ID card of someone who was eighteen, because you had to be eighteen to have that job. A lot of people use fake ID cards to get jobs. I don't think my boss knew it was not my ID. If he did they wouldn't have hired me.

I worked in a residential community for the owners of some apartments. Once, there was a thief who tried to steal some parts from a car. He'd got the hood open, but then we caught him. Four other security guards beat him up and then sent him to the police. But I didn't join the beating, because I was too young, and the other guards kept me away.

I worked there for only two months. I was getting paid only 800 yuan per month.[4] I was paid for my food and housing, too, but still, I didn't think there would be any opportunities for career development, so I quit and found a new job.

I HAD A FAKE CERTIFICATE MADE

I went to work at the paper factory where my parents worked in Hangzhou. I was using someone else's ID again. Those factories find new workers simply by introductions made by people already working there. If you know someone who works there, then it is easy to get in. The jobs there are labor intensive. They are exhausting, but you can get better pay.

I worked eight hours a day for the factory. We had three shifts, because the machines don't stop. The machines go twenty-four hours a day. At that time I was in the packaging department, where we packed the paper for shipping. I did not enjoy it, because it was so exhausting.

---

[4] 800 yuan = US$120.

But I was getting paid almost twice as much as when I was a security guard.

I worked there for more than half a year. My parents worked there too, so they were able to monitor me more strictly. And I did what I could to learn to drive the forklifts, which were operated by more skilled workers. I wasn't supposed to drive them and the factory wouldn't let me have that job. Still, I learned as much as I could and then quit that job after I felt I'd learned enough about how to operate the forklift. I thought I could get a better job.

I found a job operating a forklift in another paper factory in Hangzhou. You need a certificate for forklifts, so I had a fake certificate made. There are advertisements for making fake certificates everywhere, so it was very easy to get one. For smaller factories, it's not easy to check whether a certificate like that is fake or not. And besides, what they care about is your ability to operate the forklift. They really don't care about the certificate, as long as you have one.

After that second paper factory in Hangzhou, I worked as a salesman in the city, but that was only for about two weeks. Then I came to Shenzhen[5] and went to work as a security guard for a factory for three months before traveling north, following some leads on more permanent work. I ended up in Wenzhou,[6] and I had another security job where I was more like a temporary policeman, working for the city's administrative offices. I worked there for more than a year. At that time there was a policy that after working as a temporary police officer for ten years, you could become an official policeman. I didn't stay there though. I was arrogant, and I made some mistakes, some serious mistakes.

---

[5] Hangzhou and Shenzhen are about eight hundred miles apart.

[6] Wenzhou is a city of over nearly eight million about 750 miles north of Shenzhen. It is known as one of China's leading exporters of wholesale electronics equipment.

For us security guards, when we caught someone, we might first beat him up before arresting him or taking him to jail. This is a common practice among police and security guards in China. One time, three other temporary officers and I were trying to catch some bicycle thieves. We were wearing our plain clothes, and we followed behind one guy we thought was a thief for a whole day. He probably noticed us following him, so he didn't do anything on the first day.

We were angry about it, because for every thief we caught, we were given a bonus. We had followed that thief for a while, but because he didn't do anything, we couldn't get any bonus. So we were angry at him.

And then, the next day, around two or three in the afternoon, we caught up to him with a stolen bike on the street and gave him a heavy beating. One of the other guys kicked the thief, and he rolled under a rack of umbrellas, completely unconscious. We took him into the station. Then that night, sometime after midnight, our supervisor called us to the police station and asked us about what had happened. He told us that the thief had died.

Three of my colleagues, the ones who did most of the beating, are still in jail and haven't gone to trial yet. I had to leave the job.

FOUR DAYS OFF IN A MONTH

So after I lost my job as a security officer, I returned south in 2008. My next job was at Foxconn in Shenzhen. I started there around the end of 2008. I'd heard about Foxconn from some friends, so I tried to get a job there. I didn't know much about the company, but I'd heard that the treatment there was relatively good.

When I started, I was working ten hours a day. Eight hours was the normal working day, but I worked two hours of overtime every day. And if you worked Saturday or Sunday, you got paid overtime for that.

The basic salary for working Monday to Friday was 900 yuan, but we usually worked on Saturday and would have only Sunday off. So we would have four days off in a month and get paid 1,500 to 1,800 yuan for the month, with meals and housing included, because of the overtime.[7] Which is barely enough to live on.

Foxconn is a little more strict than the other factories. Things at other factories are a little more relaxed, but at Foxconn the work is more demanding. At that time I was living in the dorms in the factory. Ten people share one dormitory, about twenty square meters, and there's one bathroom for each dormitory. People sleep on bunk beds.

I was working in the molding department at that time, stamping sheets of metal into shape for different products. We had to do different things, including operating the machines, sometimes packing, and maybe some cleaning up. I learned to operate the machines.

But I started working there during the financial crisis, and after I'd been working there for about a month, the factory started to lay off people, and I was laid off too. I had met someone at Foxconn who became my girlfriend, but after I was laid off I went back by myself to Hangzhou and found a job operating forklifts at another paper factory. I worked there for about three months.

I FELT LIKE I COULDN'T BREATHE

And then after three months, when the financial crisis was over, I went back to Foxconn. This second time at Foxconn I was producing mobile phones for Nokia, spraying paint on the shells of the mobile phones.

We wore dust-free uniforms, which covered our whole bodies and our heads, and we wore masks. There was only a slit for our eyes. That suit

---

[7] 900 yuan = US$135. 1,800 yuan = US$270.

was so uncomfortable, and with the mask I felt like I couldn't breathe.

When we got the product into our department, we put it onto the line and there was a machine that would spray the paint over the phone automatically. After that it would go to a high-temperature area for stabilizing the paint, and then we would take out the product and see if it was okay.

I worked at Foxconn for three months, and again I lived in the dorms during that time. I left because I was going home to become engaged to my girlfriend. For the engagement, we needed to meet each other's parents, to ask them to be present at the ceremony. We were from the same area, and it just made more sense for us to quit Foxconn and go home to announce our engagement, because we couldn't invite all those people and make them travel all the way to Shenzhen. We met some of each other's relatives and had dinner together.

I didn't plan to go back to Foxconn. I was thinking I would go over to where one of my relatives was living in Hangzhou. He was working at a factory making lightbulbs. You can make 4,000 to 5,000 yuan a month there.[8] It's a small workshop. There are a lot of small workshops in that area. And I did go there, but I couldn't manage because the temperature inside the shop was really high, forty to fifty degrees Celsius.[9] I couldn't stand it.

After I quit the small workshop I found a factory nearby and went to work in the personnel department. The factory was not very big, and the job was not very demanding. But the salary was only about 2,000 yuan a month.[10]

I worked for about two and a half months, and then I went back to Foxconn in May 2010, because I didn't think there was anything that I

---

[8] 4,000 to 5,000 yuan = US$600 to $750.

[9] 104 to 122 degrees Fahrenheit.

[10] 2,000 yuan = US$300.

could get going for myself over there in Hangzhou. And for my girlfriend. She had worked in that lightbulb factory with me at that time, and I was thinking of her, because the temperature in the factory was too high and she could not handle it, either. Foxconn was much better because there was air conditioning. This is a better place for her to work as a common worker. Me, I think I can find a job anywhere.

So we both came back to Foxconn at the same time, and now we are living outside the dormitories, in our own apartment. You don't have to live in the dormitory. You get paid more when you live outside the dormitory, about 150 yuan per month more.[11] Living outside feels more free and more comfortable, but I lived in the dormitory before in order to save more money. The allowance for one person living outside the dormitory doesn't cover the whole rent, which is about 300 yuan a month.[12]

THE FIRST PRIORITY IS SPEED

Now I'm working in the storage department. On the production line they use certain materials for their jobs. They report to our department and tell us what they need, and we do the purchasing. We keep the materials in the storage area, and when they need those things, they will come to us and we distribute the materials to them.

The working hours are the same as they've always been, but this is a much easier job than the others at Foxconn.

At Foxconn, the first priority is speed, the speed of manufacturing. It's only after that they care about the quality. But I feel like a normal factory would care about the quality. Because the client is the goal, but what the clients would care about would be the quality of the product. I don't

---

[11] 150 yuan = US$22.

[12] 300 yuan = US$45.

think the clients would care much about the efficiency. But at Foxconn they think that the efficiency is more important, because they want to complete the orders that the clients make as soon as possible. They may not care very much about the quality.

But I don't think that affects the workers much. What the workers care about is that they get their salary for the job. I don't think they care much about the quality of the products.

THE MANAGEMENT IS LIKE A MACHINE

I have heard about the suicides. These are things that happen around us, but I don't know much about it. I don't have much to say about it.

It's like people say: the management at Foxconn is like a machine—no matter whether the instructions they give workers are reasonable or not, the workers have to obey them. I don't have high hopes for Foxconn's prospects. I think they will close down because the management is so poor. For example, friends of mine working in the department that produces screens for cell phones, they have to produce a thousand pieces, every day, in good condition. However, I learned that maybe half of them are not good quality. They are not up to standard. But this is not reported honestly to the upper management. Maybe out of five hundred bad products, only fifty of them will be reported.

The front-tier manager, the line leader in their department, is responsible for reporting to the upper management, but he doesn't do it honestly. Only the line workers know about that. I think this is a big waste.

But the leaders on every level of the line, they all lie to the upper levels. Because when you are being honest, you get punished. This is very common at Foxconn.

I don't plan to work at Foxconn for a long time. I'm thinking of going into business for myself. But so far I don't have a very clear idea of what

I might do. I haven't yet thought of something that would have good prospects for me. Maybe I'll try something in the IT sector. I would like to be a technician. I would like to be someone with skills.

HYE-KYEONG HAN

AGE: *36*

OCCUPATION: *Former factory worker*

BIRTHPLACE: *Chuncheon, Gangwon Province, South Korea*

INTERVIEWED IN: *Seoul, South Korea*

While manufacturing circuit boards for Samsung, where she had been employed since 1995, Hye-kyeong Han developed unusual symptoms that left her unable to continue working. After a string of visits to various specialists, Hye-kyeong was diagnosed with a brain tumor in 2004, leading her to undergo a number of surgeries and radiation treatments. She was twenty-six at the time. Although Hye-kyeong's cancer is currently in remission, the removal of her cerebellum (the part of the brain responsible for fine muscle movements and maintaining posture and balance) has made speaking and walking difficult. While Hye-kyeong is now able to walk for a few minutes at a time thanks to rehabilitation training, the road to recovery has been slow and difficult.

We interview Hye-kyeong and her mother by phone in 2011. They had arrived at a rehabilitation center in Seoul the day before our conversation. Hye-kyeong answers questions slowly and deliberately, and her mother takes over when Hye-kyeong is tired or unable to respond. Hye-kyeong speaks intently about her determination to hold Samsung accountable for the working conditions that led to her illness, as well as her wishes to prevent similar problems from befalling other young workers within the electronics industry. When we ask Hye-kyeong about her hopes for the future, she begins to sob as she shares her dreams to one day fully recover from her illness.

I WAS JUST AN ORDINARY GIRL

Hye-kyeong

I'm at the hospital right now, in Seoul. But I am originally from the suburb of Chuncheon, the capital of Gangwon Province.[1]

As a child, I was just an ordinary girl. I was healthy—I never had colds. My dream was to become a nurse, or an aerobics instructor, or a massage therapist. I enjoyed reading and listening to music—mostly ballads. I don't have many memories of my elementary school years, but in middle school and high school I had a good friend, a great friend who was like my own sister. Still today, she and I, we really are like sisters. I always think about her without even seeing her, or when I'm not calling her. I know she lives in my heart. I'm really proud of her.

One memory I have of myself as a young girl is from after my graduation from high school. My friend married early, so she, her husband, and I went on a trip to a tiny town called Wontong in the northeast. It was around my birthday, so my friend made breakfast for me, to celebrate. She made so much food—and put it all on one small table—so much food I was afraid that the table would break! This is a very happy memory for me.

---

[1] Chuncheon is a town of 275,000 about forty-six miles northeast of Seoul.

IN ONE SHIFT WE MADE SEVEN HUNDRED LAPTOP SCREENS

Hye-kyeong

I started working for Samsung before my high school graduation, in October 1995. I was eighteen. One day at school there was a job announcement posted from Samsung. It paid well and offered benefits, and Samsung was known as a good company. There were other companies posting offers but Samsung seemed to be the best. Since our class was graduating and looking for jobs, a number of companies sent notices to us. They knew we had to get jobs, but other than Samsung there weren't a lot of good options.

I remember on my first day, I went to a training institute in Gangwon. Once there, we were shut up in a room for training and not allowed to even use the phone. It practically felt like a prison. Life at the training institute felt like total hell to me. We woke up early each morning and, if there was time, had a regular meal. We had to exercise each morning as well. We were taught about semiconductors and how they work, but also about living on our own and stuff like that. It lasted about a month.

The first day at the factory was astonishing. We wore a kind of dust-free apron, a mask, gloves, and special underwear to protect from radiation. Inside the facility it was like, "You go here, and you go there." That was how the foremen talked to us, the line workers. So we went wherever they told us to go. I was told to go to the SMT, the surface-mount technology line. So I went and there were four large machines with several parts and one person was running around doing the work. My first thought was, *So that's what I'm working with.*

We had to memorize the machine parts. The names of the parts were long, too, and there were several types. I would get confused after looking at them and trying to remember them later. At first I didn't have a clue what was going on, but soon it seemed there was no need to memorize anything. I just started to learn it all after going back day after day. In the beginning I just ran around, clueless. But my co-worker told me to look over the machine parts, so I would stand in the middle of the machinery and inspect the exterior of the first one, then do the same with the second, and so on; it was mind-numbing. The machinery was so long that you had to run from one end of it to the other. There was a small opening between two of the machines that we called a dog hole, which we had to crawl in and out of. It was fun but tiring work, and time just flew by.

The product I made was a kind of circuit board called a PCB, or printed circuit board. I'd have to glue lots of tiny wires and electronics parts onto a green board using solder cream. The circuit boards I was gluing together would go into the backs of laptop computer screens. Daily output depended on the model. There must have been a quota, but we just kept working; we were never told a particular number we had to assemble. If we put together everything for one model, they'd change the model and we'd put a different one together. In one shift we made about seven hundred laptop screens.

On average we worked eight-hour shifts and usually did about four hours of overtime—so about twelve hours a day. You could work for six days, then have two days off. Or you could work for ten days doing nine-hour rotations and then get a day off. For bonuses, each individual employee was evaluated on a scale. I remember I got a fridge once. Everyone got one. At that time semiconductors were doing really, really well.

WE EVEN GOT TICKETS TO A THEME PARK

Hye-kyeong's mother

At Samsung, Hye-kyeong earned enough money so she could support herself and our family. We had no house of our own before, but after Hye-kyeong worked at Samsung for three or four years, we were able to buy a little apartment. We lived together in the apartment in Chuncheon—myself, Hye-kyeong, and my three sons.

There were other benefits, too. I went to the Samsung Seoul Hospital in Gangnam and got an endoscopy.[2] I got it for free by using a company coupon that Hye-kyeong gave me. I had blood tests done. At that time I just figured that since my daughter was working at a big company, this was just how they did things there. My friends were even a bit envious of me that I was now getting checkups through my daughter's work. Before that, I'd never had any kind of physical exam, and so I just thought that since my daughter worked at a big company, she could help her mother to live more comfortably. We even got four free tickets to Everland,[3] so Hye-kyeong, my son, my sister, and I went and rode the rides and ate lunch, all for free. At that point I just thought to myself, *Wow, Samsung really is a great company*.

Hye-kyeong

When we received health monitoring at Samsung, a bus would visit the factory from the hospital. Health personnel came to the factory to check our blood and urine and perform X-ray tests. They also tested our vision and hearing acuity. I had a health exam every year. After, I would get the results of the health monitoring, but I could not get an explanation of the results. The health personnel never told me that I was okay. They just said nothing.

---

[2] The Samsung Medical Center in the Gangnam District of Seoul boasts one of the largest cancer-treatment facilities in Asia.

[3] Everland is a theme park southeast of Seoul and is owned by Samsung Group.

LIKE THE SKY IS YELLOW

Hye-kyeong's mother

In 2001, when Hye-kyeong was twenty-three, she was sick all the time. It seemed like she always had a cold. She was so sick that she actually stopped working that year. Then, she started to notice that her menstruation was not regular. My daughter felt very strange all the time. She always had pain in her shoulders. So, in 2004, I took her to a Chuncheon hospital to have her shoulder looked at. They took an X-ray, but nothing showed up. We had absolutely no idea why she felt sick, and no one could tell us anything.

Hye-kyeong went to every kind of doctor. She saw gynecologists about her irregular periods. She went to different doctors because of the pain in her shoulders, and because of the cold or other illness she'd had for a long time. My daughter has been seen by doctors in every field and specialization. Finally, in October 2005, we went to a hospital to take an MRI. That's when we found out that Hye-kyeong had a brain tumor.[4]

When I heard the news, I was flabbergasted, shocked. In Korean, we say, "It looks like the sky is yellow." When the tests were over I stood crying at the sound of the words "brain tumor." Hye-kyeong didn't know how severe the disease was. She asked me, "Mom, what on earth is wrong with me?" I lied to her, saying, "You've got water on your spinal cord. You'll be all right once we can get that water out, just hold on until then." And the next day we went into surgery.

After the surgery, my daughter started chemotherapy. She had chemo treatments three or four times a week. She had radiation treatment forty-one times. In early February 2006, she began a rehabilitation program in

---

[4] For more on the alleged links between cancer and semiconductor manufacture, and the legal battle to obtain compensation for workers in Seoul who develop cancers linked to electronics manufacture, see Appendix III, page 364.

Chuncheon. There was a person there who cared for Hye-kyeong, but I couldn't be with my daughter at that time because I was working at the restaurant I owned. Later that year, I had to close that restaurant so that I could be with my daughter.

After her surgery, Hye-kyeong became seriously disabled in speaking, walking, and in her vision. Those disabilities were so serious she had to get more rehabilitation treatment. But in Korea you cannot stay more than three months at any one hospital and have insurance continue to cover the cost of the stay. So we just moved from hospital to hospital to get those rehabilitation treatments.

Between 2006 and 2008, it was such a difficult time for us. We were traveling very far to each hospital. We had to go to faraway cities. We lived in Chuncheon but we had to go to Wonju City and other places to find a new hospital.[5] Later, in the autumn of 2007, we had to sell our apartment to make money for Hye-kyeong's treatments and our living expenses. Now we live with the support of SHARPS, but before we met SHARPS, we were just living on our savings.[6]

THEY ARE ON THE SIDE OF THOSE WITH MONEY OR POWER

Hye-kyeong's mother

When we moved back to Chuncheon and were at the province's rehabilitation hospital, a social worker from that hospital told us about SHARPS and recommended we contact them because she knew Hye-kyeong used to work with Samsung. In this type of situation it's important to get your

---

[5] Wonju is a city of 310,000 located ninety miles east of Seoul.

[6] SHARPS (Supporters for the Health and Rights of People in the Semiconductor Industry) is a coalition of labor unions and human rights groups that seeks to protect the health and worker rights of semiconductor manufacturing workers.

story out there so I wrote some of it down and asked my son to post it online. In less than three hours I received a call from an attorney with SHARPS, Mr. Lee Jong-ran. And, in three or four days' time, attorney Jong-ran Lee and another activist, Ms. Ae-jung Jung, came and found us at the Gangwon Rehabilitation Hospital.

After we met SHARPS, we applied for the Korea Workers' Compensation and Welfare Service[7] in March 2009. The whole process has been humiliating. KCOMWEL is supposed to be there to console the worker, to take care of them, or at least that is what I thought; but what I have felt from them is that the marble walls inside the building get better treatment than we do. One time, KCOMWEL told me to bring in writing whatever it was that I had to say, so I wrote it all down on a piece of paper. When I arrived, they wouldn't give me an appointment to talk with anyone, so I stuck my paper up on the wall. A woman from KCOMWEL told me to take it down. I said to her, "My daughter can't walk, and she can't even stand up, and I can't take down this paper. Why do you want me to take it down?" Her response was that if I wouldn't take it down then she would and that she'd stick it to my face. That is the kind of treatment we received there. KCOMWEL has become a business.

At first we expected KCOMWEL to consider our case an industrial accident, at the very least. This type of cancer doesn't just appear overnight. There was no phone call or letter or anything from KCOMWEL. We learned our case had been denied from our attorney. Before that I went to KCOMWEL and spoke with one of the directors; I told him about

---

[7] In Korean, the acronym is KCOMWEL. KCOMWEL initially refused to acknowledge a possible link between circuit board manufacture at Samsung and cancer and thus refused to compensate cancer-stricken workers with occupational compensation unless clear, causal links could be established. For more on the Samsung cancer cluster, see Appendix III, page 364.

Hye-kyeong's case and begged him to approve our case. This all happened as I cried on the stairs of the lobby. All that and then we heard only from our attorney about the rejection, and my first thought was, *Of course.* That was my first thought, but I had never actually been put in a position to feel the kind of power a company like Samsung has. Since being rejected on the industrial accident application I've come to realize just what kind of power there is behind money. I can't imagine how hard it must be on our attorney Lee Jong-ran every time he has to call and say that something hasn't been approved.

KCOMWEL refused to compensate us, without giving any reason or making any investigation. They just denied our case. The facility where Hye-kyeong used to work doesn't exist anymore, so frankly speaking, an investigation of her working conditions was not possible. I think something should be done, but the government denied our case. They just refused to compensate us. And I think it's because the government, themselves, are under pressure from Samsung. They are so afraid of Samsung themselves that they don't want to decide anything against them. When I heard the news, I felt like the government is not on the side of powerless workers, only on the side of those with money or power. We were so disappointed.

Hye-kyeong thinks there are still many workers who work as she did in similar facilities doing the same kind of work that Hye-kyeong was doing. KCOMWEL decided to investigate other facilities that were producing similar products to the ones produced in the facility where Hye-kyeong worked. But these other facilities were new—they were totally automatized. They were completely different from the facility where Hye-kyeong worked. So the investigation did not have anything to do with Hye-kyeong's case.

Hye-kyeong

The first time we applied for compensation, I could not speak in public about my experience with Samsung. But later I began to speak in public when my mother and I made a protest visit to the workers' compensation agency, to meet the chairperson about our demands. This was the spring of 2009.

We went because, at some point, we realized that we had to fight this thing. It's natural. If I tell people about it, then the fight will go on. Even if it's not people who actually worked at the factory, if I just tell anybody on the street about it they'll see that Samsung is a bad company. I know since I worked there myself. I know when Samsung is lying or telling the truth.

When I began speaking about Samsung, frankly speaking, I felt like I wanted to hurt Lee Kun-hee, the chairperson of Samsung Electronics. If there are other victims like me—even just one more—then Lee Kun-hee must be punished. I feel it's ridiculous they insist Samsung is such an excellent company; there is nothing good in that company. It's a shame to call Samsung a good company.

IF YOU FIND A PROBLEM IN THE EARLY STAGES, YOU CAN CURE IT

Hye-kyeong's mother

We started rehabilitation again in the fall of 2010. We went to the rehabilitation hospital in Chuncheon for three months before she was discharged. Next she went to the welfare center as an outpatient, then to the National Rehabilitation Center in Seoul for a month for occupational therapy, and then home, and now here. We will stay until the hospital says, "Okay, time to go back home." But this time the hospital is somewhat different from before. It's a special hospital for workers, so we might be able to stay longer than three months. Hye-kyeong's body seems to be getting better and so we'd like to stay here a bit longer. But she's worried that they'll ask her to leave soon.

Hye-kyeong's doctor says that the risk of the cancer recurring is not big because there is no evidence of change, so recurrence may not come. But function in the cerebellum—that was the site of the cancer so the cerebellum was removed—cannot be recovered 100 percent. For the future, this means there are some limitations in living alone and doing things by herself. She cannot walk on her own at all, she needs assistance.

Hye-kyeong

I have something I want to tell the workers at Samsung. We cannot trust the regular health monitoring in Samsung, we cannot believe it. It is so superficial. So I want to suggest to other workers that they collect a small amount of money month by month and get independent health monitoring at least once a year because if you find a problem in its early stages, you can cure it. I want to tell this to other workers.

From my experience at Samsung, I want to tell the people that there are more important things than money, like health. Without health, we cannot live. And please be good to your parents—as good as you can be. And it's the same for Samsung. The bosses and owners at Samsung must have their own sons and daughters, so I hope they look at the workers in this company and realize they are all sons and daughters themselves. Most of them are girls—very young girls. They employ young girls and make them use such bad chemicals, even knowing it is hazardous. Can they not change the toxicity of the harmful substances that Samsung employees have to use to something that isn't harmful? If that could be changed it would make it so much better. They must take responsibility—at least, a part of the responsibility is on the company. They must not avoid it.

When I first started at Samsung, my dream, my hope, was just simple: I wanted to earn money and to learn about technology to buy a house for my family and support my younger brother in his education. I wanted to contribute to those things; I wanted to finish my work, then go back to my hometown and get a house where I hoped to live with my mother. That was my hope and my dream, but then I got this disease. In ten years, I want to walk again. I want to be normal again.

Hye-kyeong has continued to receive treatment for her disability while her family fights in courts to have KCOMWEL acknowledge the link between her illness and her former work with semiconductors. KCOMWEL has denied numerous other cancer-stricken workers' compensation claims on the grounds that establishing a causal link between possible carcinogens and specific cases of cancer is impossible. A ruling on Hye-kyeong's disability claims is scheduled in the spring of 2014.

APPENDICES

I. TIMELINE OF INDUSTRIAL MODERNIZATION

Modern agriculture, electronics, garment, and resource extraction industries all have a tightly interwoven history. The timeline below represents global technological innovations and economic shifts that are especially relevant to the narratives in this book.

1865–1 CE—At the beginning of the common era, the world's population is about 300 million and the vast majority of human industry is agricultural. The total global population grows less than .1 percent a year for the next 1,500 years before rapid growth is made possible by industrial innovation.

1492—Christopher Columbus first arrives in the Bahamas, accelerating a centuries-long competition between European nations to control access to global resources such as precious metals, agricultural goods, and human labor.

1505—The first recorded sugarcane plantation is established in the New World. Soon, enormous demand for sugar at low cost leads to the importation of thousands of slaves kidnapped from Africa.

1529—The Spanish crown grants conquistador Hernán Cortés the entire Oaxacan Valley in Mexico as personal property (an area covering the modern day state of Morelos and parts of Oaxaca). Spain considers all native inhabitants in the valley to be the property of the state. Indigenous Mexicans are forced to work in plantations (known as *haciendas* or *fincas*) and mines owned by Cortés.

1589—William Lee invents the stocking frame, the first fully mechanical loom. Queen Elizabeth I denies Lee a patent with the concern that it would displace handweavers.

1709—Abraham Darby establishes the first European business to produce metal using coke, leading to the development of the steel industry.

1735—Oil sands are mined and the oil extracted at Pechelbronn field in France.

1764—James Hargreaves invents the spinning jenny which allows one person to spin many threads at once.

1769—James Watt patents the steam engine, paving the way for the Industrial Revolution.

1773—The first all-cotton textiles are produced in factories.

1779—Failure to pass a bill regulating the frame-knitting industry in Britain leads to protesters smashing 300 frames and throwing them into the street.

1787—Global cotton production has increased tenfold since 1770. In the first major organized labor action against the garment industry, the Calton weavers of Glasgow, Scotland, go on strike to protest the drop in wages because of cheaper garment imports. After the protesters try to seize materials from strikebreaking weavers, the military opens fire on the crowd and kills six. Strikes and other labor actions by garment workers become increasingly common throughout the United Kingdom.

1790—Richard Arkwright builds the first steam-powered textile factory in Nottingham, England.

1794—Eli Whitney patents the cotton gin, a machine that speeds up the process of removing seeds from cotton fiber. This invention leads to cotton becoming a cash crop in the southern United States, creating a huge demand for slave labor.

1800—The world's population reaches 1 billion. The densest concentrations of people are in China, Europe, and India, with less than 1 percent of the world's population living in North America.

1804—Joseph Marie Jacquard invents the Jacquard loom, a machine that is able to weave complex designs by threading complex patterns of holes in strings of cards. This will later lead to the development of punch cards, a precursor of computer technology.

1808—A bill that would have guaranteed weavers a minimum wage is rejected by the British House of Commons.

1811–19—On March 11, 1811, British soldiers break up a protest for more work and better wages in the textile manufacturing center of Nottingham. That night workers smash textile machinery in a nearby village. This marks the beginning of the Luddite movement.

1812—In April, two thousand protesters mob a mill near Manchester, England. The owner orders his men to fire into the crowd, killing at least three people and wounding eighteen more. The next day, soldiers kill at least five more protesters.

1833—First documented observation of semiconductor effect on silver sulfide by Michael Faraday. Observations of materials that can be manipulated to conduct more or less electricity forms the basis of modern electronics research.

1848—First gold is found in California, marking the beginning of the California Gold Rush.

1849—Dr. Abraham Gesner distills kerosene out of crude oil. Kerosene soon replaces whale oil as a leading light source fuel and creates a new market for crude oil.

1850—Nearly two-thirds of plantation slaves in the southern United States are engaged in the production of cotton.

1854—Ignacy Lukasiewicz drills the first oil wells in Europe in Bóbrka, Poland.

1856—William Perkin invents the first synthetic dye, a petroleum product.

1858—The first oil well in North America is drilled in Ontario, Canada.

1859—Petroleum becomes a major industry in the United States after the oil discovery at Oil Creek, Pennsylvania.

1884—There are 250 coke works in the United States.

1886—Karl Benz and Gottlieb Daimler invent the gasoline-powered car in Stuttgart, Germany, creating a new market for petroleum extraction.

1910—Garment workers strike at the Hart, Schaffner, and Marx factory in Chicago. In 1911, the workers receive a wage increase, as well as a work week capped at fifty-four hours.

1911—One hundred and forty-five workers, including many teenage girls, burn to death in the Triangle Shirtwaist factory in New York City because the factory lacks adequate fire escapes. The incident launches a workers' rights movement in the U.S.

1927—The world's population reaches 2 billion, nearly double that of only one hundred years earlier.

1929—Clothing constitutes the third largest expenditure in the budget of an average American family.

1937—In the U.S., garment unions achieve collective bargaining, the legal framework to negotiate work and wage standards directly with employers.

1943—The Bengal Famine in British-ruled India costs the lives of 4 million people.

1944—The Cooperative Wheat Research and Production Program, a joint venture by the Rockefeller Foundation and the Mexican Ministry of Agriculture, begins its mission of boosting wheat production in Mexico. Norman Borlaug, the "father" of the Green Revolution, is one of the original members.

1945—Norman Borlaug becomes director of the Cooperative Wheat Research and Production Program in Mexico. Early attempts to breed high yield crops such as wheat and rice are not successful, as early varietals aren't strong enough to support the weight of their own produce.

1947—John Bardeen, Walter Brattain, and William Shockley of Bell Labs invent the transistor, an important innovation in the development of modern electronic devices like radios and computers.

1948—The United Nations releases its Universal Declaration of Human Rights, prohibiting slavery and the slave trade "in all its forms."

1954—Texas Instruments develops the first transistor radio. Gordon Teal, who came from Bell Labs, and his team at Texas Instruments develop the first commercial silicon transistor.

1955—William Shockley leaves Bell Labs and forms Shockley Semiconductor Laboratory.

1956—Bardeen, Brattain, and Shockley win the Nobel Prize in physics for their semiconductor research leading to the point contact transistor.

1956—Mexico becomes self-sufficient in wheat production by growing more than forty new high-yield wheat strains developed in part by Norman Borlaug.

1957—Sony introduces the pocket-sized TR-63 transistor radio, creating the first consumer market for transistor radios.

1958—Jack Kilby and Robert Noyce develop the first integrated circuit at Texas Instruments.

1960—The world's population reaches 3 billion, a growth of 50 percent in just over thirty years. Innovations in antibiotics and sanitation reduce infant mortality rates across the globe.

—The International Rice Research Institute (IRRI) is founded with support from the Ford Foundation, the Rockefeller Foundation, and the government of the Philippines. The IRRI will go on to breed high-yield strains of rice that are less likely to get too heavy and fall over.

1963—Norman Borlaug begins testing high-yielding semi-dwarf wheat varieties in India and Pakistan with the help of Asian scientists who had observed the development of successful strains in Mexico. The Mexican wheat varieties perform exceptionally well.

1964–66—Globally, human beings consume on average 2,358 calories per capita per day.

1965—Gordon Moore, director of Research & Development at Fairchild Semiconductor, predicts that the number of transistors on an integrated circuit doubles approximately every two years, which will later serve as yardstick for the exponential growth of technology and called "Moore's Law."

1966—Annual rice production in the Philippines increases from 3.7 to 7.7 million tons in the next two decades after the introduction of rice strains developed by the International Rice Resource Institute. India adapts the new rice strains in 1966 as well, and rice yields in India triple from two tons per hectare in the 1960s to six tons per hectare in the mid-1990s.

1968—Robert Noyce and Gordon Moore leave Fairchild Semiconductor to found Intel.

1974—The world's population adds another billion in only fourteen years. The growth rate has nearly doubled since the early 20th century.

1974–76—Globally, human beings consume on average 2,435 calories per capita per day, a 3 percent increase compared to 1964. In developing countries, humans consume on average 2,152 calories per capita per day, a 4.8 percent increase compared to 1964. In developed nations they consume 3,065 calories per capita per day, a 4 percent increase compared to 1964.

1987—The world's population reaches 5 billion.

1990s—With the emergence of biotechnology, especially genetic engineering, the origins of innovation in agriculture have shifted from public institutions to the private sector. The ability to patent artificially constructed genes and genetically modified plants is now a great profit incentive for private companies.

1998—The Consumer Electronics Association estimates that there are 1.6 billion consumer electronic devices in the country.

1997–99—Globally, human beings consume on average 2,803 calories per capita per day, an 18.8 percent increase compared to 1964. In developing countries humans consume on average 2,681 calories per capita per day, a 30.5 percent increase compared to 1964. In developed nations they consume 3,380 calories per capita per day, a 14.7 percent increase compared to 1964.

1999—The world's population reaches 6 billion.

—By the end of the twentieth century, more than 98 percent of Americans own televisions, and more than 50 percent own cell phones. By the end of the following decade, more than 80 percent of Americans own cell phones and 75 percent of Americans own computers.

2013—The world's population has surpassed 7 billion.

II. GLOSSARY

arbitration board: A panel made up of impartial but informed individuals who are tasked with resolving disputes between two or more parties such as workers and employers.

Bt crops: Crops that have been genetically modified to produce a toxin derived from the bacteria *Bacillus thuringiensis*. The toxin present in Bt crops is harmful to insects but not humans. First approved by the US Environmental Protection Agency in 1995, Bt genes have been added to numerous corn, cotton, potatoes, tobacco, and other crops throughout the world.

cancer cluster: A concentration of reported cancer diagnoses that exceeds the expectations of epidemiologists in a geographical area. Epidemiologists examine cancer clusters in an attempt to identify possible environmental carcinogens such as industrial waste or other types of pollution.

collective bargaining: Negotiation between employers and employee representatives to determine conditions of employment including wages, standard working hours, overtime pay, health and safety standards, and procedures for addressing grievances.

collective bargaining agreement: A contract negotiated directly between unionized workers and their employers. Collective bargain agreements often set terms including minimum compensation for workers, overtime pay, severance pay, and the rights of workers to have grievances addressed.

closed shop: Workplaces where membership in a union is a prerequisite for hire. Open shops are workplaces where workers can choose to be members of the union or not. Advocates of closed shops argue that non-union employees in open shops dilute the bargaining power of unions in negotiating with employers.

commodity crops/cash crops: Crops grown and sold for profit rather than subsistence. Many family-operated farms throughout the world divide their land use between cash crops such as cotton and subsistence crops such as vegetables and livestock feed.

cost of living: The expenses needed to provide a defined standard of living that may include access to food, clothing shelter, transportation, and medicine.

daywork: A compensation system where workers are paid for each day of labor, rather than an hourly wage.

developed nations: There is no broadly agreed upon definition of developed versus developing nations, though criteria used to describe developed nations include diverse industrial and economic output, high per capita income, and stable government. The list of fully developed nations often includes the U.S., Canada, much of Europe, Japan and South Korea, Taiwan, Singapore, Australia, and New Zealand.

dowry: A distribution of wealth or property to the family of the groom from the family of the bride at the time of a marriage. Dowries are an ancient custom and exist in many cultures today. Traditionally, dowries were a way to provide for the bride's livelihood in the case of widowhood, and a way to strengthen the relationships between two families joined by marriage.

Dutch Disease: An economic phenomenon whereby the discovery of valuable natural resources introduces instability into a nation's economy, ultimately limiting growth rather than expanding it. The phenomenon is named after an episode in which natural gas deposits discovered off the coast of the Netherlands damaged the country's economy by driving up the cost of currency and making the cost of other Dutch exports uncompetitive.

economies of scale: Advantages in cost of production and distribution available when producing in greater quantities. For example, large industrial farms spend less per acre to plant, fertilize, and harvest than small farms, thus allowing the large farms to sell their produce at a lower cost.

exchange rate: The value of one country's currency against another. Large international banks help determine exchange rates by trading currency in what is called the foreign exchange market. Relative values of different currencies are continuously changing and determine the costs of importing and exporting goods between countries.

export processing zones: See free trade zone.

finca: The name for a large plantation or ranch in many Latin American countries such as Guatemala. During the era of European colonization, fincas were the property of European landowners, and indigenous farm laborers known as *campesinos* or *peons* (peasants) would essentially be the property of the *patrón*, or landowner.

finished goods: Manufactured goods ready for market, distinct from raw materials and component parts that go into making finished goods.

food security: People who are neither malnourished nor in danger of starvation are described as food secure by sociologists.

fossil fuels: Hydrocarbon fuels such as petroleum, coal, and natural gas that are formed from ancient deposits of organic matter. Fossil fuels are considered a nonrenewable resource in that they can't be replaced once extracted from the earth.

free trade: A policy whereby two or more countries don't impose tariffs or otherwise interfere with imports and exports amongst themselves. Free trade agreements exist between the U.S. and numerous countries, including the North American Free Trade Agreement (1994) between the U.S., Canada, and Mexico.

free trade zone: Also called export processing zones, free trade zones are municipalities or regions within a country that are exempt from customs and tariffs and sometimes local or national laws and regulations. Free trade zones have existed for centuries, especially in port and coastal areas in Europe where they were known as free ports. Today, free trade zones exist throughout the developing world as a way to attract international investment. Examples of free trade mentioned in this book include Shenzhen, China; Butibori, India; Chambishi, Zambia; the suburbs of Dhaka, Bangladesh; and Tehuacán, Mexico.

genetically modified organism (GMO): Any organism that has had its genetic makeup altered through genetic engineering. Genetically modified foods (GM foods) have been engineered for higher yields, greater pest and drought resistance, and other advantages, but they remain controversial due to fears about risks they may pose to human health and the environment.

globalization: The integration of economies, politics, cultures, and languages between countries and peoples around the world.

grievance: In labor relations, a grievance is the formal process by which an individual union member or a group of union workers bargain with their employer to address potential violations of their labor agreement. Grievances may be brought due to safety concerns, wrongful termination, policies related to overtime pay, or individual conflicts between a worker and that worker's manager.

informal economy: Economic activity that is not taxed, regulated, or closely monitored by a governing body. In developing countries, the informal economy can make up more than half of all economic activity and include sales of produce or homemade goods at village markets.

just cause: In labor contracts, just cause refers to a defined set of reasons for dismissing or disciplining workers such as documented incompetence, insubordination, or negligence. Many countries have labor laws that outline principles of just cause, and workers that are laid off or fired without just cause may often be entitled to unemployment compensation, severance pay, or other forms of compensation.

labor contract: An agreement about conditions of labor including wages, safety precautions, overtime rules, and grievance procedures that is negotiated between employees and employers.

labor contractor: A service that manages workers for a farm or factory. Labor contractors often serve as intermediaries between workers and owners.

layoff: Termination of employees on a permanent or temporary basis when a company believes the size of its workforce is larger than needed based on consumer demand. In most jurisdictions, layoffs differ from termination with cause in that laid off employees may be eligible for severance pay or unemployment compensation.

living wage: The minimum necessary wage needed to meet basic needs such as nutrition, shelter, transportation, and medical care. Living wage standards vary from community to community depending on the cost of living in a given community.

lockout: In a labor dispute, a lockout occurs when the employer closes some or all operations and excludes workers from coming to work and earning a wage. This is opposed to a strike, in which the employees attempt to close operations by refusing to come to work or otherwise attempting to shut down a business's operations.

mega factory: A manufacturing center that uses economies of scale to produce goods more cheaply. Mega factories may have tens of thousands or even hundreds of thousands of employees within one factory compound.

maquila: A manufacturing center in a Mexican free trade zone. Products manufactured in maquilas are not subject to taxes or tariffs and are established in an attempt to lure international investment into Mexico. The maquila system is similar to the special economic zones established in China, India, and elsewhere.

mono-cropping: Dedication of farmland to a single cash crop such as cotton. Though mono-cropping allows farmers to concentrate on a single profitable crop, the practice risks depleting the soil and spreading invasive pests and disease.

non-governmental organization (NGO): An organization that has social or political goals but is not part of a political party or governmental agency.

open shop: A business where employees are not required to pay into or join a union as part of the hiring process. Businesses where this is a requirement are called closed shops.

overtime: The amount of time employees work beyond defined regular hours. In many countries, labor regulations require employers to compensate employees working overtime with a higher rate of pay, and sometimes caps are put on the amount of overtime employees can work.

pesticide: Any of a number of chemicals used to destroy invasive plants, insects, and other forms of life that might eat or damage crops. Numerous pesticides have been linked to adverse health effects in humans such as cancers, nervous system disorders, and birth defects. According to the World Health Organization, pesticide exposure may be directly responsible for as many as eighteen thousand deaths a year. Pesticides include insecticides, which are used to destroy insects, and herbicides, which kill off unwanted plants.

piecework: A system of payment based on the number of units a worker produces rather than the hours that they work. For instance, workers in a garment factory may be paid for the number of jeans they sew in a day rather than the length of their shifts.

plantation: An estate where crops are produced mostly for sale on the market rather than for subsistence. The word has no precise definition but often implies a very large commercial farming operation geared to international export.

semiconductor: A materials that can conduct energy at variable rates depending on factors such as heat, light, and other inputs. Semiconductors can be used to control and modify electrical impulses, and their manipulation is the basis of modern electronics.

severance pay: Money paid to workers who are dismissed from a company without cause.

shop steward: Representatives elected by unions who help ensure employer compliance with labor contracts. When workers file grievances, their shop stewards interview them, investigate the situation, and help them argue their case with their supervisors and managers.

slowdown: A form of worker protest in which workers continue to perform assigned work at a slower rate. Slowdowns allow workers to threaten a business's productivity while not resorting to a full strike.

special economic zone (SEZ): A region within a country that has been granted exemptions from most federal taxes and labor regulations in order to keep export prices competitive on the global market. Numerous SEZs have been established in urban manufacturing areas in China, India, Africa, and elsewhere in the developing world. See also free trade zone.

strike: In labor relations, a strike occurs when employees agree amongst themselves to stop working for a defined or undefined period of time. Strikes are meant to shut down production and pressure employers to address grievances related to wages, working conditions, or working hours.

strikebreaker: Also known as "scabs," strikebreakers are workers who refuse to join strikes or other labor actions, thus lessening their effectiveness.

subsistence farming: Crops grown to be used for the dietary needs of a farmer's family and livestock.

Superfund site: Land anywhere in the U.S. that has been designated contaminated by materials hazardous to humans or the environment and marked as a candidate for clean-up and decontamination.

tariff: A tax on imported goods. Tariffs are designed to protect the competitiveness of local industries by increasing the cost of imported goods for consumers.

tort: a civil liability or wrongdoing that is sufficient grounds for a lawsuit.

trade agreement: A formal arrangement between countries to hold down tariffs and other protections to trade and allow import and export to take place.

unemployment compensation: Temporary payments awarded by some national or local jurisdictions to workers who have been part of layoffs or who have otherwise registered as unemployed. Typically, workers who have chosen to leave companies on their own or who have been fired with cause are not entitled to unemployment compensation.

union: A group of workers who have formally organized to negotiate better wages or working conditions from employers. Unions may be as small as a group of employees working for a single company, or they may be national organizations (AFL-CIO), or even be international in scope.

workers' compensation insurance: An agreement whereby employers purchase insurance that provides some wage compensation and medical coverage in the case of workplace accidents. As part of most workers' compensation insurance agreements, workers forfeit most rights to sue employers for additional compensation.

III. HISTORICAL CAPSULES

The following are supplemental histories that offer deeper context for some of the narratives included in this book.

FACTORY ACCIDENTS IN BANGLADESH

In April 2013, the collapse of a factory in Bangladesh's Rana Plaza that had produced clothing for many Western clothing companies made headlines worldwide. Killing more than 1,100 workers, the collapse was the deadliest disaster in the history of the garment industry.

Over the past two decades, multinational companies have broken up the assembly of their goods into many small parts and distributed single, simple tasks to small factories and subfactories across the world, which the multinationals often do not directly own or operate. Rana Plaza sat at one end of one of these long supply chains of global outsourcing and subcontracting. Some factories at Rana Plaza assembled clothes for up to forty larger companies.

The creation of so many middlemen often means that the details of workers' rights and safety regulations are enforced only to local standards, or not at all—which can be part of what allows a factory to make the cheapest bid for a work contract. A large part of the shock felt in the aftermath of the collapse was due to a new awareness among American and European customers of how their clothes are made, and that there is a direct link between cheap goods at home and worker safety issues abroad.

A post-collapse investigation of Rana Plaza found that the building's structural faults were well known to authorities, and that the upper four floors had been constructed illegally, without permits. Safety violations like these are unfortunately common in many subcontracted factories, where effort is largely focused on producing the greatest number of goods in the shortest possible time. The Rana Plaza collapse was unique for its magnitude, but fires and other building collapses are not uncommon; a fire that killed 112 workers the previous November also made news across the world.

Bangladesh is the world's second-leading garment exporter, trailing only China, and has more than five thousand garment factories. Activists and labor-rights organizers had attempted to bring attention to Bangladesh's working conditions for many years, but the size of the industry and its importance to

Bangladesh's national economy made government leaders reluctant to make changes that could increase costs, and possibly cost them work from foreign brands looking to pay as little as the market would bear. And even after the collapse, most brands have been slow to pressure local governments to implement higher safety standards.

NAFTA AND THE MAQUILAS

The North American Free Trade Agreement, known as NAFTA, is an agreement between the United States, Canada, and Mexico that attempted to remove many of the barriers to trade across North America. In effect since 1994, it set out to create a broad, shared market across the three countries. In theory, each would benefit from increased exports—even though their domestic economies at the time were marked by some very significant differences. Ideally, with the removal or lowering of tariffs on a wide spectrum of consumer goods, manufacturers would be able to ship items across borders more easily, and this would result in lower prices, more jobs in places where they were needed, and a decrease in illegal immigration across North American borders.

As NAFTA took effect, however, it brought many unexpected changes, and the treaty has become not only a source of perennial debate about the implications of free trade but also a symbol of the unavoidable interconnectedness of economics with politics. Trade did increase overall, but not without creating numerous problems. In the United States, factories began to close in parts of the country that had strong histories of labor and environmental protections. Large companies found they could increase their profits by moving many U.S. manufacturing jobs to Mexico and taking advantage of local laws allowing employees to be paid less and receive fewer benefits. With workers competing for increasingly scarce jobs in some of the areas where factories closed, wages decreased. Additionally, the growth of manufacturing jobs in Mexico did not markedly decrease immigration to the United States, and the social costs of a more competitive economy were felt strongly in the two countries. (Canada's government-provided social services created a relatively resilient safety net there.) In general, NAFTA provided many advantages for multinational businesses, but few for labor. By the end of the decade, with the pull of globalization stronger than ever, many of these types of factories moved out of the NAFTA region altogether, taking the opportunities for work with them.

In Mexico, many of the new jobs were limited to low-skill factory work in maquilas, or Mexican factories that operate in free-trade zones created by Mexico's government. The concept was originally established in the mid-1960s, but NAFTA incentivized a great expansion of the maquila system, with unavoidable effects on its purpose. Factory towns began to attract workers from Mexico's faraway rural areas, many of whom left farming because they could not compete with waves of cheaper, imported produce. Additionally, the maquila workforce, which had previously been composed mostly of women, saw a rapid increase of men and children.

Although millions of Mexicans had moved to the border region by the end of NAFTA's first decade, the factories there often failed to support local growth or generate strong communities nearby. Instead, many of the benefits went to the largest, most efficient companies that could best exploit reduced trade tariffs. Many large companies that could take advantage of economies of scale would purchase raw materials cheaply and then subcontract goods manufacture to small maquilas in Mexico or nearby Latin American countries with even looser regulation of labor and wage standards.

By all measures, the gap between rich and poor in Mexico widened, and some experts began to call the industry in the maquila area "high-productivity poverty"—a new phenomenon in which industrial growth failed to produce a higher standard of living.

AGRICULTURAL TECHNOLOGY IN INDIA

In the middle of the twentieth century, a skyrocketing population coupled with a series of droughts created widespread hunger and malnutrition in India. The country's population growth began to outrun the limits of its agriculture. By the mid-1960s, India began to utilize agricultural research and technology first developed in more heavily industrialized countries, especially related to rice, wheat, and cotton. The expanded use of pesticides, fertilizers, and improved irrigation, and of seeds bred especially to create high crop yields and grow year-round, diminished the food problem as well as the percentage of the population living below the poverty line. This period of agricultural growth came to be known as the "Green Revolution."

Soon after the turn of the century, however, experts began to wonder if the benefits of the Green Revolution had run their course. Some Indian farmers, who now had access to a global marketplace, looked to increase their profits by selling cash crops rather than staples in the local markets. During economic downturns, small-scale farms reliant on cash crop sales would often fall into insurmountable debt. Environmental damage and water shortages due to the agricultural changes began to threaten future crops. Additionally, a dependence on genetically modified seeds, designed and patented by international conglomerates, limits farmers to a small number of suppliers, further constraining their choices regarding seed cost, quality, and availability.

For crops like cotton, Bt seeds, modified to be toxic to some insects, account for 95 percent of all farming in the country. Although corporate representatives and industry groups extol the benefits of GMO crops, small farmers have seen costs rise faster than crop yields. Many have begun to wonder if their overall situation has improved, and suicides of severely indebted farmers regularly make local headlines.

AGRICULTURE AND IMMIGRANT LABOR IN THE UNITED STATES

In the United States, undocumented workers make up a greater proportion of the labor force in agriculture and farming than any other field (with groundskeeping and construction close behind). Exact numbers are difficult to measure, but recent studies estimate that even when temporary workers are excluded, one-quarter to one-half of U.S. farmworkers are undocumented immigrants—though other estimates argue that because numbers like these rely on self-reporting, they are significantly deflated.

Working without legal papers, especially in rural areas, makes undocumented workers vulnerable in ways that citizens and authorized residents are not. The available reporting has found that undocumented farm workers consistently receive lower wages than documented workers performing the same jobs. Additionally, the threat of disclosure to immigration authorities, which can mean deportation and separation from children and families, has been used to prevent workers from reporting violence, sexual assault, and harassment.

The dangers are compounded for children who are undocumented agricultural workers, or who may be documented but working alongside their undocumented parents. The risk of a fatal injury for children employed as farmworkers—both documented and undocumented—is more than four times that faced by other working youth.

Undocumented workers in the U.S. are protected by a number of federal and state labor laws, and have been at the center of a long national debate about immigration reform. In addition to general constitutional protections such as equal protection and due process, undocumented workers have a legal right to minimum wage and other benefits mandated by wage laws, workers' compensation for on-the-job injuries, child labor laws, a safe workplace, and participation in a union. Workplace discrimination against undocumented workers is also illegal. Additionally, some states, rather than waiting for Congress to finalize immigration reform, have taken steps to expand undocumented workers' rights locally. In 2013, for example, California approved laws making it more difficult for state law enforcement to detain immigrants, allowing undocumented immigrants to apply for driver's licenses, and allowing undocumented workers to practice law—the latter based on the case of an undocumented immigrant who was brought to the U.S. as a baby, raised there, and graduated from a California law school.

Employer retaliation against workers who attempt to enforce any of these rights is also illegal, but the workers may be forced to disclose their status if an employment claim leads to litigation. Because of the potential consequences of this, many workplace violations remain unreported.

CHINA AND ZAMBIA

Although China has been organizing construction and finance projects in Africa since the 1970s, it has become Africa's largest trading partner over the last decade, a period when its share of the continent's exports rose from 1 percent to 15 percent. Today there are approximately five hundred Chinese companies at work in Zambia, bringing a population of one hundred thousand Chinese into the country of only fourteen million—although a language barrier means the two populations live largely separate lives. Zambia has the third-highest level of Chinese foreign investment of all countries worldwide and by 2011 its capital, Lusaka, had become the first African city to provide banking service in Chinese currency.

The current era of foreign business interest in Zambia began in 1997, when, after two decades of falling copper prices, the government began to sell state-owned mines. The next year, a state-owned Chinese enterprise bought the majority interest in the copper mine in Chambishi, updated the mine's equipment, and, in 2003, reopened it for production.

Underground mining is dangerous work, but the Chinese-run mines took on an unusually bad reputation within Zambia for health and safety. They became a source of complaints about labor abuses, including union busting and pay below the national minimum wage. Dissatisfaction over such conditions led to worker riots and protests that sometimes turned violent. Workers have allegedly been threatened with being fired for reporting dangerous conditions—including acid burns resulting from gloves or boots not replaced often enough—and many accidents go unreported. A 2005 explosion at a Chinese-owned manufacturing plant in Chambishi resulted in forty-six deaths. In 2006, management and private security at a Chinese-owned mining company shot at least six miners during riots over work conditions. Riots and work protests have continued sporadically; in 2010, when several hundred workers protested conditions at Collum Coal Mine, two Chinese managers shot thirteen protesters. Large strikes followed in 2011, and in 2012 rioting workers crushed a Chinese supervisor to death with a mining cart.

In 2007, Zambia became the first African site for one of China's "special economic zones," an area where Chinese investors could manufacture and export goods without having to pay taxes to the Zambian government. Zambia–China relations and the pros and cons of Chinese investment—jobs and economic growth on the one hand versus the dangers of pollution and unsafe working conditions on the other—have become a perennial topic in Zambian political debates, and a major campaign issue in presidential elections.

THE BOUGAINVILLE REVOLUTION

Bougainville lies at the north end of the Solomon Islands, just east of Papua New Guinea and six degrees south of the equator. The island is 40 miles across, 121 miles tip to tip. Bougainville has been inhabited for more than twenty thousand years and was settled over the millennia by a number of different migrant populations: by the time French explorer Louis-Antoine de Bougainville landed on the island in 1768, over a dozen distinct languages were in use there, spoken by the island's few thousand inhabitants.

The Germans took control of Bougainville in 1884, seizing land for huge coconut plantations and drafting Bougainvilleans as laborers. Then, after World War I, Bougainville passed into British and Australian hands. The Japanese invaded Bougainville in 1942, and Allied forces then seized control of the island over a span of two years of intense fighting. Following the war, Australia governed Bougainville as part of a mandate covering Papua New Guinea (PNG).

In 1964, prospectors from Bougainville Copper Ltd. (BCL) began exploratory drilling in the Panguna valley in central Bougainville. BCL was 56 percent owned by ConZinc Rio Tinto Australia, a subsidiary of global mining conglomerate Rio Tinto. Through a land-leasing arrangement, 20 percent of BCL was owned by the PNG government.

Once Rio Tinto learned the extent of the Panguna copper deposit, it began digging the world's largest open-pit mine. The Panguna mine operations displaced nearby residents, sliced into the mountainside, and washed debris down to the sea. Over the seventeen years of the mine's operation, from 1972 to 1989, waste from the mines dammed the Jaba and Kawerong Rivers, flooding low-lying farmlands, and tainting the island's limited fresh water supply.

Papua New Guinea gained independence from Australia in 1975, and its share of profit from the mine became its largest source of national income, after Australian aid. To develop infrastructure for Rio Tinto's operations, the PNG government appropriated thousands of acres from Bougainville landowners.

In November 1988, a small group led by Francis Ona—a landowner and surveyor for the mine, whose objections to the environmental damage caused by the mine went ignored by Rio Tinto and the PNG government—blew up the mine's electricity pylons with some of Rio Tinto's own dynamite. Shortly afterward, Ona and his supporters began gathering troops for the Bougainville Revolutionary Army. Rio Tinto shut down the mine in May 1989, but called on PNG to send troops and riot police to reopen the mine; the conflict soon escalated to open war.

In 1990, PNG imposed a total blockade of Bougainville, and an estimated fifteen thousand Bougainvilleans died as a result of the seven-year-long siege that lasted until 1997.

In 1997, PNG decided to bring in mercenaries from the British firm Sandline International. PNG defense force commander Jerry Singirok opposed the move and had the mercenaries arrested as soon as they landed on Bougainville. Singirok was himself arrested by the PNG government, but soldiers in PNG's central barracks rebelled at the decision. The rebellion, as well as broad public sympathy in both Papua New Guinea and Australia for Bougainvilleans, soon impelled the PNG government to agree to end the blockade and negotiate peace.

The peace process spanned five years and ended in 2001 with a treaty that granted Bougainville a high degree of autonomy and provided for a deferred referendum on full independence and the reopening of the Panguna mine. The date for these referendum votes has been consistently pushed back; the votes are yet to be held as of early 2014.

NIGERIA AND SHELL OIL

While the discovery of oil in Nigeria transformed the country over the second half of the twentieth century, its production has, according to Human Rights Watch, "enriched a small minority while the vast majority have become increasingly impoverished," and created power struggles among the military and government elite. One recent analysis estimated that the wealthiest 1 percent of the Nigerian population collects almost 85 percent of the country's oil revenues.

Although the Nigerian constitution states that the national government owns all oil discovered in the country, anger at the wealth imbalance has sparked protests from communities that receive little benefit from drilling on their land yet suffer the effects of severe environmental damage. In the 1990s, a protest against the federal government and Shell Oil by tens of thousands of Ogonis, an ethnic group from a major oil-producing region, began to receive international attention. Ogoni leaders founded the Movement for the Survival of the Ogoni People, known as MOSOP, which demanded political and economic autonomy for Ogoniland and accused Shell of genocide. In 1993, MOSOP organized mass protests that caused Shell to end drilling in the oil-rich region, though some of the company's pipelines that passed through the area were left in place. Security forces organized by the Nigerian government and by Shell soon cracked down on protesters, many of whom were detained, beaten, or executed. Subsequent newspaper investigations discovered that Shell tried to arrange for weapons to be imported into Nigeria.

When WikiLeaks (the international non-profit organization that publishes classified information online) released U.S. embassy communications in 2010, they revealed the relationship between Shell executives and the Nigerian government in greater depth: Shell not only employed its own security force, trained by the Nigerian government, but claimed to have staff in every main government ministry. Executives told diplomats that the company knew "everything that was being done" by officials in those ministries.

In 2011, the United Nations completed a fourteen-month environmental study of over two hundred locations in Ogoniland, concluding that many of the areas Shell had declared clean were still polluted, areas that appeared clean on the surface were severely contaminated underground, and an environmental restoration could take thirty years. In one community, drinking water was contaminated with benzene, a carcinogen, at more than nine hundred times what is generally considered the maximum safe level. Little progress has been made on the cleanup since, and most Nigerian farmers who have attempted to sue Shell in international court had their cases dismissed before a verdict could be reached (see also Alien Tort Statute, page 362).

THE BHOPAL DISASTER AND AFTERMATH

On the morning of December 3, 1984, an explosion at the Union Carbide India Limited pesticide plant in Bhopal, India, led to a massive leak of toxic gasses and other chemicals into the surrounding community. Between that night and the following few days, as many as four thousand residents of Bhopal died, largely from exposure to methyl isocyanate, a chemical used in pesticides that causes severe nerve and respiratory damage in humans.

Immediately after the leak, the "Bhopal disaster" became one of the most infamous industrial incidents ever, and news of the catastrophe introduced scores of people worldwide to the dangers of industrialization in the developing world, and the ability of foreign investment to influence local regulatory and legal environments.

The leak itself was preceded by significant corporate neglect. By 1984, famine and crop failures decreased the local demand for pesticide in the period preceding the leak, and Union Carbide, the American company that was operating the plant, had made plans to dismantle most of the facility and move production elsewhere. Until this process could be completed, the plant continued to operate below capacity, and with markedly reduced safety procedures and equipment. By the time of the leak in the early morning of December 3, many devices meant to ensure safety had already been disassembled or taken out of operation. Within the first few days, the leak had reached forty tons and killed an estimated four thousand people, blinding and injuring many others. Aside from methyl isocyanate, heavy metals such as arsenic were released into the local groundwater supply, and other toxic chemicals used in pesticide manufacture also contaminated nearby soil and water resevervoirs. Bhopal has experienced an abnormal rate of birth defects and premature deaths in the two decades since.

In the disaster's aftermath, Union Carbide attempted to avoid all legal responsibility, at first blaming an Indian subsidiary and raising the possibility of sabotage. Eventually, in February 1989, the company settled with the Indian government, agreeing to pay $470 million for victim compensation—a sum so much lower than expected that shares in Union Carbide stock rose 7 percent following the announcement. There were no criminal convictions until 2010, when a New Delhi court convicted eight former executives of Union Carbide's Indian subsidiary of neglect. In the time since the disaster, one of the executives had already died; the others are expected to appeal. At the time of the verdict, the disaster site still contained 425 tons of uncleared hazardous waste.

ALIEN TORT STATUTE

The U.S. Alien Tort Statute is a section of the U.S. Judiciary Act of 1789 that has been used by non-U.S. citizens to bring lawsuits in U.S. courts. The text of the statute reads: "The district courts shall have original jurisdiction of any civil action by an alien for a tort only, committed in violation of the law of nations or a treaty of the United States."[1]

The statute was largely unused in courts through most of the nineteenth and twentieth centuries. Then, in 1980, two Paraguayan citizens legally residing in the United States sued another Paraguayan citizen, a former police officer in Paraguay's capital, Asunción, also residing in the United States. The plaintiffs alleged that the former police officer had tortured and murdered their son in Paraguay. In *Filártiga v. Peña-Irala*, the plaintiffs successfully argued that torture was prohibited under international common law and that U.S. courts had jurisdiction to hear their claim under the Alien Tort Statute. Since the case, dozens of other claimants have used the statute as a basis for successful lawsuits.

Suits have also been brought by U.S. residents against foreign corporations for alleged crimes committed overseas. In 2000, residents of the island of Bougainville near Papua New Guinea brought suit against multinational mining conglomerate Rio Tinto in U.S. court. The suit was led by Alexis Holyweek Sarei, a California resident who had resided in Bougainville for decades, as well as other former citizens of Bougainville. In *Sarei v. Rio Tinto PLC*, the plaintiffs argued that the company's copper-mining operations had poisoned the island and made much of it uninhabitable. The Bougainvilleans successfully had their case heard in lower courts before it was taken up by the Supreme Court in 2013.

While *Sarei* was ongoing, a similar lawsuit was filed by former citizens of

---

[1] In court systems, a tort is a civil law claim of harm. For more information, see glossary, page 384.

Nigeria against Royal Dutch Petroleum in 2002. *Kiobel v. Royal Dutch Petroleum* was brought by refugees who had fled Nigeria to the United States after suffering alleged torture and the extrajudicial killing of family members by the Nigerian government with the alleged cooperation and aid of a subsidiary of Shell Oil.

In April 2013, the U.S. Supreme Court unanimously ruled in *Kiobel v. Royal Dutch Petroleum* that the U.S. courts had no authority to adjudicate claims against corporations that were based mostly outside of the United States. In light of their ruling, they also dismissed *Sarei v. Rio Tinto PLC*. Human rights organizations have claimed the Supreme Court's decision makes it difficult for victims of human rights abuses carried out with the cooperation of multinational corporations to hold those corporations legally responsible.

CHINA AND SPECIAL ECONOMIC ZONES

In the late 1970s, China began to open itself to the world market with a series of capitalist-style reforms that included the creation of special economic zones: areas the country designated with tax breaks, investment incentives, and looser regulatory requirements, meant to encourage foreign investment in China. These "reform laboratories" were located outside of China's most populated areas. Shenzhen, which had been a fishing and farming town on the China–Hong Kong border, was the first special economic zone established at the outset of the new policy.

By 2007, the official population of Shenzhen had increased from thirty thousand to 8.6 million, with possibly another four to six million uncounted, temporary workers. Shenzhen had become an "instant city," populated largely by young Chinese people who had left their hometowns to work in one of the many factories that had come to the area as China became a manufacturing superpower. Because of the rate of its growth, Shenzhen is not built around a dense city center that expanded over time, but has many dispersed "centers" connected by highway. Today China has more than a dozen special economic zones, and has designated over fifty areas for other types of economic and technological development.

As in other regions across the globe, fast industrial growth in China's special economic zones came at the cost of environmental damage and poor workplace conditions. Common challenges included twelve-hour shifts of repetitive work with intense production quotas and little room for error, and managers who often shirked rules that allowed employees to rest, socialize, or avoid excessive overtime. Awareness of these conditions began to grow in the Western world, especially around 2010 and 2011, when Foxconn, an electronics company that makes iPhones, Sony PlayStations, and Dell computers in Shenzhen, began ringing its buildings with nets after eleven separate incidents in which workers jumped to their deaths (additional workers had jumped but survived their injuries).

Around the same time, workers began to share stories of their experiences in increasingly public venues. After enduring weeks of bad publicity, companies like Apple, Hewlett-Packard, and Intel began to take a more direct role in monitoring the conditions of workers subcontracted to manufacture their products. Many of these companies encouraged reforms such as more vigorous workplace inspections and audits, a stop to illegal overtime and other violations of Chinese law, stronger safety policies, and mental health support.

THE REPUBLIC OF SAMSUNG

Around 2004, some journalists and business commentators began referring to South Korea as the "Republic of Samsung," noting the oversized influence of the company on its home country. Although known throughout the world mostly for mobile phones, semiconductors, and electronics, Samsung controls more than eighty South Korean companies, in fields as diverse as industrial machinery, home appliances, and insurance. By 2012, Samsung was generating close to 20 percent of the goods and services sold in the entire country, about the same amount as government spending.

This gives the family-run company a significant influence on South Korea's economy and politics. Despite attempts at preventative regulation, leaders of the company have been convicted of tax evasion and of bribing politicians to secure corporate advantage. Only four months after being convicted of the former, Samsung's chairman, Lee Kun-hee, received a presidential pardon; the South Korean president said he granted amnesty to benefit "national interests."

In the past few years, unusually high rates of diseases like leukemia, lymphoma, and brain cancer have begun to appear among young workers in some of Samsung's manufacturing plants, though details of chemical exposure at the facilities have not been made public. Samsung faced accusations that working conditions were designed primarily to protect sensitive equipment, not workers, from chemical contaminants; many of the Samsung employees who became ill worked at the company's older facilities.

Beginning in 2007, both Samsung and various labor groups began to release a number of conflicting studies about the dangers of the work environment at the company and in the semiconductor industry more generally, but more recently a definitive cancer link has emerged. In 2012, the Korea Workers' Compensation and Welfare Service, a government agency, ruled that there was a "considerable causal relationship" between the breast cancer of a woman who died earlier that year and her work at a Samsung plant from 1995 to 2000, and a 2013 ruling by a South Korean court determined that Samsung's earlier studies examining workplace safety had not examined health hazards sufficiently. These results have encouraged many other Samsung workers, whose cases and appeals are pending.

IV. WAGES IN DECLINE

In July 2013, the think tank The Center for American Progress released a study it had commissioned from the Worker Rights Consortium that tracked global shifts in garment worker wages over a ten-year period, from 2001–2011. "Global Wage Trends for Apparel Workers, 2001–2011" focuses on top exporters to the United States and found that in most cases, wages relative to buying power decreased for top apparel exporters to the U.S. including dramatic downward shifts in Mexico and Bangladesh. A portion of the report is reprinted here. To download the full report including methodology, visit www.americanprogress.org/issues/labor/view.

When images of poor labor conditions in the garment industries of leading apparel-exporting countries reach the global news media, it is often because those conditions seem uniquely and unjustifiably extreme. Malnourished workers working fourteen-hour days faint by the hundreds in Cambodian garment plants.[1] Hundreds more are killed in deadly factory fires in Bangladesh and Pakistan by owners who lock exit doors when fires start—presumably because they fear that fleeing workers will stop to steal clothes.[2]

Yet these images reflect a common basic reality: garment workers in many of the leading apparel-exporting countries earn little more than subsistence wages for the long hours of labor that they perform. And in many of these countries, as this report discusses, the buying power of these wages is going down, not up.

Critics of anti-sweatshop advocates often argue that concern over poor labor conditions in apparel-exporting countries is misplaced and counterproductive.[3] According to their argument, jobs in garment factories, no matter how low the wages or how difficult the conditions, benefit low-skilled workers because

---

[1] Patrick Winn, "Cambodia: garment workers making US brands stitch 'til they faint," *GlobalPost*, October 5, 2012.

[2] Farid Hossain, "Fire Exits Locked at Burned Factory," *USA Today*, January 27, 2013; and Declan Walsh and Steven Greenhouse, "Certified Safe, a Factory in Karachi Still Quickly Burned," *New York Times*, December 7, 2012.

[3] See, for example, Nicholas Kristof, "Where Sweatshops Are a Dream," *New York Times*, January 15, 2009.

they provide better conditions and compensation than jobs in the informal and agricultural sectors of developing countries. Moreover, they posit, export-apparel manufacturing offers these workers—and, by extension, developing countries—a "route out of poverty" through the expansion of the manufacturing sector.[4]

The first part of this argument is largely noncontroversial. Employment in the urban formal economy typically offers better and steadier income than informal-sector work or agricultural labor. Yet self-labeled "pro-sweatshop" pundits have not explained why the price that workers in developing countries have to pay for steady wage employment should be grueling working conditions, violations of local laws and basic human rights, and abusive treatment, except to say that there are always some workers for whom labor under any conditions will be an improvement over the status quo.

The second part of the argument, however—that employment in export-garment manufacturing offers a "route out of poverty"—rests on either an extremely low benchmark for poverty[5] or the promise that such work offers the future prospect of wages that actually do support a decent standard of living for workers and their families—that is, a "living wage."[6] In other words, for the export-garment sector to actually offer workers in developing countries a "route out of poverty," either these workers' current living conditions must not amount to poverty or, if they do, these workers must be able to expect to escape poverty in the future with the industry's further development.

Over the past decade, however, apparel manufacturing in most leading garment-exporting nations has delivered diminishing returns for its workers. Research conducted for this study on fifteen of the world's leading apparel-exporting countries found that between 2001 and 2011, wages for garment

---

[4] Ibid.

[5] See, for example, Gladys Lopez Acevedo and Raymond Robertson, eds., *Sewing Success?: Employment, Wages and Poverty Following the End of the Multi-Fibre Arrangement*, vol. 12 (Washington: The World Bank, 2012).

[6] The concept of a living wage and how it can be measured in a given country is discussed at some length in this report. For an in-depth examination of the methodological and policy issues involved in arriving at such an estimate, see Richard Anker, "Estimating a Living Wage: A Methodological Review" (Geneva, Switzerland: International Labour Organization, 2011).

workers in the majority of these countries fell in real terms.[7]

As a result, we found that the gap between prevailing wages—the wages paid in general to an average worker—and living wages[8] for garment workers in these countries has only widened. A comparison of prevailing wages to the local cost of a minimally decent standard of living for an average-sized family finds that garment workers still typically earn only a fraction of what constitutes a living wage—just as they did more than ten years ago. While these workers may not live in absolute poverty, they live on incomes that do not provide them and their families with adequate nutrition, decent housing, and the other minimum necessities of a humane and dignified existence.

To summarize briefly:

- We studied nine of the top ten countries in terms of apparel exports to the United States as of 2012 and fifteen out of the top twenty-one countries by this same measure. We only studied fifteen out of the top twenty-one countries because we were limited to those places in which we had regular field-research operations at the time of the study.[9] On average, prevailing straight-time wages—pay before tax deductions and excluding extra pay for

---

[7] As discussed, the WRC measured change in real wages in each country by estimating monthly straight-time wages for garment workers in 2001 and 2011 in local currency and then deflating the 2011 wage figure by the aggregate consumer price inflation in that country during the intervening period, using inflation data from the World Bank. See World Bank, "Data: Consumer price index (2005)."

[8] As discussed, the WRC estimated living wages in 2001 and 2011 for each country included in this report by adjusting for inflation the figure it has calculated to be the living wage for the Dominican Republic—which was derived using a market-basket research study and which has been tested through actual implementation—and converting this inflation-adjusted figure into the local currencies of the other countries using the PPP factors developed by the World Bank's International Comparison Project.

[9] For a list of the top countries exporting apparel to the United States, see *Office of Textiles and Apparel, Major Shippers Report: U.S. General Imports by Category* (U.S. Department of Commerce, 2012).

overtime work[10]—in the export-apparel sectors of these countries provided barely more than a third—36.8 percent—of the income necessary to provide a living wage.

- Among the top four apparel exporters to the United States, prevailing wages in 2011 for garment workers in China, Vietnam, and Indonesia provided 36 percent, 22 percent, and 29 percent of a living wage, respectively. But in Bangladesh, home to the world's fastest-growing export-apparel industry, prevailing wages gave workers only 14 percent of a living wage.

- Wage trends for garment workers in six additional countries among the top twenty-one countries[11] were also studied in terms of apparel exports to the United States. In four of the six countries—the Dominican Republic, Guatemala, the Philippines, and Thailand—prevailing wages also fell in real terms by a per-country average of 12.4 percent, causing the gap between workers' wages and a living wage to widen in these countries as well.

- Garment workers in Mexico, the Dominican Republic, and Cambodia saw the largest erosion in wages. Between 2001 and 2011, wages in these countries fell in real terms by 28.9 percent, 23.74 percent, and 19.2 percent, respectively.

- In five of the top ten apparel-exporting countries to the United States—Bangladesh, Mexico, Honduras, Cambodia, and El Salvador—wages for garment workers declined in real terms between 2001 and 2011 by an average of 14.6 percent on a per country basis. This means that the gap between prevailing wages and living wages actually grew.

---

[10] The term "straight-time wages" is used throughout the report to refer to "total earnings before payroll deductions, excluding premium pay for overtime and for work on weekends and holidays, [and] shift differentials." U.S. Bureau of Labor Statistics, *Glossary* (U.S. Department of Labor).

[11] For similar reasons to those stated above, the remaining five countries—Sri Lanka, Nicaragua, Italy, Egypt, and Jordan—among the top twenty apparel exporters were not included in the study. Neither was Pakistan. See Office of Textiles and Apparel, *Major Shippers Report: U.S. General Imports by Category*.

- Real wages rose during the same period in the four remaining countries among the top ten exporters that we studied—China, India, Indonesia, and Vietnam—as well as in Peru and Haiti, which were among the top twenty-one countries. Wage gains in India and Peru, however, were quite modest in real terms at 13 percent and 17.1 percent, respectively, amounting to less than a 2 percent annual gain between 2001 and 2011. Wages rose more substantially in real terms in Haiti (48.2 percent), Indonesia (38.4 percent), and Vietnam (39.7 percent) over the ten-year period. Even if these rates of wage growth were sustained in these three countries, however, it would take on average more than forty years until workers achieved a living wage. Only in China, where wages rose in real terms by 124 percent over the same period, were workers on track to close the gap between their prevailing wages and a living wage within the current decade. According to our research, Chinese apparel workers are on course to attain a living wage by 2023, but only if the rate of wage growth seen between 2001 and 2011 is sustained.

The prevalence of declining wages and persistent poverty for garment workers in a majority of the world's leading apparel-exporting countries raises doubt that export-led development strategies create a rising tide that lifts all boats in most countries pursuing these strategies.

As noted, this report examines actual trends in real wages and other related indicators between 2001 and 2011 for garment workers in fifteen of the top twenty-one countries exporting apparel to the United States. It examines whether and where prevailing straight-time wages for garment workers are actually going up or down in terms of buying power—that is, whether workers are en route out of poverty, stuck in it, or headed deeper into it. As the report discusses, the prevailing straight-time wage rate for most garment workers in most of the countries examined was the applicable minimum legal wage in their respective countries. This is due to several factors, including the widespread practice of governments setting industry- and even job-specific minimum wages, and, in many cases, a lack of worker bargaining power due to limited alternatives for formal-sector employment and low unionization rates.

The report compares levels of prevailing wages in 2001 and 2011 to the level of earnings that workers and their families need in order to afford the basic necessities of a non-poverty standard of living—a living wage—and whether garment workers are actually on a path to reach this goal or whether they are falling further behind. Our research shows that only a handful of the countries examined have achieved even modest growth in real wages over the past decade, and in only one, China, was the rate of growth significant enough that the country's workers would achieve a living wage in the relatively near term if it were to be maintained. In all of the other countries, there has either been negative real-wage growth or growth that is so slow that a living wage is decades away. Unsurprisingly, growth in real wages for garment workers tended to be most associated with those few countries that have instituted major increases in their legal minimum wages as a means of poverty alleviation and/or avoidance of social unrest and that in most cases also experienced growth in other higher value-added manufacturing sectors, not just garment production.

In sum, our research indicates that while the establishment of an export-garment-manufacturing sector may tend to expand formal employment that is more profitable than alternatives in the informal sector or agricultural labor, the growth of an export-apparel industry does not necessarily raise its workers out of poverty when left to its own workings. While the expansion of garment-sector employment may have made the very poor initially significantly less poor, it has offered limited opportunities for workers in most of the major apparel-exporting countries to make further upward progress toward an income that offers them a minimally decent and secure standard of living.

Instead, in most of the leading apparel-exporting countries, the wages for garment workers have stagnated or declined over the past decade. Wages have only risen significantly in real terms in countries whose governments have taken affirmative steps to ensure that workers share the rewards from the industry's growth and whose manufacturing sectors have diversified to put apparel factories in competition for labor with makers of higher value-added goods.

REAL WAGE TRENDS FOR GARMENT WORKERS, 2001–2011

Using the methodology discussed in the appendix, we estimated prevailing straight-time wages for garment workers in nine of the top ten and fifteen of the top twenty-one countries exporting apparel to the United States in 2001 and 2011. To observe trends in the real value of workers' wages during the intervening period, we deflated our estimate of the prevailing wage in 2011 for each country by the aggregate consumer price inflation that a country had experienced from

2001 to 2011.[12] By this measure, real wages for garment workers in nine of the fifteen countries included in this study fell over that time period.

The garment exports of the fifteen countries studied comprised nearly 80 percent of all apparel imports to the United States in 2011.[13] Prevailing straight-time wages for garment workers fell in real terms in five out of the seven countries studied in the Americas and four out of eight of the countries studied in Asia. The remaining six countries where wages increased, however, produce the majority of garments that are exported to the United States.[14]

WHERE REAL WAGES FELL IN NINE OF THE TOP TEN APPAREL EXPORTERS: BANGLADESH, MEXICO, HONDURAS, CAMBODIA, AND EL SALVADOR

In the nine countries we studied among the top ten apparel exporters to the United States,[15] wages for garment workers in five countries—Bangladesh, Mexico, Honduras, Cambodia, and El Salvador—declined in real terms during the period from 2001 to 2011 by an average of 14.6 percent on a per-country basis. These countries shipped nearly 20 percent of the total value of garments exported to the United States in 2011.[16]

Mexico registered the largest decline, seeing a 28.9 percent drop in workers' buying power over this ten-year period. This decline coincided with a much larger one in the country's market share, as the country fell from the United States's top source of imported apparel in 2001, when it accounted for nearly 15 percent of imports, to the United States' fifth-largest clothing supplier in 2011, when it had a market share of slightly less than 5 percent.[17]

Bangladesh and Cambodia, the fourth- and eighth-largest clothing exporters to the United States in 2001, respectively, dramatically expanded their apparel exports to the United States during this period, recording increases in both countries of roughly 18 percent in the value of their shipments between 2010 and

---

[12] World Bank, "Data: Consumer price index."

[13] Office of Textiles and Apparel, *Major Shippers Report: U.S. General Imports by Category.*

[14] Ibid.

[15] For reasons previously discussed, the remaining country among the top ten apparel exporters, Pakistan, was not included.

[16] Office of Textiles and Apparel, *Major Shippers Report: U.S. General Imports by Category.*

[17] Ibid.

2011 alone.[18] Since 2011 Bangladesh has overtaken Indonesia and Vietnam to become the second-largest exporter of apparel to the United States.[19]

Both Bangladesh and Cambodia, however, saw wages fall in real terms between 2001 and 2011. The decline in Bangladesh—2.37 percent over the decade as a whole—was substantially moderated by a significant increase in the minimum wage, which was instituted in 2010.[20] In Cambodia, however, the loss of buying power for workers was much more significant at 19.1 percent, particularly as the country's export-apparel industry was under the oversight of the International Labour Organization's Better Factories Cambodia program during the entire period.[21] In 2011 Cambodia and Bangladesh had the lowest prevailing monthly wages for straight-time work of any major apparel exporter to the United States at approximately $70 and $50, respectively.

The two leading Central American exporters, Honduras and El Salvador, where labor costs are considerably higher, both saw real wages for apparel workers fall. Wages for garment workers declined in Honduras in real terms by 8.76 percent from 2001 to 2011, as the country's rank among major apparel exporters to the United States fell from fifth place to seventh place during the same period.[22] Prevailing monthly straight-time wages for Honduran garment workers in 2011 stood at $245.71.

El Salvador, which failed to rank among the top ten apparel exporters to the United States throughout the first part of the decade, stood as the ninth-largest exporter in 2011.[23] Straight-time wages for its apparel workers, however, fell by slightly more than 11.5 percent during this time, to a monthly figure of $210.93.

---

[18] Ibid.

[19] Bettina Wassener, "In an Unlikely Corner of Asia, Strong Promise of Growth," *New York Times*, April 24, 2012.

[20] BBC News, "Bangladesh increases garment workers' minimum wage," July 27, 2010.

[21] Stanford Law School International Human Rights and Dispute Resolution Clinic and the Worker Rights Consortium, "Monitoring in the Dark: An Evaluation of the ILO's Better Factories Cambodia Program" (2013).

[22] Office of Textiles and Apparel, *Major Shippers Report: U.S. General Imports by Category.*

[23] Ibid.

WHERE REAL WAGES GREW: CHINA, INDIA, INDONESIA, AND VIETNAM

In the four remaining countries among the top ten exporters that were studied—China, India, Indonesia, and Vietnam—prevailing real wages for garment workers rose by an average of 55.2 percent, or slightly less than 6 percent per year between 2001 and 2011. These four countries collectively made up 57 percent of clothing imports to the United States in 2011, and all four recorded gains in market share during this period.[24]

Wage gains for garment workers in India between 2001 and 2011, however, were much more modest than in the other three countries at 13 percent, averaging only 1.3 percent per year in real terms, despite the fact that in 2011 the country stood as the sixth-largest garment exporter to the United States with its 7.23 percent market share, up from 3.2 percent in 2004.[25] Prevailing straight-time wages for Indian garment workers were $94 per month in 2011.

The buying power of workers' straight-time wages rose more substantially over this period in Indonesia and Vietnam, the third- and second-largest apparel exporters to the United States in 2011, respectively. Indonesia saw an increase of 28.4 percent, and Vietnam saw an increase of 39.7 percent. The two countries also saw their market shares increase to 6.48 percent from 3.4 percent and to 8.53 percent from 4 percent, respectively, between 2004 and 2011.[26] In the case of Vietnam, however, this figure reflects a significant minimum-wage hike that did not take effect until October 2011.[27] Even with these gains, however, prevailing straight-time wages for garment workers in Indonesia and Vietnam stood at only roughly $142 and $111, respectively, per month in 2011.

Wage gains for garment workers during this period were greatest in China, where wages more than doubled in real terms by 129.4 percent. Apparel imports from China rose dramatically from 2001 to 2011, a period in which China overtook Mexico as the leading exporter of garments to the United States and more than tripled its market share, from 10.2 percent in 2000 to nearly 38 percent in 2011.[28]

---

[24] Ibid.

[25] Ibid.

[26] Ibid.

[27] Ministry of Justice, "Increase the Minimum Wage for Businesses," August 9, 2011.

[28] Office of Textiles and Apparel, *Major Shippers Report: U.S. General Imports by Category.*

REAL WAGE TRENDS AMONG OTHER TOP APPAREL EXPORTERS TO THE UNITED STATES

Wage trends for garment workers in six additional countries that were among the top twenty-one countries[29] in terms of apparel exports to the United States were also studied. In four of these countries—the Dominican Republic, Guatemala, the Philippines, and Thailand—wages also fell in real terms from 2001 to 2011, by a per-country average of 12.4 percent. In the other two countries, Haiti and Peru, wages rose in real terms over the same period, by 48.2 percent and 17.1 percent, respectively.

WHERE REAL WAGES FELL IN REMAINING TOP FIFTEEN APPAREL EXPORTERS: DOMINICAN REPUBLIC, GUATEMALA, THE PHILIPPINES, AND THAILAND

Among the countries in the group where wages fell, the Dominican Republic saw the largest decline. Its workers' straight-time pay fell by 23.74 percent during this time period. This period also saw an equally dramatic decline in the standing of the Dominican garment industry in comparison with those of other major apparel-exporting countries. While the Dominican Republic was fifth among the top garment exporters to the United States in 2000, it had fallen to 21st by 2011, having lost 80 percent of its market share over the intervening decade.[30]

As with all but one of the countries in the Caribbean Basin that were included in this study, wages for garment workers in Guatemala fell during this period, by just more than 13 percent. Guatemala also lost a significant portion of its share of U.S. apparel imports during the past decade, with its market share declining from 3 percent in 2004 to 1.7 percent in 2011.[31]

Two other apparel-exporting countries that were studied, the Philippines and Thailand, also saw straight-time wages for apparel workers fall slightly during this period, by just more than 6 percent. These countries each also lost roughly half their share of U.S. apparel imports during the decade, with their market share

---

[29] As discussed, the remaining six countries among the top twenty-one apparel exporters were not included in this study. See Office of Textiles and Apparel, *Major Shippers Report: U.S. General Imports by Category*; Steven Greenhouse, "Factory Defies Sweatshop Label, But Can It Thrive?" *New York Times*, July 17, 2010.

[30] Office of Textiles and Apparel, *Major Shippers Report: U.S. General Imports by Category*.

[31] Ibid.

declining from roughly 3 percent each in the first half of the 2000s to approximately 1.5 percent each in 2011.[32]

WHERE REAL WAGES GREW IN REMAINING TOP FIFTEEN APPAREL EXPORTERS: HAITI AND PERU

Wages grew in real terms in two other countries in the Americas that were included in this study, Haiti and Peru. In 2011 these two countries represented the 19th- and 18th-largest exporters of apparel to the United States, respectively.[33] Wage growth for Haiti's garment workers was nearly 49 percent, much more robust than the 17 percent wage growth that Peru's workers experienced over the same period. The growth in Haiti was significantly related to substantial increases in the Haitian minimum wage that were fiercely opposed by that country's apparel industry.[34]

Yet even after the significant minimum-wage increase was implemented in 2009, Haitian apparel exports to the United States continued to rise sharply, by more than 40 percent from 2010 to 2011, compared to an 8 percent increase in Peru's apparel exports to the United States during the same period.[35] In 2011 straight-time wages for garment workers in Haiti, at $131 per month, were roughly half those earned by workers in Peru, who earned $263 per month.

---

[32] Ibid.

[33] Ibid.

[34] Dan Coughlin and Jean Ives, "Wikileaks Haiti: Let Them Live on $3 a Day," *The Nation*, June 1, 2011.

[35] Office of Textiles and Apparel, *Major Shippers Report: U.S. General Imports by Category*.

MONTHLY REAL WAGES IN FIFTEEN OF THE TOP TWENTY-ONE APPAREL EXPORTERS TO THE UNITED STATES, IN 2001 CURRENCY[36]

	Monthly real wage in 2001 currency				Percent change
	2001		2011		
	LCU	USD, PPP	LCU	USD, PPP	
Bangladesh	2,083.00	$93.67	2,033.60	$91.45	-2.37%
Cambodia*	51.00	$161.89	39.78	$126.26	-22.01%
China	480.00	$144.86	1,076.57	$324.90	+124.29%
Dominican Republic	2,698.00	$293.52	2,057.45	$223.83	-23.74%
El Salvador*	162.00	$332.44	143.34	$294.14	-11.52%
Guatemala	1,414.66	$397.62	1,230.10	$345.75	-13.05%
Haiti	1,014.00	$104.42	1,502.99	$154.78	+48.22%
Honduras	2,514.83	$359.47	2,294.53	$327.98	-8.76%
India	2,019.55	$150.20	2,281.27	$169.67	+12.96%
Indonesia	421,958.00	$134.90	583,786.75	$186.64	+38.35%
Mexico	4,766.00	$755.14	3,386.54	$536.57	-28.94%
• Mexico (Min Wage)	1,258.00	$199.32	1,297.31	$205.55	+3.12%
Peru	487.50	$335.93	570.94	$393.43	+17.12%
Philippines	4,979.00	$249.25	4,662.19	$233.39	-6.36%
Thailand	5,748.50	$360.33	5,378.25	$337.12	-6.44%
Vietnam	730,167.00	$182.43	1,019,766.50	$254.78	+39.66%

COMPARISONS OF PREVAILING WAGES TO LIVING WAGES

In this section, we compare our estimates of prevailing straight-time wages in the garment industries of the leading apparel-exporting countries—known as prevailing wages—with estimates of the income that is needed to ensure that a worker and his or her family can afford the basic elements of an adequate standard of living—known as a living wage. For each country included in this study, we compare prevailing wages to living wages in both 2001 and 2011.

These comparisons reveal that in most major garment-exporting countries, as prevailing wages declined in real-wage levels, the already large gap between

[36] In this table, LCU refers to local currency units, or the average wage calculated for garment workers in the currency of their own country or region. PPP refers to purchasing power parity, or average wages adjusted for the relative cost of common goods and services. For example, in the first row, an average wage in 2001 in Bangladesh is calculated at 2,083 taka, which would be the equivalent of just over US$20 at the conversion rate of the time, but equal to an estimated US$93.67 based on cost of living calculations.

prevailing wages and living wages only grew between 2001 and 2011. Moreover, as we discuss below, with the noteworthy exception of China, the gap between prevailing wages and living wages is still significant in the countries where prevailing wages have risen in real terms, and this is unlikely to be overcome within the next twenty to thirty years.

DEFINING A LIVING WAGE

The right of workers to earn a living wage and the obligation of business enterprises and governments to ensure its provision are enshrined in the basic instruments through which the international community has articulated basic human rights and the rights of labor.[37] Contrary to assertions sometimes made by multinational corporations seeking to avoid this responsibility,[38] there is a broad consensus on the elements of a living wage, at least as far as the types of costs that it should cover and the best practices for its calculation.[39]

A recent study on estimating living wages, conducted for the International Labour Organization, or ILO, by Richard Anker, a former senior economist with that organization, describes a living wage as one that permits "[a] basic, but decent, life style that is considered acceptable by society at its current level of economic development … [such that] [w]orkers and their families [are] able to live *above the poverty level*, and … participate in social and cultural life" (emphasis added).[40]

The ILO living-wage report notes that it is well-accepted that a living wage must provide for the basic needs of not only the individual wage earner but also for his or her family.[41]Anker points out that leading nongovernmental organizations, or NGOs, that have considered the issue, including at least one whose

---

[37] See, for example, United Nations Universal Declaration of Human Rights (1948), Art. 23; ILO, "Tripartite Declaration of Principles concerning Multinational Enterprises and Social Policy" (2006). For a discussion of ILO and other international instruments that reference living wages, see Anker, "Estimating a Living Wage: A Methodological Review," pp. 2–4.

[38] See Anker, "Estimating a Living Wage: A Methodological Review," p. 1. He quotes a 2006 statement from Nike, Inc. that says, "We do not endorse artificial wage targets or increases based on arbitrary living wage definitions."

[39] Ibid. at 25, 49–50.

[40] Ibid. at 5.

[41] Ibid. at 49.

members include many major apparel brands and retailers, are consistent in their belief that a living wage should be attainable in a regular workweek without requiring overtime work.[42]

Finally, the ILO report addresses the criticism made by some apparel firms that the process of estimating a living wage is arbitrary and/or subjective. Anker observes that, in reality, all existing measures of labor welfare are significantly based on subjective judgments, including national governments' own minimum-wage laws and their statistical estimates of unemployment.[43] The report also makes clear that there is general consensus among entities that promote payment of a living wage on the set of expenses that a living wage should cover, even though there are distinct differences in the methodologies that have been adopted in order to measure these costs.[44]

METHODOLOGY FOR ESTIMATING A LIVING WAGE IN ONE COUNTRY

To our knowledge, only one apparel factory in a developing country—the Alta Gracia factory in the Dominican Republic—has been certified as actually paying a living wage as defined using the methodological approach that the aforementioned ILO report identified to be the preferred method of making such an estimate.[45] The Worker Rights Consortium, or WRC, has verified that this factory's wages meet a living-wage standard as established through a local market-basket study last conducted by the WRC in 2010 and adjusted thereafter for inflation on an annual basis. (see box below).[46]

The WRC's market-basket study avoided a number of methodological flaws that the ILO report identified in a number of other living-wage studies conducted

---

[42] Ibid. at 50.

[43] Ibid. at 11–12.

[44] Ibid. at 49–53.

[45] Compare ibid. at 27—discussing practice of calculating costs for separate categories including food, housing, transportation, clothing/footwear, childcare, and other expenditures—to WRC, "Living Wage Analysis for the Dominican Republic" (2010).

[46] Ibid.

by other organizations in other countries.[47] Moreover, the living-wage figure that the WRC arrived at in the Dominican Republic fell roughly at a midpoint between cost-of-living estimates published by the country's central bank on the one hand and its leading labor federations on the other, suggesting that it may have succeeded in avoiding potential subjective biases.[48]

Finally, and most significantly, real world evidence at the Alta Gracia factory, including studies currently underway by public health scholars from Harvard University and the University of California, Berkeley,[49] indicate that the wage paid at the factory provides at a minimum level—neither particularly generously nor inadequately—for the basic needs of a garment worker and his or her family. The WRC has concluded, based on its original market-basket study and its ongoing monitoring of the factory since 2010, that wages paid at the Alta Gracia factory accurately reflect a minimum living wage for a Dominican garment worker residing in the area where the factory is located and his or her family.[50]

METHODOLOGY FOR ESTIMATING LIVING WAGES TRANSNATIONALLY

To estimate living-wage figures for 2001 and 2011 for the countries included in the study, we first adjusted our 2008 living-wage figure for the Dominican Republic for inflation using consumer-price-inflation data from the World Bank[51] to arrive at living-wage figures for that country for 2001 and 2011. Next, we converted this figure using purchasing power parity, or PPP conversion factors for the other countries for the same years from the World Bank's International Comparison Project[52] to arrive at figures for each country of amounts—in their

---

[47] Compare ibid. to "Estimating a Living Wage: A Methodological Review," pp. 38–40, which criticizes some living-wage studies for failing to separate categories of nonfood expenditure and failing to provide specific information regarding selection, type, price, and quantity of food items.

[48] WRC, "Living Wage Analysis for the Dominican Republic," p. 8.

[49] John Kline, "Alta Gracia: Branding Decent Work Conditions" (Washington: Walsh School of Foreign Service, Georgetown University, 2010).

[50] Ibid.; WRC, "Verification Report Re Labor Rights Compliance at Altagracia Project Factory (Dominican Republic)" (2011).

[51] World Bank, "Data: Consumer price index."

[52] World Bank, "Global Purchasing Power Parities and Real Expenditures: 2005 International Comparison Program" (2008), pp. 21–28.

respective local currencies—that provided the same buying power as the inflation-adjusted living-wage figure for the Dominican Republic.

As a general methodology for estimating living wages transnationally, relying on PPP conversions is admittedly an imperfect approach. It should be noted, however, that this is the method used by the one major multinational corporation to actually implement a living-wage policy in its global operations: the Swiss pharmaceutical firm Novartis International, AG.[53] Of particular relevance here, Anker's 2011 report for the ILO notes that this approach fails to account for variances among countries in the shares of household incomes devoted to different categories of expenditures, such as those on food, housing, utilities, and health care.[54]

For this reason, the WRC's longstanding practice has been to conduct market-basket living-wage studies in individual countries in consultation with local informants and researchers in order to arrive at living-wage figures that accurately reflect local expenditure patterns.[55] Conducting such individual studies in each of the countries included in this study, however, was beyond the scope of the research conducted for this report, which focused on the actual prevailing wages paid to garment workers during the period under study.

In this case, we determined that the value of our 2008 living wage for the Dominican Republic—as the sole living-wage figure that has been calculated using the preferred market-basket methodology and tested for real-world accuracy through implementation at an export-apparel factory in a developing country—made it a useful baseline for estimating living-wage figures for workers in the export-apparel sectors of other developing countries. Recognizing the limitations of this approach, however, we present these estimates only for the purpose of the current report and remain convinced that actual implementation of a living wage in an individual country requires a locally conducted market-basket study.

---

[53] See Anker, "Estimating a Living Wage: A Methodological Review," p. 43. He critiques this methodology generally and Novartis's living-wage studies specifically.

[54] Ibid.

[55] WRC, "Living Wage Analysis for the Dominican Republic"; WRC, "Sample Living Wage Estimates: Indonesia and El Salvador" (2006).

PREVAILING WAGES COMPARED TO LIVING WAGES

We estimated a living wage for each of the countries included in this study for the years 2001 and 2011 by using World Bank PPP conversion factors[56] to extrapolate from the living-wage figure already in use by the WRC in the Dominican Republic. We then adjusted each of these for inflation. We then compared the 2001 and 2011 living-wage figures to the figures for prevailing monthly wages for garment workers for straight-time work in each of these countries for 2001 and 2011. We then used these comparisons to calculate ratios of the current prevailing wage to the current living wage in each of these countries in both 2001 and 2011. Using these ratios, we then calculated the annual rate of convergence or divergence of the prevailing wage and living wage in each country over the intervening ten-year period. Finally, for those countries where the prevailing wage and the living wage had converged to any extent from 2001 to 2011—that is, in any countries where the gap between the prevailing wage and the living wage in percentage terms had shrunk between 2001 and 2011—we used the rate of annual convergence to calculate the number of additional years required, assuming continued convergence at the same rate, until the prevailing wage equals the living wage.

PREVAILING WAGES CURRENTLY AVERAGE A THIRD OF A LIVING WAGE

In none of the fifteen countries included in the study did the prevailing monthly straight-time wage provide garment workers with the equivalent of a minimum living wage. On average, the prevailing wage in 2011 for garment workers in each of the countries included in the study provided little more than a third—36.8 percent—of the estimated living wage in the same country, as calculated using the methodology described above.

This result is generally consistent with the WRC's prior research estimating living wages in individual countries based on local market-basket studies, which has found that achieving a living wage typically requires tripling the prevailing-wage rate for garment workers.[57] Prevailing wages for garment workers stood

---

[56] World Bank, "Global Purchasing Power Parities and Real Expenditures."

[57] See Office of Textiles and Apparel, *Major Shippers Report: U.S. General Imports by Category*; Letter from Donald I. Baker to Acting U.S. Assistant Attorney General Sharis Pozen, December 15, 2011.

in relation to a living wage in essentially the same place that they had ten years earlier, when the average share of a living wage provided by each country's prevailing wage for garment workers was 35.7 percent.

PREVAILING WAGES COMPARED TO LIVING WAGES IN FIFTEEN OF THE TOP TWENTY-ONE APPAREL EXPORTERS TO THE UNITED STATES, 2001 AND 2011

	Monthly wages, 2001 LCU		Prevailing as a percent of living
	Prevailing	Living, proxy	
Bangladesh	2,083.00	14,715.62	14%
Cambodia*	51.00	210.18	24%
China	480.00	2,950.05	16%
Dominican Republic	2,698.00	6,789.59	40%
El Salvador*	162.00	365.32	44%
Guatemala	1,414.66	2,473.31	57%
Haiti	1,014.00	6,769.50	15%
Honduras	2,514.83	4,865.92	52%
India	2,019.55	10,043.14	20%
Indonesia	421,958.00	2,708,675.43	16%
Mexico	4,766.00	5,083.61	94%
• Mexico (Min Wage)	1,258.00	5,083.61	25%
Peru	487.50	1,171.09	42%
Philippines	4,979.00	15,530.48	32%
Thailand	5,748.50	12,318.13	47%
Vietnam	730,167.00	3,167,635.39	23%

	Monthly wages, 2011 LCU		Prevailing as a percent of living
	Prevailing	Living, proxy	
Bangladesh	4,062.00	29,624.86	14%
Cambodia*	70.00	364.51	19%
China	1,363.00	3,811.25	36%
Dominican Republic	6,435.00	21,236.96	30%
El Salvador*	210.93	518.60	41%
Guatemala	2,359.64	4,721.74	50%
Haiti	5,633.00	23,908.19	24%
Honduras	4,642.64	9,845.25	47%
India	4,422.17	19,468.31	23%
Indonesia	1,287,471.00	5,814,077.48	22%
Mexico	5,200.00	7,805.96	67%
• Mexico (Min Wage)	1,992.00	7,805.96	26%
Peru	731.25	1,499.47	49%
Philippines	7,668.00	24,237.54	32%
Thailand	7,026.00	16,270.16	43%
Vietnam	2,306,667.00	7,844,895.84	29%

Not surprisingly, the country where the disparity between prevailing wages and a living wage was greatest was Bangladesh, where prevailing wages for garment workers in 2011—which were lower than those in any other country in the study—provided only one-seventh—14 percent—of a living wage. Also unsurprisingly, since real-wage levels for garment workers remained largely flat in Bangladesh from 2001 to 2011—registering, overall, a decline of 2.37 percent—the disparity between the prevailing wage and a living wage was the same in percentage terms in both 2001 and 2011.

The country where the gap between the prevailing-wage figure and the estimated living wage was the smallest was Mexico, where the prevailing wage in 2011 provided roughly two-thirds, or 67 percent, of a living wage. The narrowness of this gap, however, is largely explained by the fact the Mexico is the one country where the prevailing-wage figure used in this report includes overtime compensation. If one were to substitute as the prevailing-wage figure the legal minimum wage payable in the country's leading center of garment production, the prevailing wage would supply only 26 percent of a living wage.

Among the other countries included in the study, Guatemala, Honduras, and Peru had prevailing wages in 2011 that provided the largest proportion of a living wage—50 percent, 47 percent, and 49 percent, respectively. Unfortunately, in Guatemala and Honduras, the gap between prevailing wages and living wages actually grew slightly from 2001 to 2011 instead of narrowing.

Excluding Mexico, countries in the Americas had prevailing wages for garment workers that on average equaled 40 percent of the living wage for the same country. The gap was wider in Asia, where prevailing wages for each country provided on average 27.3 percent of a living wage. The country in that region with the smallest gap was Thailand, where prevailing wages provided 43 percent of a living wage. Again, however, this gap was slightly broader in 2011 than it was in 2001.

FUTURE TRENDS IN PREVAILING WAGES VERSUS LIVING WAGES

As would be expected, the only countries where the gap between prevailing wages and living wages narrowed between 2001 and 2011 were those countries where prevailing wages for garment workers had risen in real terms: China, Vietnam, Indonesia, India, Haiti, and Peru. Among these countries, only China saw prevailing wages make substantial gains in closing this gap, more than doubling as a proportion of the living wage—from 16 percent to 36 percent—during these ten years. In the other countries where wages for garment workers rose in real terms, such gains were more modest, representing on average an increase of 31 percent in the percentage share of the country's living wage that the prevailing wage provided.

We found that even if each of these countries maintains a rate of wage growth for garment workers comparable to that which it recorded between 2001 and 2011, attaining a living wage is still a distant prospect. This is particularly true of India, where it would take—assuming an equivalent rate of real-wage growth going forward—more than a century for workers to reach a living wage, given that prevailing wages rose in real terms from 2001 to 2011 at an annual rate of just 1.3 percent, and that the prevailing wage at the end of this period provided just 23 percent of a living wage. The situation is similar but less extreme in Peru, where despite the fact that the prevailing wage in 2001 already provided a much larger proportion of a living wage at 42 percent, a fairly modest rate of real-wage growth—1.7 percent annually from 2001 and 2011—meant that, at the same rate, the country's garment workers would not achieve a living wage for more than four decades.

Even in the cases of Indonesia, Vietnam, and Haiti, where wage rates for garment workers achieved significantly greater growth over this period—overall increases in real terms of 38 percent, 40 percent, and 48 percent, respectively, between 2001 and 2011—several decades of further growth at the same rates would be required before workers reached a living wage: 42 years for Haiti, 46 years for Indonesia, and 37 years for Vietnam. Only in China, where wage rates for garment workers have grown at a rate of 130 percent, which far surpasses the rates seen in any of the other countries included in the study, are wage rates projected to equal a living wage within the decade, assuming continued real-wage growth at the same rate. If China does manage to see such growth in real wages for its garment workers over the remainder of this decade—a possibility that seems significantly less than certain—Chinese garment workers will achieve a living wage in 2019.

CONCLUSION

We have examined the trends from 2001 to 2011 in real wages for apparel-sector workers in fifteen of the top twenty-one manufacturing countries. In nine countries—Bangladesh, Cambodia, the Dominican Republic, El Salvador, Guatemala, Honduras, Mexico, the Philippines, and Thailand—the prevailing real wage for apparel-sector workers in 2011 was less than it was in 2001. That is, apparel-sector workers in the majority of the countries studied saw their purchasing power decrease and slipped further away from receiving a living wage.

In the six countries examined in which real wages increased from 2001 to 2011, wage growth in two of the countries, Peru and India, was modest—less than 2 percent per year. While wage gains for workers in Indonesia, Vietnam, and Haiti were more substantial, it would take an average of more than 40 years for the prevailing wage rate to equal a living wage even if this rate of wage growth were sustained. Only in China did real wages for apparel-sector workers increase at a rate that would lift workers to the point of receiving a living wage within the next decade. Not surprisingly, then, the industrial centers in China where workers benefited from these gains have already seen a loss of apparel production, as manufacturers have shifted their facilities, and buyers have shifted their orders, to lower-wage areas both within China and in other countries.

One key reason that the prevailing wage increased in China is that the government substantially increased the mandated minimum wage, in part in order to limit worker unrest. Because minimum wages in most of the countries studied are both sector and job specific, this points to one possible way forward for increasing workers' compensation. Countries need to look at increasing minimum wages to help lift workers toward a living wage. Promoting greater respect for the rights of union organization and collective bargaining to empower workers to negotiate wage increases on their own could also have a similar effect.

Doing so would provide greater dignity for workers while helping to build the foundation for a strong, consumer-driven economy. But as the experience of other countries shows—particularly the higher-wage countries in Latin America that saw declines in real wages for garment workers during the last decade—such gains will only be sustainable if manufacturers and buyers are willing to absorb the added labor costs, rather than applying downward price pressure through the threat of exit.

By doing so, these manufacturers, brands, and retailers could help make apparel jobs a true route out of poverty. Raising the prevailing-wage rate for apparel-sector workers is both good for workers and good for economies. It would spark a virtuous circle in which higher wages beget increased demand and thus more and better jobs.

ACKNOWLEDGMENTS

This project is supported in part by awards from the National Endowment for the Arts and the San Francisco Arts Commission.

The editor would like to thank her friends and family for their love and encouragement throughout the production of *Invisible Hands*. Special thanks to mimi lok, Liana Foxvog, and Debbie Chan, the earliest and strongest believers in the project. Thanks also to mimi, Juliana Sloane, and to Luke Gerwe whose immense effort, talent, and patience ushered this book to publication. To my aunt Kathryn Goria, for logistical and emotional support. To my dad and his wife, for their challenging questions. To my mom and step-dad, for their interest and endless encouragement this book. To my sisters, nieces and nephew, for their joy and laughter. To my husband Accursio Lota, for his perspective, wisdom, and culinary love throughout the project. To my son, Alessandro, for being my spirited muse, and for arriving at just the right time. And thank you to the narrators: this is their book.

ART WORKS.
arts.gov

sfac
san francisco
arts commission

ABOUT THE EDITOR

CORINNE GORIA is a writer and immigration attorney. Her fiction has been featured in *The Silent History*, the *San Diego Writer's Anthology*, and the &Now Festival, and she was assistant editor of *Underground America: Narratives of Undocumented Lives* (Voice of Witness, 2008). She has lived in South Africa, Italy, and Mexico, and currently lives in San Diego, California.

The VOICE OF WITNESS SERIES

The Voice of Witness book series, published by McSweeney's, empowers those most closely affected by contemporary social injustice. Using oral history as a foundation, the series depicts human rights crises in the United States and around the world. Voice of Witness also publishes a guide for teaching oral history called *The Power of the Story*. *Invisible Hands* is the twelfth book in the series. The other titles in the series are:

SURVIVING JUSTICE

America's Wrongfully Convicted and Exonerated

Compiled and edited by Lola Vollen and Dave Eggers

Foreword by Scott Turow

"Real, raw, terrifying tales of 'justice.'" —*Star Tribune*

These oral histories prove that the problem of wrongful conviction is far-reaching and very real. Through a series of all-too-common circumstances—eyewitness misidentification, inept defense lawyers, coercive interrogation—the lives of these men and women of all different backgrounds were irreversibly disrupted. In *Surviving Justice*, thirteen exonerees describe their experiences—the events that led to their convictions, their years in prison, and the process of adjusting to their new lives outside.

VOICES FROM THE STORM

The People of New Orleans on Hurricane Katrina and Its Aftermath

Compiled and edited by Chris Ying and Lola Vollen

"*Voices from the Storm* uses oral history to let those who survived the hurricane tell their (sometimes surprising) stories." —*Independent UK*

Voices from the Storm is a chronological account of the worst natural disaster in modern American history. Thirteen New Orleanians describe the days leading up to Hurricane Katrina, the storm itself, and the harrowing confusion of the days and months afterward. Their stories weave and intersect, ultimately creating an eye-opening portrait of courage in the face of terror, and of hope amid nearly complete devastation.

UNDERGROUND AMERICA

Narratives of Undocumented Lives

Compiled and edited by Peter Orner

Foreword by Luis Alberto Urrea

"No less than revelatory." —*Publishers Weekly*

They arrive from around the world for countless reasons. Many come simply to make a living. Others are fleeing persecution in their native countries. But by living and working in the U.S. without legal status, millions of immigrants risk deportation and imprisonment. *Underground America* presents the remarkable oral histories of men and women struggling to carve a life for themselves in the United States. In 2010, *Underground America* was translated into Spanish and released as *En las Sombras de Estados Unidos*.

OUT OF EXILE

The Abducted and Displaced People of Sudan

Compiled and edited by Craig Walzer

Additional interviews and an introduction by

Dave Eggers and Valentino Achak Deng

"Riveting." —*School Library Journal*

Millions of people have fled from conflicts in all parts of Sudan, and many thousands more have been enslaved as human spoils of war. In *Out of Exile*, refugees and abductees recount their escapes from the wars in Darfur and South Sudan, from political and religious persecution, and from abduction by militias. They tell of life before the war, and of the hope that they might someday find peace again.

HOPE DEFERRED

Narratives of Zimbabwean Lives

Compiled and edited by Peter Orner and Annie Holmes

Foreword by Brian Chikwava

"*Hope Deferred* might be the most important publication to have come out of Zimbabwe in the last thirty years." —*Harper's Magazine*

The fifth volume in the Voice of Witness series presents the narratives of Zimbabweans whose lives have been affected by the country's political, economic, and human rights crises. This book asks the question: How did a country with so much promise—a stellar education system, a growing middle class of professionals, a sophisticated economic infrastructure, a liberal constitution, and an independent judiciary—go so wrong?

NOWHERE TO BE HOME

Narratives from Survivors of Burma's Military Regime

Compiled and edited by Maggie Lemere and Zoë West

Foreword by Mary Robinson

"Extraordinary." —The Asia Society

Decades of military oppression in Burma have led to the systematic destruction of thousands of ethnic-minority villages, a standing army with one of the world's highest numbers of child soldiers, and the displacement of millions of people. *Nowhere to Be Home* is an eye-opening collection of oral histories exposing the realities of life under military rule. In their own words, men and women from Burma describe their lives in the country that Human Rights Watch has called "the textbook example of a police state."

PATRIOT ACTS

Narratives of Post-9/11 Injustice

Compiled and edited by Alia Malek

Foreword by Karen Korematsu

"Important and timely." —Reza Aslan

Patriot Acts tells the stories of men and women who have been needlessly swept up in the War on Terror. In their own words, narrators recount personal experiences of the post-9/11 backlash that has deeply altered their lives and communities. *Patriot Acts* illuminates these experiences in a compelling collection of eighteen oral histories from men and women who have found themselves subject to a wide range of human and civil rights abuses—from rendition and torture, to workplace discrimination, bullying, FBI surveillance, and harassment.

INSIDE THIS PLACE, NOT OF IT

Narratives from Women's Prisons

Compiled and edited by Ayelet Waldman and Robin Levi

Foreword by Michelle Alexander

"These stories are a gift." —Michelle Alexander

Inside This Place, Not of It reveals some of the most egregious human rights violations within women's prisons in the United States. In their own words, the thirteen narrators in this book recount their lives leading up to incarceration and their experiences inside—ranging from forced sterilization and shackling during childbirth, to physical and sexual abuse by prison staff. Together, their testimonies illustrate the harrowing struggles for survival that women in prison must endure.

THROWING STONES AT THE MOON

Narratives of Colombians Displaced by Violence

Compiled and edited by Sibylla Brodzinsky and Max Schoening

Foreword by Íngrid Betancourt

"Both sad and inspiring." —*Publishers Weekly*

For nearly five decades, Colombia has been embroiled in internal armed conflict among guerrilla groups, paramilitary militias, and the country's own military. These oral histories describe a range of abuses, including killings, disappearances, rape, and the displacement of more than four million from their homes.

REFUGEE HOTEL

Compiled and edited by Juliet Linderman and Gabriele Stabile

"There is no other book like *Refugee Hotel* on your shelf." —*SF Weekly*

Refugee Hotel is a groundbreaking collection of photography and interviews that documents the arrival of refugees in the United States. Evocative images are coupled with moving testimonies from people describing their first days in the U.S., the lives they've left behind, and the new communities they've since created.

HIGH RISE STORIES

Voices from Chicago Public Housing

Compiled and edited by Audrey Petty

Foreword by Alex Kotlowitz

"Joyful, novelistic, and deeply moving." —George Saunders

In the gripping first-person accounts of *High Rise Stories*, former residents of Chicago's iconic public housing projects describe life in the now-demolished high rises. These stories of community, displacement, and poverty in the wake of gentrification give voice to those who have long been ignored.

THE POWER OF THE STORY

The Voice of Witness Teacher's Guide to Oral History

Compiled and edited by Cliff Mayotte

Foreword by William and Richard Ayers

"A rich source of provocations to engage with human dramas throughout the world." —*Rethinking Schools Magazine*

This comprehensive guide allows teachers and students to explore contemporary issues through oral history, and to develop the communication skills necessary for creating vital oral history projects in their own communities.